Chis 1-7

SCHOOL PROGRAMS IN SPEECH-LANGUAGE

ORGANIZATION AND MANAGEMENT

second edition

Elizabeth A. Neidecker
Bowling Green State University

PRENTICE-HALL, INC., ENGLEWOOD CLIFFS, NEW JERSEY 07632

Library of Congress Cataloging-in-Publication Data

Neidecker, Elizabeth A.
    School programs in speech-language.

    Bibliography: p. 276
    Includes index.
    1. Speech therapy for children—United States—
Curricula.   2. Speech therapy—Vocational
guidance—United States.   I. Title.
LB3454.N44   1987   371.9′14   86-22572
ISBN 0-13-794330-X

Editorial/production supervision: Dee Amir Josephson
Cover design: Karen Stephens
Manufacturing buyer: Harry P. Baisley

PRINTED IN THE UNITED STATES OF AMERICA

10   9   8   7   6   5   4   3

ISBN 0-13-794330-X   01

PRENTICE-HALL INTERNATIONAL (UK) LIMITED, *London*
PRENTICE-HALL OF AUSTRALIA PTY. LIMITED, *Sydney*
PRENTICE-HALL CANADA INC., *Toronto*
PRENTICE-HALL HISPANOAMERICANA, S.A., *Mexico*
PRENTICE-HALL OF INDIA PRIVATE LIMITED, *New Delhi*
PRENTICE-HALL OF JAPAN, INC., *Tokyo*
PRENTICE-HALL OF SOUTHEAST ASIA PTE. LTD., *Singapore*
EDITORA PRENTICE-HALL DO BRASIL, LTDA., *Rio de Janeiro*

In memory of my family . . .
Fred, Alpha, John, Nancy

CONTENTS

**Chapter Six: TOOLS OF THE TRADE:
SPACE, FACILITIES, EQUIPMENT,
AND MATERIALS 78**

**Chapter Seven: CASE FINDING, CASE SELECTION,
AND CASELOAD 91**

**Chapter Eight: SCHEDULING AND IMPLEMENTING
THERAPY 135**

Chapter Nine: WORKING WITH OTHERS: THE SCHOOL SPEECH-LANGUAGE PATHOLOGIST AS A CONSULTANT 174

Chapter Ten: ORGANIZING AND MAINTAINING RECORDS AND REPORTS FOR ACCOUNTABILITY AND EVALUATION 203

Chapter Eleven: STUDENT TEACHING 223

Chapter Twelve: LIFE AFTER COLLEGE   240

PREFACE

Since the publication of the first edition of this book in 1980, the role of the speech-language pathologist in the schools has expanded considerably. New challenges have prompted new ways of looking at service delivery models, the scope of the profession, the storing and retrieving of information, the prevention of communication problems, and also working relationships with parents and allied health and education professionals. Much of this was brought about by Public Law 94-142, the Education for All Handicapped Children Act.

Although the future of the law may be uncertain, there will be no turning back from its path. The implementation of Public Law 94-142 has sometimes been difficult, but the intent of the law was good. It was never meant to supplant common sense, and the criterion for making decisions must always be: "What is best for the child?"

This book is written for students preparing for positions as speech-language pathologists in the schools. It can also serve as a source of information for students who may be thinking about becoming school pathologists or for individuals already working in the schools as speech-language pathologists who wish to augment their store of information. It may also serve as a source book for those responsible for school programs in speech, language, and hearing—including superintendents, assistant superintendents, principals of elementary, middle, or high schools, and administrators of programs for handicapped children.

The school speech-language pathologist is committed to the idea that communication skills are prerequisite to the acquisition of educational skills and knowledge of a subject. The role of the school speech-language pathologist is to prevent, alleviate, and remove communication barriers that hinder the student from profiting from the instruction offered in the classroom.

Over 40 percent of the speech, language, and hearing professionals are employed in the schools. They are truly the front line of the profession. They daily face many challenges. They are conscientious, competent, and dedicated individuals. It is my sincere hope that this book will meet some of the needs of present and future speech-language pathologists in the schools and will assist them in their day-to-day activities.

Chapters 1, 2, and 3 provide basic information for the school speech-language pathologist. The early growth, development, and later expansion of the profession in the schools is discussed against the background of the profession as a whole. The present and future roles of the school speech-language pathologist are examined. The topics of professionalism, accreditation, and organizations are also considered in Chapter 2. In Chapter 3 the foundations of the programs in the schools are discussed, including Public Law 94-142, litigation and due process, mainstreaming, the financing of school programs, and the prevalence of communication problems.

Chapter 4 provides a detailed discussion of the continuum-of-service model and the various delivery-of-service models. These models are the framework for school programs.

Chapter 5 examines the role of the school SLP as a manager of time, facilities, and resources, including paraprofessionals and computers.

In Chapter 6 the topics of space, physical facilities, equipment, and materials are examined.

Case finding, case selection, and caseload—three important tasks of the school clinician—are discussed in detail and include recent findings that reflect developments in the profession. The responsibilities of scheduling and implementing therapy in various settings and with various communication problems are dealt with in Chapter 8.

Chapter 9 includes information on other education and health-related professions and how they interact with the expanding role of the school speech-language clinician.

Chapter 10 discusses generating, managing, storing, and retrieving information in records and reports. The relationship of record and report systems is viewed in the light of providing ongoing evaluation of programs.

Student teaching is the subject of Chapter 11. The roles and responsibilities of the student clinician, the cooperating clinician in the schools, and the university supervisor are outlined, as well as the supervising process.

Chapter 12 discusses what goes on in the world of work after student teaching, including publications, research, and the importance of continuing education. A valuable part of this chapter is information on how to get one's first job.

At the end of each chapter there are discussion questions and projects. They are included to help students make practical applications of theoretical knowledge and factual information and to stimulate dialog with each other and with the instructor of the course.

ACKNOWLEDGMENTS

Throughout my professional life I have been fortunate to have been associated with school programs in one way or another: as a public school clinician, a university professor teaching the public school methods course in speech-language pathology, and as coordinator of student teaching programs. I have found it enjoyable and challenging, and I especially cherish my association with students and with my colleagues in the public schools, state education departments, and universities. I am indebted to all of them for enriching my experience. It would be impossible to list all their names; however, in the preparation of this second edition, I owe a special debt to professional colleagues throughout the United States who shared with me their knowledge, research findings, ideas, criticisms, and encouragement. This is a way of saying thank you to Faith Jackson, June Sweede, William Heob, Mark Zoback, Virginia Bingham, Kathleen Bartels, Karen Buhrer, Debra Greenfield-Furman, Carol Flaherty, Hortencia Kayser, Gail Harris, Carole Donnelly, Amy B. Harris, Denise Wray, Tom C. Ehren, Colleen J. Marks, Marilyn S. Finn, Salvatore DeMarco, Arthur H. Schwartz, Ann Wilson-Vlotman, Jean Blosser, Roberta DePompei, Jean Silbar, Phyllis Evans, Elmer C. Cameron, Barbara Winzenreid, Jerry Whittaker, Jerry Johnson, Dolores Gelfand, Mary Beach, Nancy Schroeder, Elizabeth Matthews, Stan Dublinske, William Healey, and Mary Clare Torpey. I also wish to thank the following reviewers for their comments on the manuscript: Elaine L. Brown-Grant, Northwestern University, and Deidre K. Clugston, Michigan State University.

My list of persons to be thanked would be incomplete without acknowledging two of my teachers whose help, confidence, and encouragement were an inspiration to me. They are Dr. Virginia S. Sanderson, professor emerita, Ohio State University, in whose class I first learned about public school speech and hearing programs; and the late George Fortune, first director of the Cleveland Hearing and Speech Center, who gave me my first opportunity to teach the public school programming course and supervise student teachers in communication disorders.

Robert Thoreson of Prentice-Hall initially provided the necessary encouragement for embarking on the task of writing a book, and I am very grateful to him.

In addition, I would like to thank Sue Schwartz and Kathy Crudele for the typing and for help in bringing order out of chaos in putting the manuscript together.

Elizabeth A. Neidecker

ONE
THE GROWTH
AND DEVELOPMENT
OF THE PROFESSION
IN THE SCHOOLS

INTRODUCTION

This chapter provides a historical background of the profession of speech, language, and hearing and the development of programs within the schools of the United States. The philosophy of education that invited speech, language, and hearing programs into the schools is described. Also discussed is the expansion of school programs, both professionally and geographically. The chapter points out the role of the school pathologists in the early days and changes in that role, as well as the factors that influenced those changes. It also considers the prevailing philosophy and legislation mandating equal educational opportunities for all handicapped children and its implications for both the programs of the future and the roles and responsibilities of the school pathologist.

EARLY HISTORY

Although speech, language, and hearing problems have been with us since the early history of humankind, rehabilitative services for children with communication handicaps were not realized until the early part of the twentieth century. The growth of the profession and the establishment of the American

Academy of Speech Correction in 1925 reflect the realization of the needs and special problems of the handicapped population.

According to Moore and Kester (1953), the educational philosophy that invited speech correction into the schools was expressed in the preface to a teacher's manual published in 1897, which contained John Dewey's "My Pedagogic Creed." The preface, written by Samuel T. Dutton, superintendent of schools, Brookline, Massachusetts, stated

> The isolation of the teacher is a thing of the past. The processes of education have come to be recognized as fundamental and vital in any attempt to improve human conditions and elevate society.
>
> The missionary and the social reformer have long been looking to education for counsel and aid in their most difficult undertakings. They have viewed with interest and pleasure the broadening of pedagogy so as to make it include not only experimental physiology and child study, but the problems of motor training, physical culture, hygiene, and the treatment of defectives and delinquents of every class.
>
> The schoolmaster, always conservative, has not found it easy to enter this large field; for he has often failed to realize how rich and fruitful the result of such researches are; but remarkable progress has been made, and a changed attitude on the part of the educators is the result.

Moore and Kester (1953) suggested that child labor laws influenced the growth of speech programs in the schools. Barring children from work forced both the atypical and the normal child to remain in school, and teachers soon asked for help with the exceptional children. A few got help, including assistance with children having speech defects.

According to Moore and Kester (p. 49), it was in 1910 that the Chicago public schools started a program of speech correction. Ella Flagg Young, the superintendent of schools, in her annual report in 1910 said

> Immediately after my entrance upon the duties of superintendent, letters began to arrive filled with complaints and petitions by parents of stammering children—complaints that the schools did nothing to help children handicapped by stammering to overcome their speech difficulty, but left them to lag behind and finally drop out of the schools; and petitions that something be done for those children. It was somewhat peculiar and also suggestive that these letters were followed by others from people who had given much attention to the study of stammering and wished to undertake the correction of that defect in stammerers attending the public schools. Soon after the schools were opened in the fall, I sent out a note, requesting each principal to report the number of stammerers in the school. It was surprising to find upon receiving the replies that there were recognized as stammerers 1,287 children. A recommendation was made to the committee on school management to the effect that the head of the department of oral expression in the Chicago Teachers' College be authorized to select ten of the members of the graduating class who showed special ability in the training given at the college in that particular subject and should be further empowered to give additional training of these students preparatory to their undertaking, under the direction of the department, the correction of the speech defects of these 1,287 children. The Board appropriated $3,000.00 toward the payment of

these students who should begin their work after graduation at the rate of $65 a month during a period extending from February 1 to June 30.

Instead of gathering the children into one building or into classes to be treated for their troubles, a plan was adopted of assigning to the young teacher a circuit and having her travel from school to school during the day. The object of this plan was to protect the young teacher from the depression of spirit and low physical condition that often ensue from continued confinement in one room for several successive hours at work upon abnormal conditions. It was soon found that the term "stammering" had been assumed to be very general in its application and many children who had been reported as stammerers had not the particular defect reported but some other form of speech defect.

The superintendent of schools in New York City in 1909 requested an investigation of the need for speech training in the schools, and two years later the following recommendations were presented to the board of education: First, the number of speech handicapped children was to be ascertained and case histories obtained; second, speech centers were to be established providing daily lessons of from 30 to 60 minutes; third, English teachers were to be given further training and utilized as instructors; and fourth, a department for training teachers was to be established. It was not until four years later, however, that a director of speech improvement was appointed to carry out the recommendations (Moore & Kester, 1953).

EARLY GROWTH

During this same decade there was an increasing number of public school systems employing speech clinicians. Among them were Detroit, Grand Rapids, Cleveland, Boston, Cincinnati, and San Francisco (Paden, 1970). In 1918, Dr. Walter B. Swift of Cleveland wrote an article entitled "How to Begin Speech Correction in the Public Schools" (reprinted in *Language, Speech and Hearing Services in Schools,* April 1972).

To the state of Wisconsin goes the credit for establishing at the University of Wisconsin the first training program for prospective specialists in the field and for granting the first doctor of philosophy degree in the area of speech disorders to Sara M. Stinchfield in 1921. Wisconsin was also the first state to enact enabling legislation for public school speech services and to appoint in 1923 a state supervisor of speech correction, Pauline Camp. Meanwhile, other universities throughout the United States were developing curricula in the area of speech disorders. Until 1940, however, only eight additional states added similar laws to their statute books (Irwin, 1959). By 1963, a study by Haines (1965) indicated that 45 of the states had passed legislation placing speech and hearing programs in the public schools. These laws provided for financial help to school districts maintaining approved programs, supervision by the state, responsibility for administering the law, and the establishment of standards. The laws described minimum standards, which the programs were expected to exceed (Haines, 1965).

The first state supervisors, in cooperation with the school clinicians in their respective states, did a remarkably far-sighted job in establishing state-wide programs in regard to the organizational aspects. With no precedents to follow, they established standards that have retained merit through many years. The Vermont program (Dunn, 1949), providing speech and hearing services to children in rural areas, and the Ohio plan (Irwin, 1949) furnish two such examples. They addressed themselves to such topics as finding children who need the services, diagnostic services, caseload, the scheduling of group and individual therapy sessions, rooms for the therapist, equipment and supplies, coordination day, summer residence programs, in-service training of parents and teachers, and periodic rechecks of children.

Development of Programs for the Hearing Impaired

The concern for the hearing handicapped has long been an issue both with the families of those individuals and with professionals. The history of the education of the deaf had its beginning in Europe in the sixteenth century. Educational programs for the deaf were first established in the United States in 1817 with the founding of the American School for the Deaf at Hartford, Connecticut (Bender, 1960).

Initially, programs in this country were designed for deaf children, and the needs of the hard-of-hearing child were for the most part neglected. Deaf children were educated in residential schools or institutions until the establishment of classrooms in regular schools. More recently, hearing-impaired children as well as profoundly deaf children have been helped in preschool classes, special classrooms, and regular classrooms as well as in residential schools. The educational programs are individualized, and wherever appropriate, mainstreaming is the case. The program for the hearing-impaired child is bolstered by the coordinated efforts of parents, classroom teachers, otologists, educational audiologists, psychologists, and speech-language pathologists.

A PERIOD OF EXPANSION

The decades of the 1940s and the 1950s were times of growth for all aspects of the profession. In 1943 the American Medical Association requested that a list of ethical speech correction schools and clinics be provided for distribution to physicians. During World War II the entire membership was listed in the National Roster of Scientific Personnel. The organization that started life in 1926 as The American Academy of Speech Correction with 25 dedicated and determined individuals changed its name in 1948 to The American Speech and Hearing Association and in 1979 to The American Speech-Language-Hearing Association. Its membership had increased to 1,144 persons in 1948 (Paden, 1970), in 1978 the membership was reported to be 27,642 and in 1985 over 45,000.

The official publication, *Journal of Speech Disorders,* was first published in 1936 at Ohio State University with G. Oscar Russell as editor. In 1957 the American Speech and Hearing Association established a permanent national office and appointed a professional executive secretary, Kenneth Johnson. In 1959 an employment bulletin, *Trends,* and a monthly professional magazine, *Asha,* were published.

Speech Improvement

School programs designed to help all children develop the ability to communicate effectively in acceptable speech, voice, and language patterns were first called *speech improvement* programs. Such programs were usually carried out by the classroom teacher, with the speech-language specialist serving as a consultant and doing demonstration teaching in the classroom. Many such programs were initiated in the 1920s, 1930s, and 1940s and were concentrated on the kindergarten and first-grade levels. One of the purposes was to reduce the number of minor speech problems.

The programs were not considered part of the school clinician's regular duties in many states. However, in some cities, speech improvement programs were carried out successfully despite lack of state support. According to Garrison and colleagues (1961), the communities of Arlington County, Virginia; Brea, California; Des Moines, Iowa; Hartford, Connecticut; Hingham, Massachusetts; New York City; Wauwatosa, Wisconsin; Wichita, Kansas; and Youngstown, Ohio, were recognized as having well-organized speech improvement programs.

In recent years the philosophy of the speech, language, and hearing profession has expanded to include prevention of problems. Programs may be carried out on the kindergarten and the primary-grade level or on the high-school level. They are usually planned and implemented cooperatively with the classroom teacher.

It was also during these decades that the public school programs increased and expanded, both professionally and geographically. School clinicians found themselves wearing many hats. In addition to selling the idea of such a program to the school system and the community, the clinician had to

Devise a set of forms to be used for record keeping and reporting

Locate the children with speech and hearing handicaps

Schedule them for therapy after talking with their teachers for the most convenient time for all concerned

Provide the diagnosis and the therapy

Work with the school nurse on locating the children with hearing losses

Counsel the parents

Answer hundreds of questions from teachers who were often totally unfamiliar with such a program

Keep the school administration informed

Confer with persons in other professional disciplines

And, at the same time, remain healthy, well groomed, trustworthy, modest, friendly, cheerful, courteous, patient, enthusiastic, tolerant, cooperative, businesslike, dependable, prompt, creative, interesting, and unflappable

Furthermore, the clinician had to keep one eye on the clock and the calendar and the other eye on state standards.

IMPROVEMENT IN QUALITY

The growth in numbers of clinicians serving the schools was steady during the 1950s and the 1960s. That era concentrated on the improvement of quality as well as quantity by emphasizing increased training for clinicians through advanced certification standards set by the American Speech and Hearing Association.

A major project geared toward improving speech and hearing services to children in the schools was undertaken by the U.S. Office of Education, Purdue University, and the Research Committee of the American Speech and Hearing Association (Steer et al., 1961). The major objectives were to provide authoritative information about current practices in the public schools and to identify unresolved problems. On the basis of these findings, priorities were established for identification of urgently needed research. With the cooperation of hundreds of clinicians, supervisors, classroom teachers, and training institution personnel, a list of topics for further study and research was distilled by the work groups. Given highest priority were the following topics: the collection of longitudinal data on speech; comparative studies of program organization (with special attention to the frequency, duration, and intensity of therapy); and comparative studies of the use of different remedial procedures with children of various ages presenting different speech, voice, and language problems.

Six additional topics were also identified and assigned a high priority: the development of standardized tests of speech, voice, and language; the development of criteria for selection of primary-grade children for inclusion in remedial programs; comparative studies of speech improvement and clinical programs; comparative studies of group, individual, and combined group and individual therapy programs; studies of the adjustment of children and their language usage in relation to changes in speech accomplished during participation in therapy programs; and comparative studies of different curricula and clinical training programs for prospective public school speech and hearing personnel.

The study also addressed itself to such topics as the professional roles and relationships of the school clinician, the supervision of programs, diagnosis and measurement, and the recruitment of professional personnel to meet the growing needs of the communicatively handicapped in the schools.

THE QUIET REVOLUTION

Things were changing rapidly in the late 1960s and early 1970s for school programs, and the "quiet revolution" referred to by O'Toole and Zaslow (1969) became less quiet as the school speech-language specialists talked about breaking the cycle of mediocrity, lowering caseloads, giving highest priority to the most severe cases, scheduling on intensive cycles rather than intermittently, extending programs throughout the summer, utilizing diagnostic teams, and many other issues. The emphasis had shifted, slowly but surely, from quantity to quality.

The appointment in 1969 by the American Speech and Hearing Association of a full-time staff member to serve as Associate Secretary for School/Clinic Affairs; the publication in 1971 of *Language, Speech and Hearing Services in Schools;* and the appointment by ASHA of a standing committee on Language, Speech and Hearing Services in Schools all attest to the recognition of the public school speech-language specialist as a large and important part of the profession.

It was not the professional organization's thinking alone that brought about the many changes. Outside influences—mainly the changes in the philosophy and conditions surrounding the American educational system—began to effect changes in the profession. Increased populations, tightened school budgets, focus on the lack of reading skills in the elementary school, more attention to special populations such as the mentally retarded and the socially and economically disadvantaged child—all had an impact.

FEDERAL LEGISLATION

In 1954 the U.S. Supreme Court's decision in the case of *Brown* vs. *Board of Education* set into motion a new era and struck down the doctrine of segregated education. This decision sparked such issues as women's rights; the right to education and treatment for the handicapped; and the intrinsic rights of individuals, including blacks and minority groups.

Parent organizations have long been a catalyst in bringing about change, and in the case of handicapped children they were certainly no exception. According to Reynolds and Rosen (1976)

> Parents of handicapped children began to organize about thirty years ago to obtain educational facilities for their offspring and to act as watchdogs of the institutions serving them. At first, the organizations concentrated on political action; since 1970, however, they have turned to the courts. This fact may be more important than any other in accounting for the changes in special education that are occurring now and are likely to occur in the near future.

The PARC Case

An extension of the *Brown* vs. *Board of Education* decision, according to Reynolds and Rosen, was the consent decree established in the case of the Pennsylvania Association for Retarded Children. This decree stated that no matter how serious the handicap, every child has the right to education. The PARC case established the right of parents to become involved in making decisions concerning their child and stipulated that education must be based on programs appropriate to the needs and capacities of each individual child.

Mainstreaming

One of the unexpected aftermaths of the PARC case was to place the stamp of judicial approval on *mainstreaming*. According to Reynolds and Rosen (p. 558)

> Mainstreaming is a set or general predisposition to arrange for the education of children with handicaps or learning problems within the environment provided for all other children—the regular school and normal home and community environment—whenever feasible.

The intent of mainstreaming is to provide handicapped children with an appropriate educational program in as "normal" or "regular" an environment as possible. Thus, depending on the nature and/or severity of the handicapping condition, the child may be in a self-contained classroom or a regular classroom for all or part of the educational program, in other words, in the "least restrictive environment."

Mainstreaming has special implications for the regular classroom teacher as well as other personnel involved in the education of children with handicaps. Reynolds and Rosen (pp. 557–58) say

> Obviously, mainstreaming makes new demands on both regular classroom and special education teachers. In the past, a regular education teacher was expected to know enough about handicapping conditions to be able to identify children with such problems for referral out of the classroom into special education settings. At the same time, special education teachers were trained to work directly with the children with certain specific handicaps (as in the days of residential schools) in separate special settings.
>
> Under mainstreaming, different roles are demanded for both kinds of teachers. The trend for training special education teachers for indirect resource teacher roles rather than narrow specialists is well established in many preparation centers. Concurrently, programs are underway to provide regular education teachers with training in the identification of learning problems. At the local school level, regular and special education teachers in mainstreamed programs are no longer isolated in separate classrooms. They work together in teams to share knowledge, skills, observations, and experiences to enhance the programs for children with special problems, whether the children are permanently or temporarily handicapped. Thus, it has become essential for special teachers to learn the skills of consultation and for both teachers to learn techniques of observation as well as communication.

Bureau of Education for the Handicapped

In 1967 the Congress created the Bureau of Education for the Handicapped and began a program of grants to speed the development of educational programs.

In 1974, Edwin W. Martin, then director of the Bureau of Education for the Handicapped, in an address to the members of the American Speech and Hearing Association, stated that he did not feel we were successfully integrating our roles as speech and hearing specialists in the educational system.

He urged that speech-language pathologists and audiologists in schools must be actively involved in interdisciplinary efforts with parents, learning disability specialists, administrators, guidance counselors, classroom teachers, and all educational colleagues.

FEDERAL LEGISLATION: PUBLIC LAW 94-142

On November 29, 1975, the most sweeping and significant change concerning the education of handicapped children took place when President Gerald Ford signed Public Law 94-142. The law, usually referred to as the Education for All Handicapped Children Act, defined the scope of speech-language pathology and audiology services within the public schools. These services were summarized by Dublinske and Healey (1978) as follows:

1. Identification of children with speech or language disorders
2. Diagnosis and appraisal of specific speech or language disorders
3. Referral for medical or other professional attention necessary for the habilitation of speech or language disorders
4. Provision of speech and language services for the habilitation or prevention of communicative disorders
5. Counseling and guidance of parents, children, and teachers regarding speech and language disorders

Audiology services include

1. Identification of children with hearing loss
2. Determination of the range, nature, and degree of hearing loss including referral for medical or other professional attention for the habilitation of hearing
3. Provision of habilitative activities such as language habilitation, auditory training, speech reading, hearing evaluation, and speech conversation
4. Creation and administration of programs for prevention of hearing loss
5. Counseling and guidance of pupils, parents, and teachers regarding hearing loss
6. Determination of the child's need for group and individual amplification, selection, and fitting an appropriate aid and evaluating the effectiveness of amplification

The regulations also cover the provision of appropriate administrative and supervisory activities necessary for program planning, management, and evaluation.

Changes in PL 94-142

Since the passage of PL 94-142 those concerned with the education of handicapped children have been busy not only with the implementation of the bill but also with the interpretation of it. As a result, amendments to the bill have been added and in some cases the bill has been challenged in the courts.

In 1983, The Education of the Handicapped Amendments (PL 98-199) changed the category of "speech impaired" to "speech or language impaired."

PL 98-199 also expanded the age range of children who may receive services under the PL 94-142 preschool incentive grant program, adding children from birth to three years of age; however, it does not allow the state to include these children in the child count. Nor does this change require states to serve children from birth to age three, although it does allow states to use federal funds if permitted by state policy.

Therefore, all handicapped individuals from birth to age 21 must be provided special education and/or related services unless this requirement conflicts with state policies.

As we can see from the history and development of school programs in speech, language, and hearing, although many changes were underway, PL 94-142 has given a definite boost to school programs and has provided financial assistance as well as a legal basis for services. Before this time individual states had enacted legislation *permitting* speech services in the schools. PL 94-142, however, *mandated* services.

Section 504

Under the Vocational Rehabilitation Act of 1973, Section 504 (PL 93-112), the individual states must adequately provide for all handicapped persons according to federal regulations and statutes. Because of the fiscal restraints it imposes on agencies and schools that are in noncompliance, Section 504 provides a source of enforcement of PL 94-142.

A more detailed discussion of PL 94-142 is included in Chapter 3.

The impact of PL 94-142 on both the state and the local school district is pervasive and profound. According to Ratliff* PL 94-142 was "conceived by petition, born of legislation and nurtured through litigation." An understanding of PL 94-142 is important to the school speech-language pathologist.

THE CHANGING ROLE OF THE SCHOOL
SPEECH-LANGUAGE PATHOLOGIST

The changes in descriptive terminology are a reflection of the changing role of the school pathologist; indeed, they also reflect the perceptions of the school pathologist's role as viewed by others in the profession.

Ainsworth (1965, p. 495) examined two possible roles of the school pathologist—participant and separatist. He described the separatist role as one that

> looks upon the speech specialist as an independent professional person who is responsible for diagnosing and treating the speech disorders of children in public schools. This point of view assumes that the responsibilities of the specialist are

*Dr. Leslie Ratliff, Identification and Program Development Coordinator, Northwest Ohio Special Education Regional Resource Center, Bowling Green, Ohio, private conversation.

fulfilled when he successfully carries out the clinical activities for which he has been trained.

Regarding the participant's role he stated

This concept is similar to the first in that it views the role of the speech specialist to be that of an independent professional who provides a remedial and therapeutic service to the children in the schools. However, it conceives of additional responsibilities which can be summarized by saying that the speech specialist is obligated to make a direct contribution to, and thus be an integral part of, the on-going educational program. In addition to conducting himself appropriately as a speech pathologist, this specialist is obligated to carry out this work in such a way that it will reinforce and, in turn, be reinforced by appropriate educational activities in the total school program.

After examining both roles, Ainsworth felt that it was neither desirable nor possible for the school clinician to maintain a separatist position and that the child who would be treated as part of the school program would receive better quality care if therapy were integrated into the educational process. Indeed, he felt that an entirely new concept of funding speech therapy would need to be developed if the separatist role were to be the school pathologist's role.

Ainsworth explained that through the years the clinical speech program (under a variety of designations) has been enthusiastically welcomed into the public schools on the basis that it contributed substantially to the total program. He further pointed out that even before the profession emerged as such, public schools were employing such specialists because alleviation of disorders of communication was vital if the child was to be able to take advantage of educational opportunities.

Ainsworth's participant versus separatist article was written in response to two position statements issued by the American Speech and Hearing Association in the publication *Asha*. The first article, issued in April 1962, described the basic services and functions of the school clinician and differentiated this individual from the instructional, curriculum personnel, such as the classroom teacher. The second article, issued in June 1964, also dealt with basic responsibilities. It delineated the speech clinician's role with respect to speech improvement and the broad language-arts skills as being in a consultative relationship with the classroom teacher.

These articles seemed to be directed more to the world outside the profession; hence, Ainsworth felt it appropriate and crucial for the profession as a whole, the pathologists in the schools, and the major professional organization, to look more deeply into the roles and the responsibilities of the speech specialist in the schools.

TERMINOLOGY: WHAT'S IN A NAME?

The historical development of school programs in speech, language, and hearing is interestingly revealed in what titles have been used over the years. The earliest professionals called themselves "speech correctionists." Some who had previously worked in school systems in this capacity were known as "speech teachers," although they were more concerned with habilitation than with elocution. During the 1950s and the 1960s we became "speech and hearing therapists" and "speech and hearing clinicians." All these changes caused no end of trouble, especially in trying to explain ourselves to others.

During the 1970s we became known as "speech pathologists," and in 1977 The American Speech-Language-Hearing Association in a preference survey found that "speech-language pathologist" was the choice of professionals in the field.

How did we get from "speech correctionist" and "speech teacher" to "speech-language pathologist"? The answer is not simple, but perhaps a review of clinical practices may shed some light.

In the 1930s a few universities began programs to train people for clinical roles in public schools and universities. We were "speech correctionists" and "speech teachers." Stuttering problems were the major focus during the earliest days, along with articulation problems. Clinicians were aware of language systems, but problems in that area were treated as speech problems. When faced with children who did not talk, clinicians attempted to stimulate speech by targeting vocal play and babbling. Speech clinicians weren't without their Bryngelson-Glaspey Speech Improvement Cards (1941) or Schoolfield's book *Better Speech and Better Reading* (1937).

Children who did not talk or who had little speech were viewed as having "organic" problems, those related to the brain or neurologic system. Children whose problems in communication yielded to therapy were said to have had "functional" problems. Children who had even minimal vocalization, such as cerebral palsied children or hearing-impaired children, were treated as speech problems. It was at this time the titles of "speech therapist" and "speech and hearing therapist" were used.

Very young children with "delayed speech" and mentally retarded children were excluded from therapy as it was thought they had not reached the proper stage of development to benefit from treatment.

This clinical model was followed for about 30 years, until the late 1950s and early 1960s, when Noam Chomsky's "generative grammar" theories set the stage for the beginning of the profession's understanding of language and language behavior. Although Chomsky offered little help in solving clinical problems, it was at this time that B.F. Skinner's behavioral theories appeared. Speech clinicians still used the functional approach to therapy; however, they did include language-handicapped children on their caseloads for the first time.

One result of these two widely divergent schools of thought was to move the speech clinician's focus away from concentration on phonemes and articulation.

During the 1960s and the 1970s the stimulus-response and reinforcement pattern and "precision therapy" were used to elicit language and speech. These behavior modification methods were widely accepted, and speech clinicians dispensed a great deal of candy.

Chomsky's grammar and Skinner's behaviorism systems prepared the way for the profession's move into semantics and pragmatics and the area of child language. During the 1970s the profession expanded the knowledge base and built on the foundations developed in the 1960s. This had the effect of developing new concepts about language behavior and its component parts.

During the early 1980s children previously excluded from therapy were now included. Children with articulation problems, although still a large part of the speech-language pathologist's caseload in the public schools, now included individuals with severe language deficiencies, language-learning disabilities, mental retardation, motor handicaps, and hearing handicaps. Adding impetus to this development was the passage and implementation of Public Law 94-142.

The U.S. Department of Labor (1979) uses the title "speech pathologist" as its official designation. The American Speech-Language-Hearing Association prefers "speech-language pathologist."

Although some may view the trouble with terminology as an identity crisis affecting an entire profession, it might also be construed as symptomatic of a gradual shift in focus from a preoccupation mainly with articulation problems to an interest in language-learning behavior. It also indicates a widening of the scope of services to include prevention as well as remediation, to hone and fine-tune our individual professional skills, and to see that these skills are delivered in the most efficient and effective way to the appropriate consumer.

THE ROLE OF THE SCHOOL PATHOLOGIST NOW

It is probably safe to say that pathologists in the schools often have been viewed as itinerant workers dealing mainly with functional articulation problems and working with children in groups rather than individually because of high maximum caseload requirements set by state law. Unfortunately, this stereotype has persisted although the school pathologist's role is continually changing. Let us look at the roles and responsibilities of the school speech, language, and hearing specialist.

The school pathologist plans, directs, and provides diagnostic and remediation services to communicatively handicapped children and youth. The pathologist works with articulation, language, voice, disfluency (stuttering), and hearing impairments, as well as speech, language, and hearing problems associated with such conditions as cleft palate, cerebral palsy, intellectual impairment, visual impairment, emotional and behavioral disturbances, autistic behavior, and aphasia.

An important aspect of the school pathologist's duties is cooperation with other school and health specialists, including audiologists, nurses, social workers, physicians, dentists, special education teachers, psychologists, and guidance counselors. Cooperative planning with these individuals on a periodic basis results in effective diagnostic, habilitative, and educational programs for children with communication problems.

The school pathologist works with classroom teachers and resource teachers to implement and generalize remediation procedures for the handicapped child. Working with parents to help them alleviate and understand problems is also a part of the pathologist's function. School administrators are often the key to good educational programming for children, and the school pathologist works with both principals and superintendents toward that end.

The school pathologist may also be a community resource person, providing public information about communication problems and the availability of services for parents and families and for the personnel in both public and voluntary community agencies.

Many school pathologists are engaged in research related to program organization and management, clinical procedures, and professional responsibility. The field of language, speech, and hearing is constantly broadening, and the school pathologist must keep abreast of new information by reading professional journals and publications; attending seminars and conventions; enrolling in continuing education programs; and sharing information and ideas with colleagues through state, local, and national professional organizations.

Frequently school pathologists are asked to help university students by serving as supervisors of student teaching and by providing observational opportunities for students-in-training. The supervision of paraprofessionals and volunteers in school programs is also the responsibility of the school pathologist.

Because the school pathologist is considered an important part of the total educational program, the size, need, and structure of the local school district will have much to do with the organizational model used as well as the nature of the services provided. Many school pathologists work as itinerant persons. Some will be assigned to a single building, whereas others may work in special classes, resource rooms, or self-contained classrooms. Often the school pathologist will be either a full- or part-time member of the pupil evaluation team or a resource consultant to teachers, administrators, or other staff members. Many school pathologists are employed as supervisors or administrators of speech and language programs.

The speech, language, and hearing pathologist also serves high-risk infants in school-operated child development centers; preschoolers in Head Start programs; severely handicapped children in special schools, centers, classes, or home settings; multiply handicapped students in special schools; and elementary-, middle-, and secondary-school pupils.

The role of the school pathologist is changing from that of an itinerant clinician who works with large numbers of children with articulatory problems to that of the specialist in communication disorders. The consultative role is becoming more and more important, and more is required of the school pathologist in the way of diagnosis of speech, language, and hearing problems. Classroom teachers, special teachers, and personnel in other specialized fields will depend on the school pathologist to provide information on diagnoses, assessment, and treatment.

Some school SLPs may be sensitive about the term *specialist.* Freeman (1969) pointed out that the term *special* should not be equated with *superior,* as it implies no superiority over the other school personnel. The school pathologist is a professional specialist in the school, whose role is similar to that of the speech, language, and hearing specialist in the hospital or community agency.

THE FUTURE ROLE OF THE SCHOOL
SPEECH-LANGUAGE PATHOLOGIST

What is the future role of the speech-language pathologist (SLP) in the schools? Undoubtedly a catalyst to programs in the schools and the role of the school pathologist is PL 94-142. In a study of the effectiveness of the law by Hyman (August 1985), seven out of ten respondents having five or more years of experience with children in the schools agreed that the law had improved the quality of speech, language, and hearing services. Approximately 80 percent of this group believed that the law had enhanced the communicatively handicapped child's access to services and that it had served to augment parental involvement in the educational process.

Although the future of the law is uncertain, there is reason to believe that it has set the course of events toward positive goals and that there will be no turning back. There are still many problems to be solved and challenges to be met, and these need to be identified by school SLPs and the profession as a whole.

Donnelly (1984) identified several of these problems, including the following three main areas: first, the changing size and composition of the caseload and how it has led to burnout; second, the imbalance between monies generated by SLP services and those actually spent to support these programs; and third, the professionally compromising position that SLPs often find themselves in because of the school administrator who is unaware of their professional responsibilities, which often include referral to services outside the school.

Donnelly has offered some strategies for coping with these professional problems. In the area of burnout she has suggested that the school SLPs get out of the isolated speech therapy room and work more with pupils in their classrooms, to work more closely with classroom teachers, and to demand from school administrators smaller caseloads in order to offer to any given child the therapy required.

Regarding the amount of money generated by SLP services, Donnelly suggests that the school SLPs should keep abreast of the political information that affects their programs. Communicatively handicapped children constitute the second largest category of handicapped children, second only to learning-disabled children, and therefore generate a very substantial amount of money for school districts. These funds, however, are not always used for SLP services. Donnelly says that these facts should be brought tactfully but knowledgebly to superintendents and others who make budgetary decisions.

The third problem, that of the professionally compromising position, calls for a combination of solutions. First, the school SLP must do what is professionally appropriate and ethical. In addition, the SLP should inform the parents that if the condition in question does not interfere with educational performance, the school district is not liable for payment for treatment by an outside agency. The SLP must also assume the responsibility of educating school personnel concerning the appropriateness of the recommendation. Along this same line, the SLP needs to keep school personnel advised of the availability of services that exist outside the school.

Although there are many problems to be faced by school SLPs and the profession as a whole, there are also exciting and challenging developments. It is difficult to predict how speech-language pathology will be different in the future, but we can make some educated guesses. The makeup of caseloads in the schools will be shifting from a preponderance of articulation problems to language and learning disabilities. More and more children with severe handicaps will be in regular classrooms and many of these children will have speech and/or language problems. There will be an extension of services to preschool children. The role of the SLP as a consultant will be greatly expanded, as will the role as a team member in the school in diagnosis, assessment, and placement. The school SLP will be more and more involved in overall education, in the communicative skills of reading, writing, and spelling as well as in speaking and listening. As has been true in the fields of medicine and dentistry, there will be an emergence of specialists in speech-language pathology and audiology.

Strategies for coping with these changes will have to be met by the school SLP and audiologist as well as by the profession as a whole, and certainly by the professional organization, the American Speech-Language-Hearing Association, and the state speech, language, and hearing groups. At this writing several mitigating developments are emerging for dealing with the expanding roles of the school SLP and audiologist. One is the use of computers and their potential for record keeping and retrieval, for writing programs, and for therapy application.

Another development is the use of paraprofessionals, or communication aides or supportive personnel, as they are also known. The use of supportive personnel has been described by a number of professionals (Alpiner, 1970; Moncur, 1967; Ptacek, 1967) but at this writing has not been fully exploited by SLPs in the schools.

The future of speech-language pathology and audiology in the schools looks bright. Traditionally in the United States, speech, language, and hearing services for children have been offered as a part of the school program, and the bulk of the profession has been employed in the schools. Although in this country we have followed the *educational model,* speech, language, and hearing professionals in other countries have followed the *medical model* and have provided services through health and medical facilities. This is not to say that there are not numerous health, medical, and community agencies throughout the United States providing excellent speech, language, and hearing services. Our system is undoubtedly a reflection of our democratic philosophy of education that children have a right to education and that our function in the schools is to prevent, remove, and alleviate communicative barriers that interfere with the child's ability to profit from the education offered.

In an article originally presented as a paper at an ASHA Regional Workshop for School Specialists, Knight (1970) sounded a confident note for the future of school speech pathology and audiology programs:

> But I have faith in the resilience of the school clinician. I am confident, also, that if we keep our work child-centered instead of clinician-centered, if we capitalize on the elements of our setting which are assets rather than wasting our

energies in complaining about those which are liabilities, and if we demonstrate that we are clinically competent by the excellence of our performance rather than by our insistence on the trappings, we shall continue to improve status both for ourselves and for our profession.

DISCUSSION QUESTIONS AND PROJECTS

1. How does an understanding of the early role of the school speech-language clinician help in understanding the current role?
2. Trace the focus of the profession on specific problems throughout the years. Do you think this has had any relationship to professional terminology?
3. Read Swift's (1972) article. How relevant is it today?
4. Ask ten of your friends, not in the speech-language or hearing field, to comment on the titles by which we have called ourselves and what these titles convey to them. Ask the same questions of elementary education majors at your university.
5. Do you think the changes in the profession were brought about by outside pressures or by internal factors?
6. Read the two position statements by the American Speech and Hearing Association in *Asha* (Committee on Definitions of Public School Speech and Hearing Services, 1962, and Committee on Speech and Hearing Services in Schools, 1964). Then read Ainsworth's (1965) article. Why do you think Ainsworth felt it important to publish this article? How relevant is it today?

TWO
THE PROFESSIONAL SCHOOL SPEECH-LANGUAGE PATHOLOGIST

INTRODUCTION

The Code of Ethics of the American Speech-Language-Hearing Association has established the ground rules for the entire profession. The principles include conduct toward the client, the public, and fellow professionals. Accreditation is the stamp of approval issued by a responsible agency to the individual meeting specific requirements. It confers the right to practice and the right to be recognized as a professional. It also carries with it the responsibility of exemplary professional behavior.

Organizations are important links facilitating the exchange of new ideas, information, research, recent developments, materials, and professional affairs. School pathologists will need to be aware of the various organizations and their functions in order to choose the ones with which they will affiliate.

THE CODE OF ETHICS

One of the first tasks of the American Academy of Speech Correction, as the professional organization was first called, was the establishment of a Code of Ethics. Mindful of the fact that there were unscrupulous individuals who would take advantage of persons with handicapping conditions by making rash promises of cures and by charging exorbitant fees, the earliest members of the profession felt it necessary to maintain professional integrity and encourage high standards by formulating a Code of Ethics. As may be expected, it was a difficult task, and throughout the history of the organization the code has been periodically updated to meet current problems; however, it has remained substantially the same. The code outlines the ASHA member's professional responsibilities to the patient, to co-workers, and to society. Thus, it might be said that accountability has always been one of the profession's highest priorities.

Although the code was adopted for an association, it serves the entire profession. In the language of the code the term *individuals* refers to all members of the American Speech-Language-Hearing Association and those non-members who hold the Certificate of Clinical Competence.

The basis of the code is comprised of six principles of ethics which define professional conduct and form the underlying moral groundwork. The ethical proscriptions are the "thou shalt not" statements of the code. Under Matters of Professional Propriety are listed guidelines of conduct toward the public and potential consumers of the services.

The code has no legal basis except in states where it has been adopted as part of the licensing requirements.

The American Speech-Language-Hearing Association has established an Ethical Practice Board whose major responsibility is the enforcement of the Code of Ethics. A member of ASHA who is a holder of the Certificate of Clinical Competence and who is found guilty of noncompliance may be dropped from membership and have the certificate revoked. A nonmember who is found guilty of noncompliance would face revocation of the certificate. The loss of membership status and/or the revocation of the Certificate of Clinical Competence would follow procedures of due process set up by the Ethical Practice Board. There is also an appeals procedure. A copy of the board's practices and procedures as well as the appeals procedures are printed in the Directory of the American Speech-Language-Hearing Association, 10801 Rockville Pike, Rockville, Maryland 20852. In addition, the association's Code of Ethics is reprinted each year in the January issue of *Asha.* Effective January 1985, that issue also lists all issues in ethics statements that the Board has published to interpret sections of the code. (At the end of this chapter is a list of problems, the solutions to which may be found in the Code of Ethics.)

Following is the revision of the ASHA Code of Ethics, January 1, 1986. Read it carefully.

Code of Ethics of the American Speech-Language-Hearing Association 1986 (Revised January 1, 1986)

Preamble

The preservation of the highest standards of integrity and ethical principles is vital to the successful discharge of the professional responsibilities of all speech-language pathologists and audiologists. This Code of Ethics has been promulgated by the Association in an effort to stress the fundamental rules considered essential to this basic purpose. Any action that is in violation of the spirit and purpose of this Code shall be considered unethical. Failure to specify any particular responsibility or practice in this Code of Ethics should not be construed as denial of the existence of other responsibilities or practices.

The fundamental rules of ethical conduct are described in three categories: Principles of Ethics, Ethical Proscriptions, Matters of Professional Propriety.

1. *Principles of Ethics.* Six Principles serve as a basis for the ethical evaluation of professional conduct and form the underlying moral basis for the Code of Ethics. Individuals* subscribing to this Code shall observe these principles as affirmative obligations under all conditions of professional activity.
2. *Ethical Proscriptions.* Ethical Proscriptions are formal statements of prohibitions that are derived from the Principles of Ethics.
3. *Matters of Professional Propriety.* Matters of Professional Propriety represent guidelines of conduct designed to promote the public interest and thereby better inform the public and particularly the persons in need of speech-language pathology and audiology services as to the availability and the rules regarding the delivery of those services.

Principle of Ethics I

Individuals shall hold paramount the welfare of persons served professionally.

A. Individuals shall use every resource available, including referral to other specialists as needed, to provide the best service possible.
B. Individuals shall fully inform persons served of the nature and possible effects of the services.
C. Individuals shall fully inform subjects participating in research or teaching activities of the nature and possible effects of these activities.
D. Individuals' fees shall be commensurate with services rendered.
E. Individuals shall provide appropriate access to records of persons served professionally.
F. Individuals shall take all reasonable precautions to avoid injuring persons in the delivery of professional services.
G. Individuals shall evaluate services rendered to determine effectiveness.

Ethical Proscriptions

1. Individuals must not exploit persons in the delivery of professional services, including accepting persons for treatment when benefit cannot reasonably be expected or continuing treatment unnecessarily.
2. Individuals must not guarantee the results of any therapeutic procedures, directly or by implication. A reasonable statement of prognosis may be made, but caution must be exercised not to mislead persons served professionally to expect results that cannot be predicted from sound evidence.
3. Individuals must not use persons for teaching or research in a manner that constitutes invasion of privacy or fails to afford informed free choice to participate.
4. Individuals must not evaluate or treat speech, language or hearing disorders except in a professional relationship. They must not evaluate or treat solely by correspondence. This does not preclude follow-up correspondence with

---

*"Individuals" refers to all members of the American Speech-Language-Hearing Association and non-members who hold a Certificate of Clinical Competence from this Association.

persons previously seen, nor providing them with general information of an educational nature.

5. Individuals must not reveal to unauthorized persons any professional or personal information obtained from the person served professionally, unless required by law or unless necessary to protect the welfare of the person or the community.
6. Individuals must not discriminate in the delivery of professional services on any basis that is unjustifiable or irrelevant to the need for and potential benefit from such services, such as race, sex, age, or religion.
7. Individuals must not charge for services not rendered.

Principle of Ethics II

Individuals shall maintain high standards of professional competence.

A. Individuals engaging in clinical practice or supervision thereof shall hold the appropriate Certificate(s) of Clinical Competence for the area(s) in which they are providing or supervising professional services.
B. Individuals shall continue their professional development throughout their careers.
C. Individuals shall identify competent, dependable referral sources for persons served professionally.
D. Individuals shall maintain adequate records of professional services rendered.

Ethical Proscriptions

1. Individuals must neither provide services nor supervision of services for which they have not been properly prepared, nor permit services to be provided by any of their staff who are not properly prepared.
2. Individuals must not provide clinical services by prescription of anyone who does not hold the Certificate of Clinical Competence.
3. Individuals must not delegate any service requiring the professional competence of a certified clinician to anyone unqualified.
4. Individuals must not offer clinical services by supportive personnel for whom they do not provide appropriate supervision and assume full responsibility.
5. Individuals must not require anyone under their supervision to engage in any practice that is a violation of the Code of Ethics.

Principle of Ethics III

Individuals' statements to persons served professionally and to the public shall provide accurate information about the nature and management of communicative disorders, and about the profession and services rendered by its practitioners.

Ethical Proscriptions

1. Individuals must not misrepresent their training or competence.
2. Individuals' public statements providing information about professional services and products must not contain representations or claims that are false, deceptive or misleading.
3. Individuals must not use professional or commercial affiliations in any way that would mislead or limit services to persons served professionally.

Matters of Professional Propriety

1. Individuals should announce services in a manner consonant with highest professional standards in the community.

Principle of Ethics IV

Individuals shall maintain objectivity in all matters concerning the welfare of persons served professionally.

A. Individuals who dispense products to persons served professionally shall observe the following standards:
    (1) Products associated with professional practice must be dispensed to the person served as a part of a program of comprehensive habilitative care.
    (2) Fees established for professional services must be independent of whether a product is dispensed.
    (3) Persons served must be provided freedom of choice for the source of services and products.
    (4) Price information about professional services rendered and products dispensed must be disclosed by providing to or posting for persons served a complete schedule of fees and charges in advance of rendering services, which schedule differentiates between fees for professional services and charges for products dispensed.
    (5) Products dispensed to the person served must be evaluated to determine effectiveness.

Ethical Proscriptions

1. Individuals must not participate in activities that constitute a conflict of professional interest.

Matters of Professional Propriety

1. Individuals should not accept compensation for supervision or sponsorship from the clinical fellow being supervised or sponsored beyond reasonable reimbursement for direct expenses.
2. Individuals should present products they have developed to their colleagues in a manner consonant with highest professional standards.

Principle of Ethics V

Individuals shall honor their responsibilities to the public, their profession, and their relationships with colleagues and members of allied professions.

Matters of Professional Propriety

1. Individuals should seek to provide and expand services to persons with speech, language and hearing handicaps as well as to assist in establishing high professional standards for such programs.
2. Individuals should educate the public about speech, language and hearing processes, speech, language and hearing problems and matters related to professional competence.
3. Individuals should strive to increase knowledge within the profession and share research with colleagues.
4. Individuals should establish harmonious relations with colleagues and mem-

bers of other professions, and endeavor to inform members of related professions of services provided by speech-language pathologists and audiologists, as well as seek information from them.

5. Individuals should assign credit to those who have contributed to a publication in proportion to their contribution.

Principle of Ethics VI

Individuals shall uphold the dignity of the profession and freely accept the profession's self-imposed standards.

A. Individuals shall inform the Ethical Practice Board when they have reason to believe that a member or certificate holder may have violated the Code of Ethics.
B. Individuals shall cooperate fully with the Ethical Practice Board concerning matters of professional conduct related to this Code of Ethics.

Ethical Proscriptions

1. Individuals shall not engage in violations of the Principles of Ethics or in any attempt to circumvent any of them.
2. Individuals shall not engage in dishonesty, fraud, deceit, misrepresentation, or other forms of illegal conduct that adversely reflect on the profession or the individuals' fitness for membership in the profession.

It is important that you read the Code of Ethics because it is there that you will find the answers to many of the vexing problems you will encounter in your day-to-day work.

Under Principles of Ethics I is a statement that says, "Individuals shall hold paramount the welfare of persons served professionally." There is hardly a professional problem that cannot be solved by asking yourself, "What is best for the client?"—not "What is best for me?" or "What is best for the school?" Your role as a speech-language pathologist puts you in the position of a child advocate. In other words, you are on the side of the child, whose best interests are your professional responsibility and for whom you speak.

Deciding what is best means that you will have to look at the needs of the *whole* person. A communication problem cannot be separated from the rest of the individual. The educational, health, psychological, and social aspects will have to be taken into consideration. Fortunately you do not always have to make decisions by yourself because in a school system you will be working closely with the classroom teacher, psychologist, school nurse, physician, social worker, educational audiologist, and other professionals. The decision concerning what is best for the student is therefore a consensus of those in the school, who hold paramount the best interests of that individual.

Another important ethical consideration is confidentiality. You will have access to much information about the student with whom you are working and the child's family. This information is given in trust and should be regarded as confidential. The only other persons with whom you might share this information are other professionals in the school who may be working with the child. Within a school system the school policies usually state that pertinent information may be shared among interested professionals, whereas information that may be conveyed to professionals or agencies *outside* the school system must have the written consent of the parents or guardians.

"Shared information" does not mean idle gossip. A conference with a classroom teacher is not to be carried on in the hallways, over lunch in the teachers' lunchroom, or in the teachers' lounge. When I was supervising student clinicians in the schools, one of the nicest compliments from a classroom teacher about a student was the following: "We like your student teacher very much; she's friendly, professional, and gets along well with everyone, but she certainly is close-mouthed!"

PERSONAL QUALIFICATIONS

The communications disorders profession is a multifaceted one. Some members teach university courses, some supervise in clinics, some administer programs, some provide therapy, some do research, and some are diagnosticians. The SLP who chooses to work in education has the responsibility of preventing, removing, and alleviating communication barriers that may hinder a student from receiving the instruction offered in the classroom. In addition, the school clinician is a resource person to others in the school system. Another role of the school clinician is counselor to the family of the student who has the communication disorder or to that individual.

In addition to the appropriate education and specialized knowledges and skills, what personality traits are desirable for the school SLP, who must wear so many hats? Among the most frequently mentioned are patience, understanding, honesty, adaptability, flexibility, sense of humor, warm and friendly nature, respect for others, acceptance of others, dependability, resourcefulness, and creativity.

The speech-language clinician in the schools is a decision maker. Knowing who you are and what you are and knowing where you fit in will provide the basis from which to make decisions and plans for the school's speech, language, and hearing program and the students enrolled in it.

UNDERSTANDING ACCREDITING AGENCIES

Understanding the various forms of accreditation in speech-language pathology and audiology is part of each person's professional responsibility. To the neophyte pathologist the task of understanding accreditation may seem formidable; however, some basic information may help clarify the situation.

Prerequisite to understanding accreditation is a knowledge of the types of agencies in the United States and their roles in relation to the profession of speech-language pathology and audiology.

The Voluntary Agency

Voluntary agencies have developed in countries with a democratic form of government. The voluntary agency is more clearly identified with the United States than with any other nation and has usually evolved out of an unmet need and a concern for one's fellows. The unmet need may be related to social issues, to leisure time and recreation, or to health. Voluntary health agencies may be related to specific diseases or handicapping conditions. Usually the membership of voluntary agencies is made up of both lay persons (in many cases, parents) and professionals. Examples of voluntary health agencies are the Society for Crippled Children and Adults, the United Cerebral Palsy Association, and the National Multiple Sclerosis Society.

Voluntary agencies are not accrediting agencies in the usual sense of the word; however, they perform extremely vital functions for the handicapped individual.

The Official Agency

The official agency is tax-supported and may be on the city, county, regional, state, state and federal, or federal level. Official agencies cover a myriad of categories, including health, education, welfare, vocation, recreation, and social, and they are interested in the prevention of problems, in research, and in the specific disease category. Examples of official agencies are the city or county health department and the Office of Vocational Rehabilitation. Some official agencies may be accrediting bodies, such as a state department of education.

The Professional Organization

In addition to official and voluntary agencies there are also professional organizations. These, as the name implies, are made up of individuals sharing the same profession. Their goals are the establishment and maintenance of high professional standards, research, recruitment of others into the field, sharing of professional information, and accreditation. Examples are the American Speech-Language-Hearing Association, the American Medical Association, and the American Dental Association.

These various types of agencies often work together in a unique fashion, sometimes motivating each other to carry out specific tasks, often supporting each other financially and in other ways, frequently exchanging services and information and preventing duplication of services. The official agencies and the professional organizations are often accrediting bodies in addition to their other functions.

Accreditation by the American Speech-Language-Hearing Association

One type of accreditation is that issued by the American Speech-Language-Hearing Association (ASHA). Unlike licensing and state certification, it has no legal status, but nevertheless it is recognized by various states and by other professions as authenticating the holder as a qualified practitioner or supervisor. ASHA certification is known as the *Certificate of Clinical Competence* (CCC) and can be obtained by persons who meet specific requirements in academic preparation and supervised clinical experiences and who pass a national comprehensive examination. It may be granted in speech pathology or audiology, and some individuals hold certification in both areas. It permits the holder to provide services in the appropriate area and also to supervise the clinical practice of trainees and clinicians who do not hold certification. In 1977 it was decided that persons who were not members of the association could also obtain the certificate by complying with the requirements.

The CCC is held by individuals who provide services in schools, universities, speech-language and hearing centers, hospitals, clinics, private practice, and other programs throughout the United States, Canada, and many foreign countries.

Information on how to apply may be obtained from the American Speech-Language-Hearing Association, 10801 Rockville Pike, Rockville, Maryland 20852.

State Certification

The SLP who wishes to be employed in the public schools of a specific state must obtain a certificate issued by that state's department of education. The qualifying standards are set by each state and include following a prescribed course of study and fulfilling the practicum requirements. These include both clinical practice in the university clinic or one of its satellites under qualified supervision and student teaching under the supervision of the cooperating school pathologist and the university supervisor. The certification is awarded at the master's level in an increasing number of states and at the bachelor's level in the remainder. Each state has various levels of certification, and moving from one level to another requires additional experience and course work. Information on the certification requirements of each state can be obtained by writing to the office of the state's commissioner of education or its equivalent.

Where requirements are the same, there is reciprocity among the states in regard to certification, and individuals may move from one state to another with a minimum of difficulty. However, there is no state-by-state uniformity in certification standards for public school SLPs, nor is there always conformity to the American Speech-Language-Hearing Association standards (Taylor, 1980). In a survey by Bullett (1985) the results indicated that the majority of the states and the District of Columbia required a bachelor's degree as the minimum degree for certification. The Bullett survey also indicated that minimum clinical practicum hours and certification renewal criteria varied greatly from state to state. A comparison of the Taylor (1980) and Bullett (1985) report indicates a trend toward the requirement of a master's degree for state certification.

Some states have developed their own set of certification standards for professionals in the schools, whereas others have adopted ASHA's. These standards may or may not include a master's degree for certification in states where they have not used the ASHA prototype. It should be pointed out, however, that the local education agencies in cities, towns, or counties may require a master's degree for employment. It is also the perogative of the local education agency (LEA) to require the Certificate of Clinical Competence from ASHA as a condition of employment.

Commenting on the obvious shortcomings in many state certification standards, Flower (1984) stated

> If . . . our profession believes that ASHA certification standards represent "the minimal requirements to train a general practitioner," it is obvious that many state requirements do not reach that minimum. Two equally untenable conclusions are likely. One is that school speech, language, and hearing specialists are subprofessionals. The other is that the delivery of acceptable and appropriate speech, language, and hearing services to students in schools is less demanding of professional competence. Since neither conclusion has any acceptable basis in fact, obviously we must continue efforts to strengthen state education agency credentialing programs.

Licensing

A license to practice a business or profession within the geographical bounds of a specific state is issued by that state's legislature, usually through an appointed autonomous board or council. Licensing came about originally to protect the consumer from unqualified and unscrupulous persons. It is also viewed by some as a way to control growth and income of professional interest groups. Obviously, the laws to create licensure are unique to each state.

In the speech, language, and hearing profession, the licensure board may establish rules for obtaining and retaining a license, continuing one's education, and setting standards for ethical conduct; administer examinations for applicants; and enforce the license law. Usually a fee is charged for the license, which may be renewed yearly.

Another aspect of licensing is the "sunset law," which means that periodically the legislature may review the licensing agency (and other regulating agencies) and recommend whether or not it should be terminated.

Registration

An alternative to licensure is registration, a process by which an individual must meet defined qualifications in order to use a title. Nonqualified persons are not barred from practice but are prevented from presenting themselves to the public as qualified (Grossman, 1979).

In most states school speech-language pathologists are not required to be licensed to practice in the public schools.

Inasmuch as laws regarding licensure change not only from state to state but also from year to year, it is a good idea for the speech-language pathologist and the audiologist who plan to seek employment in a particular state to write to that state's department of education or department of health and human services to learn the current credentialing qualifications.

SUMMARY OF ACCREDITATION AND ACCREDITING AGENCIES

Briefly, those are the four types of certification that directly affect the profession. Certification of one type does not preclude certification in the other three. In fact, most individuals hold several types of accreditation.

In looking at the academic, clinical, and experience requirements of all types of accrediting agencies, you will note that they are almost identical. The academic requirements follow the same pattern, and specific courses can be utilized to fulfill requirements in several types of accreditation. For example, a course in articulation problems can fulfill the requirements for ASHA's Certificate of Clinical Competence, for school certification from the state's department of education, and for a state license.

Table 2–1 may help to clarify the various forms of accreditation in speech-language pathology and audiology.

ORGANIZATIONS

The school SLP has a professional responsibility to keep abreast of new ideas, research, recent developments, materials, publications, and professional affairs. This is a lifelong commitment, and it is part and parcel of what being "professional" means. One way of keeping current and informed is through organizations. Organizations have meetings with speakers, publish journals and newsletters, and provide an excellent way to get to know fellow professionals. Speech-language pathologists in schools often feel isolated even though they are in daily contact with clients and school personnel. This sense of isolation comes from not having enough contact with other speech-language specialists, with whom they can share ideas, information, frustrations, and triumphs.

The oldest professional organization in the field of speech, language, and hearing is the American Speech-Language-Hearing Association, which at this writing has over 45,000 members. This organization has been one of the chief agents for growth and development in the profession. The association publishes *The Journal of Speech and Hearing Disorders; The Journal of Speech and Hearing Research; Language, Speech and Hearing Services in Schools;* and *Asha.* Students are encouraged to affiliate with the National Student Speech-Language-Hearing Association (NSSLHA), which offers many opportunities not otherwise available to individuals in training. It is an affiliate of ASHA, with chapters in colleges and universities.

The Public School Caucus is an organization comprised of individuals in private and public school settings. It serves as a support group and information network that focuses on relevant school issues on the local and national levels. The group maintains a close working relationship with the American Speech-Language-Hearing Association's Committee on Speech, Language and Hearing Services in the Schools and is represented on ASHA's legislative council. PSC publishes a quarterly newsletter, holds membership meetings annually at the ASHA convention, and a PSC representative from each state is appointed to serve as an advocate for and liason between local and national memberships. Public School Caucus members are committed to increasing the school professionals' voice in matters that concern their work and recognition of the school speech-language pathologist's contribution and role. Information concerning membership may be obtained from the national office of ASHA.

TABLE 2-1 Accreditation and Accrediting Agencies

ACCREDITING AGENCY	FORM OF ACCREDITATION	POSSIBLE HOLDER
American Speech-Language-Hearing Association	Certificate of Clinical Competence in Speech-Language Pathology and/or Audiology	Person who wishes to be identified by the American Speech-Language-Hearing Association as a qualified practitioner and/or supervisor in speech-language or audiology. Requires meeting ASHA standards, including a master's degree and passing an examination.
State of _____ Department of Education	Certificate to practice in the public schools of the State of _____	Person who wishes employment in the State of _____ as a speech-language pathologist and/or audiologists in an educational facility. Requires meeting state certification standards.
State of _____ Board of Speech-Language Pathology and Audiology	License to provide speech, language, and/or audiology services in the State of _____	Person wishing to practice in a voluntary or official agency (except specifically named educational facilities) or practice privately in the State of _____. Requires meeting state board standards and passing an examination.
State of _____ Board of Health or Health Occupations Council	Registration to use title of Speech-Language Pathologist and/or Audiologist	Person who wishes to use title of Speech-Language Pathologist and/or Audiologist in the State of _____. Does not bar a person from practicing but does require defined qualifications for registration.

Another organization with which the school speech-language pathologist may want to affiliate is the Division for Children With Communication Disorders, an associate of the Council for Exceptional Children. This organization publishes the *Journal of Childhood Communication Disorders,* holds state and national meetings, and is organized as a state group in many states. The business of DCCD is conducted by officers elected by the membership and has representation on the CEC's Board of Governors and Delegate Assembly. There are student chapters on many college campuses.

Every state has its professional organization, which holds conventions, publishes journals, sponsors continuing education programs, and offers short courses. The state organizations also publish directories of members' names and professional addresses. A listing in a professional directory authenticates the member.

In addition to the state organizations, the state may contain regional organizations. Affiliation with the regional group provides an invaluable opportunity for exchange of information and offers support to individual members. Involvement in such groups is both rewarding and enjoyable.

The national as well as state and local speech, language, and hearing professional organizations are concerned with such things as research, the study of human communication and its disorders, the investigation of therapeutic and diagnostic procedures, and the maintenance of high standards of performance. The professional organizations are also interested in the dissemination of information among its members and the upholding of high ethical standards to protect the consumer. There are other benefits to be derived from affiliating with a professional organization. Such a group can provide a forum for discussion of issues and can speak with a concerted voice on matters of professional interest. If the professional individual wishes to have a voice in decisions and opinions, the best way to do so is through a professional organization on the state, local, or national level.

There are a number of other professional organizations with which the school clinician may wish to become affiliated. Membership in other professional groups provides opportunities for valuable exchanges of information and enhances cooperation and understanding. Here are the names and addresses of some of the organizations you may wish to know more about:

Acoustical Society of America, 335 East 45th Street, New York, New York 10010

Alexander Graham Bell Association for the Deaf, Inc., 3417 Volta Place NW, Washington D.C. 20007

American Academy for Cerebral Palsy, University Hospital School, Iowa City, Iowa 52240

American Cleft Palate Association, Administrative Office, 331 Salk Hall, University of Pittsburgh, Pittsburgh, Pennsylvania 15261

American Speech-Language-Hearing Association, 10801 Rockville Pike, Rockville, Maryland 20852

Association for Children with Learning Disabilities, 5225 Grace Street, Pittsburgh, Pennsylvania 15236

Bureau for Education of the Handicapped, 400 6th Street, Donohoe Building, Washington D.C. 20202

Council for Exceptional Children, 1920 Association Drive, Reston, Virginia 22091

Division for Children with Communication Disorders, 1920 Association Drive, Reston, Virginia 22091

Division for Children with Learning Disabilities, 1920 Association Drive, Reston, Virginia 22091

Down's Syndrome Congress, 8509 Wagon Wheel Road, Alexandria, Virginia 22309

National Association for Hearing and Speech Action, 814 Thayer Avenue, Silver Springs, Maryland 20901

National Easter Seal Society for Crippled Children and Adults, 2023 West Ogden Avenue, Chicago, Illinois 60612

National Society for Autistic Children, 169 Tampa Avenue, Albany, New York 12208

United Cerebral Palsy Association, 66 East 34th Street, New York, New York 10016

DISCUSSION QUESTIONS AND PROJECTS

1. You are the school SLP. What do you do in these situations:

   A parent asks you to continue therapy with a child even though the child has reached optimum improvement. The parent says that the child enjoys therapy and it would be traumatic to terminate the therapy. The parent offers to pay you for continuing to see the child.

   A local hearing-aid dealer asks you to supply a list of the students in the school with hearing losses.

   An elementary teacher asks if she may see the records and reports of a junior high-school student enrolled in therapy. She asks your opinion concerning whether or not the student is mentally retarded. (The child isn't.) She doesn't tell you that she is the student's aunt.

   You are asked to do private after-school therapy with a child enrolled in a school in which you are working. The child is already receiving therapy and is on your caseload.

   The parents of a student referred for medical evaluation ask you to recommend a doctor.

   You are asked to do therapy in the school with a student who is currently receiving therapy at a nearby private speech, language, and hearing center. You are aware of this, but the parents did not provide you with this information.

2. Find out what your state department of education standards are in relation to what is required for certification as a speech-language pathologist in the schools.

3. Find out if your state has licensing or registration for school speech, language and hearing professionals. If so, what are the requirements?

4. Find out what speech, language and hearing organizations are active in your area. Check to learn how often meetings are held and what types

of programs are presented. Invite an officer of a local organization to speak to your class.

5. Is there a state speech, language and hearing organization in your state? When do they hold meetings? Do they publish journals and newsletters?

6. What are the advantages in joining the National Student Speech-Language-Hearing Association?

THREE
FOUNDATION
OF THE PROGRAM

INTRODUCTION

This chapter contains basic information about the factors that need to be considered in planning and organizing a school speech-language program. It should be understood that the information about the structure of the school system is general. You, as the school speech-language pathologist, should acquaint yourself with the structure of the educational system in the state in which you live and work. The same is true about the city, county, or district school system in which you are employed. In fact, if you are considering a specific site for future employment it is a good idea to learn as much as possible before you sign a contract; then continue to increase your knowledge as you go along.

Public Law 94-142 has had a tremendous effect on school programming. As you read through this book you will find frequent references to it. The future of the law may be uncertain, and changes are occurring even as you are reading this book. But the essence of the law will remain. Your task will be to keep abreast of the changes and developments of PL 94-142 and the state laws affecting your school speech, language, and hearing program.

Public schools are supported by state and local taxes as well as federal flow-through funds. It is important to be knowledgeable about how your program is supported, how budgets are determined, and the process by which funds are allocated. In some cases the input of the SLP is required or expected and in some instances you may wish to have input. Without a knowledge of how schools and programs are financed the SLP is at a serious disadvantage.

Another factor in planning a speech, language, and hearing program is the number of students with whom you will be dealing. It would be nice if these figures were conveniently available, but unfortunately determining prevalence figures is a complex and slippery matter. The best we can do is to rely on all the current information at hand and make generalizations that apply to individual school systems. Much more attention is given to determining prevalence figures at the present time than in the past, and the developments in this area are promising.

THE ORGANIZATIONAL STRUCTURE OF THE SCHOOL SYSTEM

The Program on the State Level

Because of our democratic philosophy of education we are committed to the idea of education for all. The major responsibility for education rests with each state rather than with the federal government. Through a state board of education, policies, regulations, rules, and guidelines are set. The laws for education in each state are enacted through the state legislatures, and money is appropriated through this body. A state superintendent of instruction is the chief education officer in each state. A state department of education is responsible for carrying out and developing policies, regulations, and standards related to schools. Figure 3–1 depicts the jurisdictional relationship between the state and the local educational agencies (Rebore, 1984).

State departments of education provide state consultants in various areas of special education. The responsibilities of the consultants in speech, language, and hearing may vary slightly from state to state, but in general the tasks are similar throughout the nation. A major task of the professional staff on the state level is to monitor and enforce minimum standards in local programs that are partially or fully reimbursed with state money. Along with this local programs are encouraged to approach optimal goals in serving the needs of handicapped students. The state staff may provide leadership and assistance in identifying, developing, and maintaining optimal standards. Some of the ways in which professional leadership may be exerted by the state consultants in assisting local programs include the following (*Rules for the Education of Handicapped Children* 1982):

A.   Professional literature and materials
  1.   Establish procedures by which local materials can be exchanged.
  2.   Periodically prepare a selected bibliography of significant materials.
  3.   Write or prepare materials that are needed but not available.
B.   Preservice education programs
  1.   Identify unmet needs in university and staff program.
  2.   Serve as an instructor on an emergency basis.

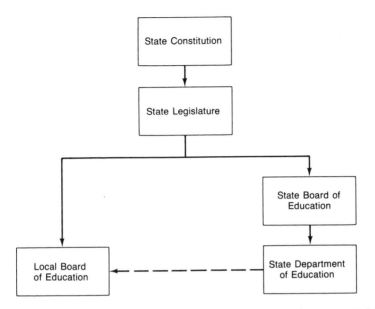

FIGURE 3-1   Jurisdictional Flow Chart. From Ronald W. Rebore, Sr., A HANDBOOK FOR SCHOOL BOARD MEMBERS, 1984, p. 5. Reprinted by permission of Prentice-Hall, Englewood Cliffs, New Jersey.

    3. Serve as a resource person for university students and instructors.
    4. Assist in the development of new professional curricula.
    5. Assist in the evaluation and improvement of existing professional curriculum.
C. Inservice education programs
    1. Provide professional field services.
    2. Conduct and encourage area professional meetings.
    3. Encourage and assist professional organizations.
    4. Encourage and stimulate development of appropriate non-credit workshops and courses.
D. Research studies and experimental projects
    1. Identify research needs.
    2. Initiate and conduct research studies and experimental projects.
    3. Promote and encourage research studies and experimental projects.
    4. Interpret and disseminate findings and conclusions.
E. Professional relations at the local state and national level
    1. Maintain membership in professional organizations.
    2. Attend meetings of professional organizations.
    3. Contribute to journals of professional organizations.
    4. Provide leadership for professional organizations.
F. Appropriate and desirable criteria for optimal special education
    1. Initiate procedures by which these criteria can be identified.
    2. Encourage schools to use the criteria in self-evaluation.
    3. Utilize criteria in professional field services.

G. Extension of present programs in special education
    1. Identify unmet needs within present standards.
    2. Assist local district in establishing new programs or expanding established program.
H. Identification of emerging needs for new programs in special education
    1. Identify unmet needs not now provided for within existing standards.
    2. Encourage and stimulate the development of pilot studies and experimental programs.
    3. Evaluate results of studies and submit recommendations for needed modifications in existing law and standards.

Public Law 94-142 requires each state to submit an annual plan, which is to be approved by the U.S. Department of Education. Each of the components of the act is addressed in the state's plan with a description of the process by which the requirements will be met. One of the responsibilities of the state education agency is to monitor and evaluate the activities of the local education agency to assure compliance with the federal statutes.

In addition, the state education agency is responsible for the proper use of federal funds in the administration of local programming for handicapped children. The state education agency is also responsible for the following activities in regard to PL 94-142: (1) the adoption of complaint procedures, (2) the disbursement of federal funds, (3) an annual report on the number of children served and the criteria for counting them, (4) the establishment of a state advisory committee on the education of handicapped children, (5) a comprehensive system of personnel development, and (6) records on all the activities related to PL 94-142.

REGIONAL RESOURCE CENTERS

An important linkage between the state and the local school districts is the regional resource center. The Ohio Division of Special Education, for example, recognized that a state agency cannot relate to each individual teacher, supervisor, and school district. Under PL 94-142, Title VI-B, Amended Annual Program Plan, the Ohio Department of Education utilized the discretionary portion of Title VI-B to fund the Special Education Regional Resource Center (SERRC) system (*Operation and Management Plan for the Northwest Ohio Special Education Regional Resource Center,* 1983). The SERRCs:

> Assist school systems in the initiation and expansion of programs and services for handicapped children through joint planning and cooperation among school systems to serve an increased number of handicapped children.
>
> Serve as the mechanism by which school systems will plan, organize and implement an effective regional identification and child find strategy to insure that all handicapped children residing in Ohio who need special education will be identified, located, and evaluated so that appropriate programs and services can be planned and provided.
>
> Provide school systems with resources designed to improve the quality of in-

struction for handicapped children through a materials delivery and inservice training based on newly developed instructional materials and methodologies.

Provide school systems with technical assistance in interpreting, implementing, and complying with legislative mandates, rules and regulations.

Serve as a catalyst for product development and dissemination of information which meets the needs of special educators, parents and the handicapped.

Serve as a clearing house for information pertaining to special education.

THE PROGRAM ON THE LOCAL LEVEL

On the local level, school systems are organized into school districts. In some states these are known as *intermediate units*. The district, or intermediate unit, is a geographical area and may cross county lines. It is governed by a superintendent, who is the chief administrative officer, and a district board of education, which is elected by the people of the district and is responsible for developing and establishing policies.

The superintendent is the chief personnel officer for the school system in that he or she makes recommendations to the board concerning the hiring, promotion and dismissal of staff members. The superintendent is responsible for the total operation and maintenance of the school system; leadership of the professional staff; and administration of the clerical, secretarial, transportation, and custodial staffs.

The basic responsibility for each school system rests with the citizens of that community inasmuch as they elect the school board. The school board selects the superintendent, who recommends the needed staff to operate the schools.

Depending on the size of the school system, there may be assistant superintendents who have specific areas of responsibility, such as finance or buildings and grounds.

The structure of individual school systems may vary from state to state and from community to community. Usually there are directors of elementary education and of secondary education. There may be directors of pupil personnel services, instructional program services, special education services, child accounting and attendance, guidance and health services, and others.

Each principal is responsible for supervising the professional and support-services staff assigned to that building. The role and function of the elementary-school principal will differ from that of the middle- and secondary-school principal. In addition, roles and functions of principals will vary according to the unique characteristics of the community and will reflect the various cultural backgrounds of the students and their parents. The principal is responsible for managing the school's instructional program, pupil personnel services, support services, and community relations.

Figure 3–2 is a partial organizational chart of the school system on the local level.

An understanding of the structure of the school system is necessary for the speech, language, and hearing specialist to function effectively. Obviously

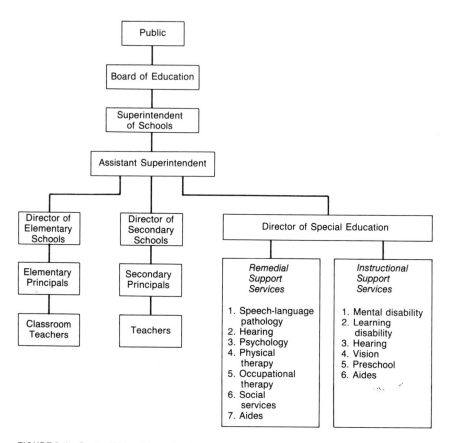

FIGURE 3-2   Partial Table of Organization on the Local Level.

there will be variations in organizational structures throughout the country; thus in addition to having a general knowledge of the school system, you, as the SLP, will need to be familiar with the educational facility in which you are employed.

PUBLIC LAW 94-142

The Education for all Handicapped Children Act of 1975 mandates a free, appropriate public education for all handicapped children and youth. Special education and related services must be provided at no cost to the child or parents.

The act provides:

1. All handicapped children and their parents are guaranteed due process with regard to identification, evaluation, and placement.

2. A written individualized education plan must be developed and implemented for each child receiving special services.
3. To the greatest extent possible handicapped children should be educated with nonhandicapped children in the least restrictive environment appropriate to the child's needs.
4. There are two priorities among handicapped children: (a) those not currently receiving any education and (b) those with the most severe handicaps within each disability who are receiving an inadequate education.
5. The federal government is committed to assuming up to 40 percent of the excess costs incurred in providing the programs for handicapped children.
6. The local education agencies are responsible for providing the appropriate educational programs.
7. The local education agencies are responsible for periodic review and monitoring of such programs.
8. Local education agencies must file a written plan clearly stating the procedures involved in meeting the provisions of the mandatory law. These include (a) a child-find process, (b) nondiscriminatory testing and evaluation, (c) the goals and timetable of the plans, (d) guarantee of complete due process procedures, and (e) a guarantee to protect the confidentiality of data and information.

Not only are handicapped children eligible for appropriate educational programs but they are also eligible for all extracurricular activities such as music, art, and debate. The costs of educating handicapped children are borne by the school system. When the child's school cannot provide the appropriate educational placement, the local school system must pay for transportation, tuition, and room and board if the child is enrolled in a residential or tuition-based program.

Public Law 94-142 also states that the handicapped child has the right to a nondiscriminatory evaluation of educational needs. Tests and evaluation materials must not be culturally discriminatory and must be administered in the predominate language spoken in the home. The evaluation is administered by a team of professionals and must include the child's parents and/or guardians.

The heart of PL 94-142 is the Individualized Education Plan, or as it is more familiarly known, the IEP. The concept of the IEP is hardly new because over the years competent clinicians have been doing what the law now mandates. Essentially the law requires that an IEP be developed for *each* handicapped child and reviewed jointly by a qualified school official, the student's teacher or teachers, the parents or guardians, and when appropriate, the student.

Parents as Team Members

Public Law 94-142 clearly gives parents a much greater voice than they previously had in the decisions regarding the education of their children.

The rights and responsibilities of the parents are described under the *due process* section of the handicapped child law in the various states. Due process gives the parents the right to have full status at the meeting. They have a right to question why any one procedure is necessary, why one may be selected over another, how a procedure is carried out, and whether or not there are alternative procedures. If parents disagree with the recommended procedures they have the right of review with an impartial judge. The purpose of due process is to give parents the right to have the school system explain to them and defend the recommended procedures. It does not necessarily make the parents adversaries to the system.

On the other side of the coin, the parents have the responsibility of dealing openly and honestly with the school system, accurately describing their child's behavior and reasonably and realistically requesting services (Sherr, 1977).

Under due process the parents are entitled to the following procedures:

1. A written notice before any action is taken or recommended that may change the child's school program
2. A right to examine all records related to the identification, evaluation, or placement of the child
3. A chance to voice any complaints regarding any matters related to the educational services the child is receiving
4. An impartial hearing before a hearing officer or a judge in the event that the school and the parents cannot agree on the type of school program for the child
5. An adequate appeals procedure if parents are not satisfied with the due process procedure. The case may be taken to the state department of education or finally to a court of law.

Each state has its own guidelines relating to due process, and a copy of these may be obtained either from the state's special education department or from a concerned citizens group within the state. A copy of PL 94-142 may be obtained by contacting your senator or member of congress or by writing to the Superintendent of Documents, U.S. Government Printing Office, Washington, D.C. 20402.

FUNDING FOR SCHOOL SPEECH, LANGUAGE, AND HEARING SERVICES

Who pays for speech, language, and hearing services in the schools? Not surprisingly the answer is that everyone who pays taxes pays for the schools and their many services. Local education agencies are supported in part from local taxes, with reimbursement from state foundation programs. In recent years the federal government through PL 94-142 has reimbursed states for a portion of the expenditures for special education.

States have set minimal standards for speech education programs including speech, language, and hearing. The standards may cover such areas as personnel qualifications, housing, facilities, equipment, materials, transportation, caseload, and case size. Failure to comply with state standards may result in the loss of foundation money to the school district.

According to Jones and Healey (1975) there are three types of reimbursement to the local education agency; unit per pupil, and special. Each state has its unique features in funding patterns, but according the Healey they fall within these three categories.

A. Unit reimbursement
    1. Pure unit
        a. Per professional
        b. With stipulations (class size, number of regular class units)
    2. Percentage
        a. Salaries, transportation, materials, equipment, and so on
        b. Provision for proration
    3. Straight sum
        a. Specified personnel-type allotments
        b. Provision for materials and equipment
B. Per-pupil reimbursement
    1. Straight sum
        a. Specific sum for each disability area
        b. ADA-based or ADM-based
    2. Excess cost
    3. Weighted formula
C. Special reimbursement
    1. Instructional materials and equipment
    2. Transportation
    3. Facilities
    4. Research and experimentation
    5. Personnel training
    6. Pupil assessment
    7. Residential care
    8. Extended school year
    9. Specific personnel
        a. Administrators and supervisors
        b. Teachers and specialists
        c. Paraprofessionals
        d. Ancillary services (physicians, audiologists,* psychologists, social workers, and so on)

"ADA-based" refers to average daily attendance, and "ADM-based" means average daily membership. The terms are identical in meaning. Because school attendance is compulsory all schools must report the attendance each day. At some point in the school year, usually in October and February, the ADA is determined.

A "unit" may be defined as a specific number of students or a special class. In Ohio, for example, (*Rules for the Education of Handicapped Children,* 1982) a unit for a speech-language pathologist may be approved on the basis of 2,000 children in "average daily membership." Therefore, a school system with a total population of 6,000 students would be eligible for three

---

*In states where audiologists are not employed in the schools and services by these professionals are obtained through contractual arrangements.

full-time SLPs. Or a school system with a population of 5,000 students would be eligible for two and one-half units, which would be two full-time and one half-time SLP.

"Per pupil reimbursement" means that the local education agency is compensated for each student receiving special education services. This could be based on ADA or ADM.

A "special reimbursement" plan usually supplements a unit or per-pupil reimbursement. For example in Ohio a special unit for speech-language pathology may be approved on the basis of 50 multihandicapped, hearing handicapped, or orthopedic and/or other health handicapped children in special class or learning center units.

PREVALENCE AND INCIDENCE:
HOW MANY CHILDREN ARE WE TALKING ABOUT?

The prevalence figures of speech, language, and hearing problems, or the number of persons affected at a given time, are difficult to obtain. Incidence figures, the number of new cases occurring during a given time period, are usually not available. The terms *prevalence* and *incidence* are often used interchangeably, and persons reading reports should be aware of this.

Why is it important for prevalence figures to be known? One of the most crucial reasons is that programs for children to 21 years of age are based on the number presently being served and those to be served in the future. Because the infusion of money into states by the federal government under PL 94-142 is based on prevalence figures, these figures should be available and as accurate as possible.

Not only is it important for planners on the state and national levels to have prevalence information but it is important on the local level as well. The school speech-language pathologist needs to know approximately how many students in a given school population can be expected to be eligible for speech, language, and hearing services. The principal needs to know because of space requirements. The superintendent needs to know so that an adequate number of speech-language pathologists may be hired.

The problem of attempting to ascertain the numbers of school-age children with speech and hearing handicaps was a huge one in the early days of school programs. As Milisen (1971) stated, "Early workers had to demonstrate the number of people who had disabling speech handicaps before superintendents would hire clinicians and before college presidents would allow courses in speech pathology to be listed in their curricula." Milisen further suggested that once the need for speech rehabilitation was established by incidence figures, the study of incidence could then be directed toward the solutions of other problems.

Unfortunately, determining the number of speech-disordered individuals is not simply a matter of taking a head count. The complicating factors present in the early days of the profession are still with us today and have become even more complex.

Johnson (1959), stated that 4 percent of school-age children have severe speech and hearing impairments. His report stated that the figures were based on a total estimate of 40 million school children (5 to 17 years of age inclusive) in the United States as of October 1957. He cautiously advised that this was probably an underestimate but that he felt it better to be conservative in view of the fact that the data currently available were not adequate to support precise estimates.

In a study prepared by the Committee on Legislation of the American Speech and Hearing Association (1959), it was estimated that 5 percent of school-age children and 1.3 percent of children under five have speech problems. In addition, 0.7 percent of school-age children and 0.3 percent of preschool-age children were estimated to have handicapping hearing problems. These populations did not include Alaska, Hawaii, or Puerto Rico.

The committee stated, "The above estimates are believed to be conservative, and in each instance err on the side of underestimating the number of children with speech and hearing problems. For example, it should be noted that only children with significant or handicapping hearing losses are included above. An additional one million school children have non-handicapping reductions in hearing acuity."

A national study of disorders among school-age children (Hull, 1969) included 40,000 pupils and was based on a random demographic sample. It covered overall speech patterns, articulation, voice, fluency, and hearing and was also broken down by grade levels. Despite some limitations this survey has provided us with important information about the communication disorders in public schools (see Table 3-1).

In regard to the incidence of language problems, Jones and Healey (1973) observed, "The incidence and prevalence of language and language learning problems are not known. Only recently has there been increased awareness of

**TABLE 3-1   Communication Disorders
in the Public Schools**

DEGREE AND TYPE OF DEVIATION	PERCENT
Acceptable overall speech pattern	34.8
Mild overall speech deviation	53.1
Moderate overall speech deviation	10.6
Extreme overall speech deviation	1.5
Acceptable articulation	66.4
Moderate articulation deviation	31.6
Extreme articulation deviation	2.0
Acceptable voice	50.1
Moderate voice deviation	46.8
Extreme voice deviation	3.1
Acceptable fluency	99.2
Dysfluent	.8
Normal bilateral hearing	88.8
Reduced hearing	11.2

the problems many children have in using linguistic symbols in comprehension, transformation and/or expression for communication."

The difficulty in ascertaining the incidence of children with language delay and language deviations continues to be a problem, not only for speech, language, and hearing clinicians but also for all workers in the field of special education. As indicated earlier the number is probably larger than we suspect.

Reports on incidence and prevalence of speech and hearing handicaps among school-age pupils have not been complete for several reasons. Sometimes the data were based on too few children, and sometimes the surveys were based on the reports of persons with little or no training in identifying speech problems. Often bilingual children, institutionalized children, children in special classes, and school dropouts were not included in the survey. Because of wide discrepancies in obtaining language samples, very little if any information was obtained on the incidence of language problems. Many children who might have died at birth are today being saved through improved medical care, and this points to an increase in communication problems.

Despite the difficulties in obtaining incidence figures, it is safe to assume that although speech, language, and hearing problems have always been with us, the number of them is increasing in both the preschool and the school-age population.

Jones and Healey (1973) stated, "Estimates of the number of children with communicative problems and needs vary, but present information available indicates that the number of children of all ages with all kinds and degrees of communication disorders exceeds three million."

Numerous studies have taken place in the United States regarding incidence and prevalence, but a reliable data base has not yet been established. Fisher (1977) reported that among the ten highest priorities determined at the 1975 Colorado Evaluation Conference was the need to collect reliable incidence and prevalence data.

Phillips (1975) stated, "Based on the majority of recent studies, it is probably safe to judge that between 8 and 10 percent of the children now enrolled in school exhibit some kind of oral communication disorder." I would tend to agree with Phillips. There are even indications that the figure of 10 percent is a conservative one. There are possible reasons for this. In reporting it is often common practice to report the presence of only one handicapping condition. For example, a learning-disabled child may also have accompanying speech, language, or hearing problems, but in a survey that child is reported as being learning-disabled only.

Another reason is that definitions and terminology regarding handicapping conditions may vary from state to state and from person to person so that the reporting of various conditions is not consistent.

Table 3–2 (Healey et al., 1981) presents data from the school years 1978–79, 1979–80, and 1980–81. One portion pertains to children receiving special education in the public schools under PL 94-142. A second portion pertains to those children trained under PL 89-313 in state-supported schools and institutions for the handicapped, including schools for the deaf, schools for the mentally retarded, and similar institutions. The final section of each table combines the numbers and percentages of the two major sections.

Table 3–3 (Karr & Punch, 1984) reports on the number of speech im-

TABLE 3-2 Report of Handicapped Children Receiving Special Education and Related Services as Reported by State Agencies Under PL 94-142 and PL 89-313 School Year 1980–1981: National Summary

	PL 94-142					PL 89-313				COMBINED		
	AGES 3-5	AGES 6-17	AGES 18-21	TOTAL	% POP	STATE	LOCAL	TOTAL	% POP	TOTAL	% POP	% HDCPD.
Mentally Retarded	17,626	651,688	69,195	738,509	1.52	88,440	22,941	111,381	0.23	849,890	1.75	20.3
Hard of Hearing	3,309	32.575	2,032	37,916	0.07	2,479	817	3,296	0.00	41,212	0.08	0.9
Deaf	2,136	14,722	907	17,765	0.03	22,395	1,212	23,607	0.04	41,372	0.08	0.9
Speech Impaired	164,953	995,708	6,045	1,166,706	2.41	8,588	2,498	11,086	0.02	1,177,792	2.43	28.1
Visually Handicapped	1,932	19,278	2,460	23,670	0.04	9,127	834	9,961	0.02	33,631	0.06	0.8
Emotionally Disturbed	7,222	293,247	12,163	312,632	0.64	31,639	7,189	38,828	0.08	351,460	0.72	8.3
Orthopedically Impaired	6,863	36,796	4,656	48,315	0.10	9,904	2,476	12,380	0.02	60,695	0.12	1.4
Other Health Impaired	4,604	86,052	3,880	94,536	0.19	3,747	963	4,710	0.00	99,246	0.20	2.3
Learning Disabled	19,839	1,383,963	36,024	1,439,826	2.98	12,075	3,234	15,309	0.03	1,455,135	3.01	34.7
Deaf-Blind	246	1,531	172	1,949	0.00	810	196	1,006	0.00	2,955	0.00	0.0
Multi-Handicapped	8,360	47,001	4,183	59,544	0.12	8,674	3,470	12,144	0.02	71,688	0.14	1.7
Total	237,090	3,562,561	141,717	3,941,368	8.16	197,878	45,830	243,708	0.50	4,185,076	8.66	100.0

Data by individual states are available from either the ASHA National Office or the Office of Special Education.

TABLE 3-3 **PL 94-142 State Child Counts—Handicapped Children, Ages 3-21, Receiving Special Education Services Under PL 94-142 and PL 89-313: School Year 1982-83**

Each year Special Education Programs (SEP) of the Department of Education reports the number of children served under Public Law 94-142. These data, referred to as "child count" data, are collected by states on December 1 of each year and used as the basis for allocating funds to states to educate the nation's handicapped children. Counts are nonduplicative, representing the number of handicapped children served rather than the prevalence of handicapping conditions. Services provided for the primary handicap are referred to as special education and are included in the count. Services provided for concomitant conditions are designated as related services and are not included in the child count. Thus, for example, the "speech-impaired" category includes only those with speech impairment as a primary handicap, and not the total number of children served by speech-language pathologists in schools.

The accompanying table shows the number of children ages 3–21 served in 1982–83 under PL 94-142 and PL 89-313 (State Operated Programs for Handicapped Children) in four handicap categories of interest to speech-language pathologists and audiologists. The "Total Handicapped" column reports totals for all handicap categories, including the four selected categories, plus mentally retarded, visually handicapped, emotionally disturbed, orthopedically impaired, deaf-blind, multihandicapped, and other health impaired. Speech-impaired, hard-of-hearing, deaf, and learning-disabled children account for 2.47%, 0.08%, 0.07%, and 3.80% of the total school age population, respectively.

The ratio of handicapped children in a given category to the total handicapped represents the percentage of PL 94-142 funding generated by that particular category. Speech-impaired children, therefore, accounted for 26.4% of funds generated in 1982–83.

Other important points not shown in the table are that:

- Nationally, speech-impaired children comprise approximately 71% of the total handicapped served in the 3–5 year age range.
- The number of handicapped children served under PL 94-142 has steadily increased from 3,935,119 in 1978–79, the first year of the Act, to 4,297,812 in 1982–83.
- Despite this overall increase, the numbers of speech-impaired, hard-of-hearing, and deaf children served, respectively, have declined by 6.6%, 5.5%, and 19.7% since 1978–79. These reductions are consistent with an increased emphasis on service to moderately and severely impaired children, as required by PL 94-142.
- The number of learning-disabled children served has increased from 1,154,430 in 1978–79 to 1,745,791 in 1982–83, an increase of 51.2%.

For further information, contact the Governmental Affairs Department of the ASHA National Office.

STATE	SPEECH IMPAIRED	HARD-OF-HEARING	DEAF	LEARNING-DISABLED	TOTAL HANDICAPPED
Alabama	16,235	418	718	20,899	81,609
Alaska	3,374	130	70	6,826	12,017
Arizona	11,195	1,043	0	25,710	51,862
Arkansas	10,493	358	381	19,436	48,962
California	92,056	2,871	4,346	198,696	364,318
Colorado	7,796	1,018	0	19,654	45,126
Connecticut	13,896	532	454	29,352	66,010
Delaware	1,747	149	145	6,670	14,405

STATE	SPEECH IMPAIRED	HARD-OF-HEARING	DEAF	LEARNING-DISABLED	TOTAL HANDICAPPED
District of Columbia	1,780	77	6	1,629	5,809
Florida	46,256	1	2,085	58,105	155,609
Georgia	26,782	749	1,098	35,722	112,555
Hawaii	1,962	166	82	8,189	12,876
Idaho	4,350	201	229	8,233	17,673
Illinois	75,784	2,350	1,843	96,805	261,683
Indiana	41,360	772	590	27,434	100,228
Iowa	14,656	718	343	21,340	56,109
Kansas	14,274	487	284	16,190	44,159
Kentucky	24,922	524	419	20,064	73,170
Louisiana	20,701	518	1,189	39,707	86,009
Maine	6,136	227	176	8,974	26,485
Maryland	24,209	744	756	48,366	90,879
Massachusetts	31,848	1,108	831	48,884	138,480
Michigan	44,081	2,790	269	55,467	155,771
Minnesota	19,013	1,440	195	34,748	77,658
Mississippi	16,797	308	326	16,714	50,570
Missouri	33,202	621	554	36,224	99,984
Montana	4,790	126	121	7,208	15,215
Nebraska	9,246	366	148	12,227	30,448
Nevada	3,232	65	110	7,041	13,326
New Hampshire	2,325	147	129	8,220	14,143
New Jersey	61,280	957	1,071	62,736	161,481
New Mexico	6,789	226	196	12,237	26,334
New York	41,661	1,533	3,553	116,753	264,835
North Carolina	25,808	1,461	844	49,019	120,586
North Dakota	3,600	173	84	4,340	10,802
Ohio	56,932	2,609	174	72,031	202,234
Oklahoma	20,389	357	495	28,625	65,819
Oregon	11,614	624	784	23,459	46,200
Pennsylvania	61,684	2,882	1,283	63,413	196,277
Rhode Island	3,337	92	148	11,729	18,571
South Carolina	19,596	957	234	20,930	71,705
South Dakota	5,413	301	3	3,563	11,841
Tennessee	32,996	1,528	658	42,804	106,091
Texas	66,544	427	4,441	150,768	289,343
Utah	8,375	296	533	13,611	38,968
Vermont	2,695	127	79	2,973	9,309
Virginia	30,703	744	871	38,614	100,713
Washington	13,511	607	778	31,286	64,295
West Virginia	12,774	291	199	14,719	42,418
Wisconsin	17,991	774	465	27,218	72,164
Wyoming	3,184	107	20	5,095	11,144
U.S. Territories	2,791	1,493	925	5,134	43,534
Total	1,134,165	39,590	35,735	1,745,791	4,297,812

Total includes children in four selected categories as well as mentally retarded, visually handicapped, emotionally disturbed, orthopedically impaired, deaf, blind, multihandicapped and other health impaired.

U.S. Department of Education, 1983. Special Education Programs, Report of Handicapped Children Receiving Special Education and Related Services as Reported by State Agencies under PL 94-142 and PL 89-313 School Year 1982–83.

paired, hard-of-hearing, deaf, and learning-disabled children served under PL 94-142 during the school year 1982-83.

DISCUSSION QUESTIONS AND PROJECTS

1. Why is it necessary for the school pathologist to know the structure of the school system on the local level?
2. What questions would you ask about the structure of the school system if you were being interviewed for a position as SLP?
3. What relationship do you see between the prevalence figures for speech-language handicapped students and program planning?
4. Why are most prevalence figures for language-handicapped children difficult to obtain?
5. Public Law 94-142 states that test and evaluation materials must be nondiscriminatory. Give examples of what this means.
6. Find out the minimum standards for speech-language programs in your state.
7. Find out if there is a regional resource center in your area. What services does it provide? Visit the center.
8. Interview a school SLP to find out to whom this individual is directly responsible in the school structure.
9. Invite the state department of education consultant in speech-language pathology to speak to your class. Prepare a list of questions to ask.

FOUR
PROGRAMMING
AND PROGRAM
ALTERNATIVES

INTRODUCTION

Garrard (1979) in her article entitled "The Changing Role of Speech and Hearing Professionals in Public Education" stated:

> In the past decade, the role of speech and hearing professionals in public education has undergone tremendous change. Public school speech and hearing personnel continue to function as specialists who identify children having communication problems, assess communication skills, formulate and implement therapeutic strategies, and evaluate children's progress on an individual basis. In recent years, though, it has been increasingly necessary for speech and hearing professionals to reevaluate their responsibilities and competencies in relation to the entire public education structure and the needs of all communicatively handicapped children.

Public Law 94-142, a legislative landmark, had the greatest impact on the role of speech-language pathologist in education.

In this chapter we will examine the continuum-of-services model developed by the American Speech-Language-Hearing Association. The model presents programming alternatives for communicatively and educationally handicapped children and youth. This chapter also presents definitions of terms that are generally agreed on and used by all professionals in the field. The definitions of communication disorders and an understanding of the continuum-of-services model are basic tools for the school speech-language pathologist and may be considered the building blocks of good program development and management.

THE DEFINITION OF TERMS

A good place to start any process is to come to an agreement on the definition of terms. In 1978 the Committee on Language, Speech, and Hearing Services in the Schools (1982) began work on a revision of terminology and submitted the definitions of communicative disorder and variations to the membership of ASHA. The definitions were accepted by the association and disseminated for use by federal, state, and local agencies and others concerned with programs for the communicatively handicapped. The school pathologist must be able to define and interpret the terminology to parents, teachers, medical personnel, and legislators.

The definitions are as follows:

Definitions:* Communicative Disorders and Variations

I. A *COMMUNICATIVE DISORDER* is an impairment in the ability to (1) receive and/or process a symbol system, (2) represent concepts or symbol system, and/or (3) transmit and use symbol systems. The impairment is observed in disorders of hearing, language, and/or speech processes. A communicative disorder may range in severity from mild to profound. It may be developmental or acquired, and individuals may demonstrate one or any combination of the three aspects of communicative disorders. The communicative disorder may result in a primary handicapping condition or it may be secondary to other handicapping conditions.

    A. A SPEECH DISORDER is an impairment of voice, articulation of speech sounds, and/or fluency. These impairments are observed in the transmission and use of the oral symbol system.

        1. A VOICE DISORDER is defined as the absence or abnormal production of vocal quality, pitch, loudness, resonance, and/or duration.

        2. An ARTICULATION DISORDER is defined as the abnormal production of speech sounds.

        3. A FLUENCY DISORDER is defined as the abnormal flow of verbal expression, characterized by impaired rate and rhythm which may be accompanied by struggle behavior.

    B. A LANGUAGE DISORDER is the impairment or deviant development of comprehension and/or use of a spoken, written, and/or other symbol system. The disorder may involve (1) the form of language (phonologic, morphologic, and syntactic systems), (2) the content of language (semantic system), and/or (3) the function of language in communication (pragmatic system) in any combination.

*Various definitions and eligibility criteria may exist for determining degree of handicap and disability compensation. The definitions in this document are not intended to address issues of eligibility and compensation.

1. Form of language
    a. PHONOLOGY is the sound system of a language and the linguistic rules that govern the sound combinations.
    b. MORPHOLOGY is the linguistic rule system that governs the structure of words and the construction of word forms from the basic elements of meaning.
    c. SYNTAX is the linguistic rule governing the order and combination of words to form sentences, and the relationships among the elements within a sentence.
2. Content of Language
    a. SEMANTICS is the psycholinguistic system that patterns the content of an utterance, intent and meanings of words and sentences.
3. Function of Language
    a. PRAGMATICS is the sociolinguistic system that patterns the use of language in communication which may be expressed motorically, vocally, or verbally.

C. A HEARING DISORDER is altered auditory sensitivity, acuity, function, processing, and/or damage to the integrity of the physiological auditory system. A hearing disorder may impede the development, comprehension, production, or maintenance of language, speech, and/or interpersonal exchange. Hearing disorders are classified according to difficulties in detection, perception, and/or processing of auditory information.

Hearing-impaired individuals frequently are described as deaf or hard of hearing

1. DEAF is defined as a hearing disorder which impedes an individual's communicative performance to the extent that the primary sensory avenue for communication may be other than the auditory channel.
2. HARD OF HEARING is defined as a hearing disorder whether fluctuating or permanent, which adversely affects an individual's communication performance. The hard of hearing individual relies upon the auditory channel as the primary sensory avenue for speech and language.

II. *COMMUNICATIVE VARIATIONS*
A. COMMUNICATIVE DIFFERENCE/DIALECT is a variation of a symbol system used by a group of individuals which reflects and is determined by shared regional, social, or cultural/ethnic factors. Variations or alterations in the use of a symbol system may be indicative of primary language interferences. A regional, social, or cultural/ethnic variation of a symbol system should not be considered a disorder of speech or language.
B. AUGMENTATIVE COMMUNICATION is a system used to supplement the communicative skills of individuals for whom speech is temporarily or permanently inadequate to meet communicative needs. Both prosthetic devices and/or nonprosthetic techniques may be designed for individual use as an augmentative communication system.

Prepared by:
Committee on Language, Speech, and Hearing Services in the Schools.

CONTINUUM-OF-SERVICES MODEL

Before a comprehensive speech, language, and hearing program is organized by the pathologist, some basis must be established for its implementation. We will call this basis a *model*.

A model is an approximation of the real world and is meant to be used, manipulated, changed, added to, diminished, and expanded. The speech-language pathologist in any school district is the decision maker who must take into account all the information available, and using the model as a guide, construct the program in speech, language, and hearing for that particular community.

The Council for Exceptional Children (1971) issued a policy statement on some of the major principles on which a special education program should be organized and administered. The statement included recommendations on *delivery models* for all handicapped children. Utilizing this as a basis, ASHA described a *delivery-of-service model* for communicatively handicapped children. The model includes a variety of options and covers the range of communication handicaps from severe disorders to developmental problems. It also makes provision for the prevention of communication problems.

The delivery-of-services model allows implementation of many options and tends to discourage the sole use of the itinerant model or any other single model for delivering services. The provision of service commensurate with need and adaptive behavior should be the primary concern in establishing intervention programs. Organizational models used to deliver services should allow adequate frequency and intensity of help for optimum progress.

Examples of various delivery-of-service models can be found throughout the United States. Some models are described in the publication *Language, Speech and Hearing Services in Schools*, and some descriptions are found in the journals published by the various state associations. As the impact of PL 94-142 is felt on the state and local levels, programs are changing to meet better the needs of handicapped students.

The American Speech-Language-Hearing Association (1973–1974), has developed a *continuum model*, which can be used as a framework to assist the school pathologist in planning a program that will meet the needs of the communicatively handicapped in any school district. This model defines the population served and the program goals in respect to various segments of the population. Further, it helps the pathologist in planning the program, in carrying out the program, in evaluating the program, and in providing ideas for future directions of the program. The model is shown in Table 4-1.

The children included in the *communicative disorders* component include those with severe to moderately severe problems in language, voice, articulation, fluency, or hearing. These are the children who would require intensive individual or small-group intervention by the pathologist and other specialists. Also involved in the habilitation of these children would be the parents and the classroom teacher. Some of these children would be those who had never acquired language for causes unknown and those with serious language delay because of other handicapping conditions such as profound hearing loss, mental retardation, or serious emotional disturbances.

Those in the *communicative deviations* section of the continuum would include children with somewhat less severe but significantly handicapping problems in communication such as nonmaturational misarticulations, mild language delays, or mild hearing losses. Children with developmental lags and mild intellectual retardation would also be included.

The intervention would include less intensified direct or indirect services by speech-language pathologists as well as parents, teachers, aides, counselors, psychologists, physicians, nurses, social workers, psychiatrists, and dentists.

The *communicative development* component has two major goals. One is the prevention of communication problems in young children. The other is the enrichment of the total use of language for children who may be proficient in a dialect or language other than English.

The *communicative development* program is primarily the responsibility of the classroom teacher, whereas the role of the language, speech, and hearing clinician is that of consultant who works closely with the teacher in such areas as

1. Providing information on normal speech and language development
2. Screening or developing screening procedures to be used by others to determine specific needs or class groups and individual pupils
3. Helping teachers to define goals, plan activities, and select materials appropriate for groups of children
4. Demonstrating procedures and techniques for the teacher
5. Planning, providing, and evaluating in-service programs for teachers, administrators, parents, and others who will be expected to participate in the program.

Does the continuum model suggest guidelines for the future for speech, language, and hearing programs in the schools? Would the school specialist be able to utilize it as a workable base for planning, implementing, and evaluating programs?

The American Speech-Language-Hearing Association has provided practical suggestions for the school pathologist. The continuum-of-services model is not intended to answer all questions, however, and this becomes obvious as the model is carefully examined. The major ingredient in the model is the school pathologist, who must become the information processor and the decision maker. The model, or portions of it, may be applied to any school district and utilized appropriately. But the appropriateness can best be determined by the speech-language pathologist.

Traditionally, speech and language services have been provided on an itinerant basis and have been based on state regulations that define caseload, number of child-contact hours per week, and ratio of clinicians to school populations. Historically, the hearing-impaired and the deaf have received treatment in residential or day schools and special classes in regular schools. By providing more options for delivery of services instead of relying solely on the itinerant model, more children who need help can be reached. This does not imply that the itinerant model is not a good model when it is used in the appropriate circumstances; however, it does mean the speech, language, and hearing profession must break the habit of thinking of it as the only option.

TABLE 4-1 The Continuum of Language, Speech, and Hearing Services for Children and Youth

CONTINUUM COMPONENTS

	COMMUNICATIVE DISORDERS - - - - - ➤	DEVIATIONS - - - - - ➤	DEVELOPMENT
Population Served	Pupils with severe language, voice, fluency, articulation or hearing disorders.	Pupils with mild-moderate developmental or non-maturational deviations in language, voice, fluency, articulation, and those with mild hearing loss requiring minimal oral rehabilitation procedures.	All pupils in regular or special education classes.
Program Goals	1. Provide direct, intensive, individualized clinical-educational services to effect positive change in communication behavior of pupils with handicapping disorders. 2. Provide information and assistance to other participants.	Provide direct and/or indirect clinical-educational services to stimulate and/or improve pupils' communication skills and competencies.	Provide prevention-oriented, sequenced curricular activities to help pupils develop communicative behaviors in appropriate social, educational and cultural contexts.

Services Provided by Language/Speech or Hearing Specialists

1. Identification
2. Comprehensive Assessment (diagnostic evaluation) — Assessment and Evaluation of Communicative Skills.
3. Referral (for additional services)
4. Parent Counseling and Instruction
5. Pupil Counseling and Placement
6. Teacher Counseling and inservice orientation/instruction
7. Direct Clinical-Educational Management — Direct or Indirect Clinical-Educational Management.
8. Program Evaluation — Demonstration Lessons
9. Pupil Re-assessment
10. Dismissal and Follow-up — Consultation (for individual pupils or groups).
11. Research

Program Types and Alternatives

1. Diagnostic center placement
2. Special class placement
3. Regular classroom placement with:
   a. Itinerant services
   b. Resource room services (emphasis on individual—small group) — Regular classroom placement with: a. Itinerant services b. Resource room services (emphasis on group services) — Regular classroom placement with: a. Supportive services from other participants.
4. Home or hospital services
5. Parent/Infant Instruction
6. Residential placement

(Transportation, Purchased services-May be required to facilitate provision of a service continuum.)

Other Participants (most common)

Parents, teachers, administrators, aides, counselors, psychologists, physicians, psychiatrists, social workers, nurses, occupational therapists, physical therapists, dentists. — Parents, teachers, administrators, aides, counselors, physicians, psychologists, psychiatrists, social workers, nurses, dentists. — Parents, teachers, administrators, aides, counselors, curriculum specialists.

Delivery-of-Services Options

In the publication *Project Upgrade: Model Regulations for School Language, Speech and Hearing Programs and Services* (Jones & Healey, 1973) the following recommendations for delivery-of-service options for school speech, language, and hearing programs, are presented:

Recommendations: The following types of options constitute component parts of a continuum model appropriate for pupils with communicative disorders, deviations or needs:

I. Diagnostic center placement. This option may be employed to provide thorough diagnostic assessments and appropriate educational plans for pupils enrolled in the center on a short-term basis. Services are given by speech pathologists, audiologists, teachers of the hearing impaired and other support personnel in a inter-disciplinary team approach. Such centers may operate on either a local, cooperative or regional basis.

II. Special classroom placement. This option should be considered when the diagnostic assessment indicates that the pupil's needs cannot be met by placement in the general education program. The special classroom program should be designed to serve small groupings of pupils with severe communicative disorders. In some instances, these classes may be housed in special schools. When the classrooms are located in or near regular school facilities, pupils may be programmed into regular classes and activities for part of their instruction and related services as they demonstrate potential for successful performance.

III. Regular classroom placement with supportive services. This option may be used for pupils with communicative development needs. Supportive services provided by language, speech, and hearing specialists include:

A. Direct/indirect services to pupils enrolled in regular or special classrooms from a language, speech, or hearing specialist and/or a team operating on:

1. Itinerant basis - the specialist provides continuous, on-going services to pupils in more than one school or center. Scheduling options for this type of service include: intermittent sessions on a regular basis, or intensive cycling, which provides daily service in a particular school or center for a specified block of time. Flexibility of operation and scheduling is desirable in itinerant programming in order to provide for the varying needs of individual pupils.

2. Single building basis - the specialist is assigned full-time to one building or center. Services may be provided by either intermittent or intensive scheduling.

B. Direct/indirect service to pupils provided through a resource room within a school staffed with language, speech, and hearing program personnel. Pupils remain in regular or special classrooms for the major part of the day, but are scheduled into the resource room for one or more periods of individualized attention.

C. Consultative services to regular or special classroom teachers, curriculum specialists, parents, etc., to provide them with information on communicative skill development, specialized materials and procedures, demonstration sessions and other activities organized to help pupils develop appropriate communicative behaviors in social, educational, and cultural contexts.

IV. Home and/or Hospital Services. Language, speech and hearing specialists may use this option to serve pupils who are unable to attend school because of confinement to their homes or to a hospital setting.

V. Parent/Infant Instruction Services. In this option, parents are provided with guidance and instruction for assisting infants and pre-schoolers to develop appropriate communicative behaviors and skills. The guidance and instruction provided by language, speech and hearing specialists may be given in schools, centers, homes or other approved facilities as appropriate. This model is considered most applicable for children who, because of organic, behavioral, or other symptoms, are determined to be actually or potentially handicapped in developing necessary communicative skills.

VI. Residential Placement. This option is usually reserved for pupils with severe disorders. Education and specialized services are provided in addition to residential care.

CHARACTERISTICS OF GOOD SERVICE-DELIVERY MODELS

According to Flower (1984) the essential characteristics of good service-delivery models fall under five headings: efficacy, coordination, continuity, participation and economy.

1. The first obvious criterion, efficacy, is whether the service makes any difference to the consumer. Screening services can usually be judged in fairly objective terms; however, other services are often more difficult to assess. Evaluation by the clinician and the insights of families, clients, and other professionals all provide information of a subjective nature, but it is frequently difficult to determine whether achievements have, in fact, occurred.

2. Clients with communicative disorders are served by several different professionals. Some of these may provide services that are directly related to the communicative disorder, for example, the learning disabilities specialist working with a child with problems in language acquisition. Other professionals provide services with only peripheral relevance to the communicative disorder, for example, the teacher of a classroom in which a young stutterer is enrolled. Whenever multiple professional services are provided to the same client, the effectiveness of any of those services will often depend on the *coordination* with all other services.

3. Good care depends on the *continuity* of sequential services over a period of several months or sometimes several years. This often requires multiple professional services, that is, a total plan for services, with each phase staged and integrated into an uninterrupted sequence toward the ultimate goal.

4. Professional services carried out with little regard for the clients' wishes or little concern for their understanding of what was occurring seriously impair the effectiveness of those services. *Participation* by the client and the family in all decision-making processes ensures the opportunity for excellent services.

5. *Economy* does not only mean spending as little money as possible. It refers also to the conservation of time and energy. The conservation of financial resources, as well as the orderly management of services to avoid waste, and

the achievement of efficiency through careful planning constitute the broader definition of economy.

Each school system is unique. The school speech-language pathologist needs to implement the delivery-of-services models that best fit that particular school system and the needs of the students. Flower's five criteria will be helpful in assessing delivery-of-service models.

DISCUSSION QUESTIONS AND PROJECTS

1. Read Garrard's (1979) article. What does she mean by the term *total communication*? What competencies does she suggest are needed by the SLP? Garrard's article was written in 1979. What are the implications for school SLPs today?

2. Why is it important to have definitions of communicative disorders that are uniform and agreed on by professionals in the field?

3. Why do you think definitions of "communication variations" are included in the list?

4. Study Table 4–1 (Continuum Components) carefully. How does this model help the school SLP in planning a program?

5. You are the school SLP. How would you utilize the continuum model in explaining your program to a meeting of elementary teachers in a specific school?

6. You are the school SLP. What specific activities would you suggest to the kindergarten and first-grade teachers in carrying out the "communicative development" program?

7. Can you give examples of the various delivery-of-service options in your community?

8. Interview some SLPs presently working in the various delivery-of-service modes.

9. Using Flower's list of essential characteristics of good service-delivery models, devise a list of questions under each of the five headings. The purpose of the questions would be to evaluate the delivery-of-service models found in a typical school.

FIVE
THE SCHOOL SPEECH-LANGUAGE PATHOLOGIST AS A MANAGER

INTRODUCTION

When school speech-language clinicians are asked about their programs, services, and job performances, they are quite likely to make the following responses: "We need more time to plan," "There are too many children on my case roster," "We need more staff members," "I have trouble scheduling students because of all the other school activities," "My room is too small and not well ventilated," and so on. Interestingly enough, the school clinician is generally pleased with the progress of the children in the program, and the school administration is pleased with the program. Why, then, the complaints? Very possibly the reason is that each school pathologist is constantly faced with the challenge of providing the highest caliber of services with the most efficient expenditure of time, money, and resources, including physical, technical, and human resources.

In this chapter we will examine how the school SLP, in the role of manager, may utilize time more efficiently and expand human resources more effectively to provide optimal services to students. Topics covered include planning ahead, establishing goals, managing time and paperwork, utilizing supportive personnel, and using computers to carry out administrative functions.

THE IMPORTANCE OF PLANNING

The school SLP, although responsible to another person in the hierarchy of the administration, is responsible for the management of the school's speech, language, and hearing program. The school system may be a large urban system, a small community system, or a sprawling countywide system, and the school SLP must assess the needs in light of the local situation and plan accordingly.

If the school system employs more than one SLP, there must be coordination of their activities. If it is a large or moderately large system, one SLP may be designated as the coordinator of the program. But even the school SLP who is working alone in a small school system needs to have a plan of action.

Planning ahead is the key to a successful program. Setting goals and objectives is one of the most critical elements of the planning process. Once the goals and objectives have been determined, the next step is writing them down in such a form that they clearly communicate their intent to all the persons concerned and involved in the program.

The utilization of written goals and objectives has many potential advantages in the school speech, language, and hearing program. First, it allows for change, because through the system of periodic review, objectives will need to be revised and rewritten. Also, it creates a positive pressure to get things done. Communication among professionals will be improved. There will be more precise definitions of the roles and responsibilities of the school speech, language, and hearing clinician. A system for evaluating and assessing the overall program is inherent in the written goals and objectives. Better utilization of each staff member's time and capabilities will be encouraged. And finally, there will be a better basis for understanding the program both within the school system and in the community.

Applying Management Principles

Although it is beyond the scope of this book to provide a crash course in management principles and practices, let us look at what the field has to offer the struggling speech-language and hearing clinician about to organize a program in the schools.

Accordingly to Coventry and Burstiner (1977), a common core of problems exists for any organization to be dealt with by its management. First, there is a need to establish major objectives and major policies. What is the purpose of the organization, and how can that purpose be attained? Does everyone involved understand clearly the objectives and policies?

Second, a structure must be set up to determine the responsibilities for the various tasks that must be accomplished in order to achieve the objectives. The relationships between these jobs must be established.

Third, there must be resources such as space, equipment, furniture, staff, supporting services, and supervisors, to mention only a few.

Finally, there must be long-term and short-term programs of work that conform effectively to the objectives and policies that have been laid down.

TABLE 5-1   The MBO Process

THE ESSENTIAL ELEMENTS   THE MAJOR STEPS

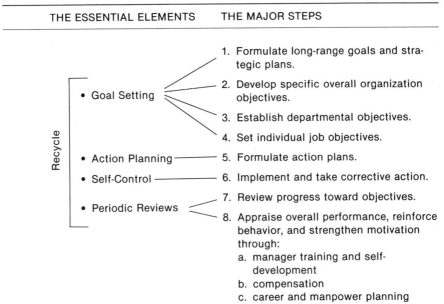

1. Formulate long-range goals and strategic plans.
2. Develop specific overall organization objectives.
3. Establish departmental objectives.
4. Set individual job objectives.
5. Formulate action plans.
6. Implement and take corrective action.
7. Review progress toward objectives.
8. Appraise overall performance, reinforce behavior, and strengthen motivation through:
   a. manager training and self-development
   b. compensation
   c. career and manpower planning

From *Managing by Objectives* by Anthony P. Raia. Copyright © 1974 by Scott, Foresman and Company. Reprinted by permission.

These basic principles seem fairly obvious, but sometimes the obvious is overlooked. For example, how many organizations know *exactly* their real objectives, as opposed to assumed objectives?

Management is the process of getting things done by people in the most efficient and effective way. It involves setting goals and objectives that are both understood and accepted, and then coordinating the activities of people toward the attainment of these goals.

In 1954, a system known as *management by objectives* (MBO) was developed by Peter F. Drucker. This system has been utilized, in its various forms, by business, industry, governmental agencies, and educational systems concerned with efficient and effective organization and management. Table 5-1 illustrates the MBO process (Raia, 1974).

ESTABLISHING GOALS FOR THE PROGRAM

Let us examine Table 5-1 with the idea of applying it to the organization and management of a school program. The first essential element is *goal setting,* and the major steps are formulating long range goals and strategic plans, developing specific overall organizational objectives, establishing departmental objectives, and setting individual job objectives.

Goals are long-term and short-term, tangible, measurable, and verifiable. They are not nebulous statements but specific statements of a desired future condition or accomplishment. Ideally, goals should be set by all persons involved in the structure so there is a commitment on their part. Once the goals have been determined it is crucial to get them down in writing. The language must be clear and concise and must communicate the intent to all relevant parties.

Once specific overall goals have been established, the step-by-step process of translating them into required action begins. This brings us to the second essential element, which is *action planning.* Action planning involves determining *when, who, what, to whom,* and *how much* is needed to reach the given objective. It also includes the criterion and the evaluation. It is a way of providing a connecting link between the statement of a goal and the more complete program of implementation. Another way of stating action planning is *setting program objectives.*

The third element is *self-control* and is based on the idea that the individual and not the superior will control his or her own behavior. According to Raia (1974, p. 18),

> Self control requires meaningful participation in the goal-setting and action-planning process, resulting in a better understanding and a higher level of commitment to the objectives. The individuals must also, however, be given feedback and information he needs to assess progress and to take corrective action on his own.

The fourth element is *periodic reviews.* The purpose of the reviews is to evaluate progress and performance in the light of the established objectives. The problem areas can be identified and the obstacles removed so that new objectives can be established. It is a method of systematic stock-taking on the way to reaching the goal.

In setting up goals and objectives for speech-language and hearing programs, we would also include a statement of the criterion and the evaluation. The criterion indicates how successful you want to be in accomplishing the *what.* The evaluation indicates a method that will be used to find out whether or not the *what* was accomplished.

Also, keep in mind that in this chapter we are talking about *program* goals and objectives. The same general principles could be applied to *instructional* goals and objectives.

WRITING GOALS FOR THE PROGRAM

Let us look at some examples of writing goals and objectives. We will first consider writing long-range program goals, assuming that you have already evaluated the existing situation and have determined the overall needs of the program. Keep in mind that although these are long-range and broad in focus, they still need to be stated specifically and concretely.

Example: One year from (date) the clinician will have developed and written a language curriculum guide for teachers of the adjusted curriculum classes in Ottawa County.

Example: By (date) the clinician will have completed a research project related to case selection at the kindergarten level.

Example: By (date) 90 percent of the pupils in Danbury School identified as having communication problems and needing therapeutic intervention will be receiving services.

Some goals and objectives may be narrower in focus and have a shorter time frame.

Example: By (date) the clinician will have administered audiometric screenings to 95 percent of the second-grade pupils in the Port Clinton School district.

Example: By (date) the clinician will have conducted group parent meetings for parents of all children enrolled at Lakeside School.

Some objectives are very short-term and have a very narrow focus. Sometimes they may be considered subgoals, that is, contained within a goal or objective and contributing to its attainment.

Example: During the second week of school in September 19__, the clinician will acquaint teachers at Jefferson School with referral procedures through an in-service meeting.

Example: By (date) the clinician will write an article for the local newspaper and prepare items for the local radio and television stations regarding the prekindergarten communication evaluation program to be held during the first week in May at Catawba and Danbury schools.

A *criterion*, or *standard of performance,* is the description of the results of a job well done. It should always be a number or an indication of quantity, that is, *how much* and *by when.* It should be realistic, control-oriented, and high enough so that when the task is completed it will have been of value to the program.

Example: Dismiss 30 percent of the pupils enrolled as functionally corrected and 50 percent as greatly improved by the end of the school year.

Example: By (date) the clinician will provide three demonstration language-development sessions in 50 percent of the kindergarten classrooms of Bataan School, and receive positive feedback, in written form, from 90 percent of the teachers involved.

The *evaluation* is an indication of the method to be used to determine if the goal or objective has been accomplished. An indication of the evaluation may be a report sent to the coordinator of speech-language and hearing services. Or it may be a list of posttest scores, a list of referrals made, or a chart indicating that change has occurred.

Example: By (date) the clinician will have administered speech-language screening tests to 95 percent of the third-grade pupils in Marblehead School, and a report will be submitted to the school principal and the director of speech-language and hearing services.

Occasionally, objectives are difficult to measure or confirm, even though they are activities or events that when accomplished lead to the overall improvement of a situation or condition.

Example: The clinician will attempt to improve communication with the classroom teachers by
1. Eating lunch with the teachers at least two times per week or more often if possible
2. Inviting teachers to observe therapy sessions
3. Attending as many school meetings and social functions as time permits.

MANAGEMENT: BASIC PRINCIPLES

Perhaps the best place to start is to admit to ourselves that in the field of management we need to acquire new skills, new techniques, and new instruments, as well as an understanding of the principles of the management process: planning, organizing, staffing, directing, and controlling. The goal of comprehensive services for all handicapped children points out the need for appropriate managerial skills at the local level as well as at the state and national levels.

The American Speech-Language-Hearing Association's manual on management (Jones & Healey, 1973), utilized the management-by-objectives system. In the foreword to the publication it is stated,

The present trend toward implementation of formal systems for program planning, development, management, and evaluation appears to be gaining acceptance at national, state, and local levels. Although the principles on which most systems operate have some commonality, their application in special programs requires interpretation and definition of specific procedures.

Many colleges and universities through their continuing education programs offer courses in supervision and management. Sometimes they are general courses in supervision, management, leadership, and communication and may be geared to specific professions or businesses or particular groups of individuals. Seminars in management techniques are being offered at many places throughout the country, usually in addition to the regularly scheduled university courses in management. The proliferation of these courses and seminars in recent years points out the fact that state and local government agencies and departments are enlisting the aid of local universities and business people in developing and improving management techniques in the public sector.

The need to examine closely the school programs, what they are attempting to do, how they are doing it, and how effective they are is vital. The school speech, language, and hearing clinician today and in the future will need to be acquainted with sophisticated tools and systems for evaluation and measurement of programs and personnel. A "cookbook" approach is not the answer because there is no single "recipe" for a good program.

THE MANAGEMENT OF TIME

The management of time is an important factor in considering the role of the school SPL. Public Law 94-142 has been blamed for creating increased amounts of paper work in the implementation of its procedures. Although this has undoubtedly accounted for an increased expenditure of time, there are ways of managing time that can lead to increased productivity.

Let us look first at what the school clinician's job entails.

1. *Screening.* In this activity the clinician identifies children with speech, language, and hearing problems. The bulk of it may take place at the beginning of the school year; however, many clinicians carry out preschool screenings in the summer or the end of the school year. Sometimes kindergarten and first-grade children are screened throughout the school year.
2. *Diagnosis and assessment.* This task includes formal and informal testing and is carried on throughout the school year.
3. *Staffing and placement.* This procedure is often carried out by a placement team and involves reviewing the data on individual students to develop individualized educational programs for each student.
4. *Intervention.* These are the actual therapy and instructional activities provided by staff members to develop, improve, or maintain communicative abilities.
5. *Record keeping.* This task includes all activities involved in maintaining information on the delivery of services to each student.
6. *Consultation.* These activities include the exchange of information with parents, teachers, psychologists, nurses, and others in regard to individual students.

Other services, not directly related to the communicatively handicapped students, maintain, promote, and enhance the speech, language, and hearing program. These activities are of an indirect nature, but at the same time, are essential to the program. They include in-service training programs provided by the speech, language, and hearing staff, as well as in-service training received by them for the purpose of upgrading their skills. Travel to provide services is a necessary part of many school clinicians' programs, and many specialists are engaged in research related to the school programs. Time is also spent organizing, planning, implementing, analyzing, and evaluating programs. Some school specialists spend time supervising student teachers in speech pathology and audiology as well as paraprofessionals assigned to the program. Conservation and prevention programs may be carried out by the school clinicians, as well as public information activities such as talks to various groups, radio and television programs, and newspaper articles.

Planning for the Year

After the school clinician has taken a good look at what the job entails, he or she determines long-range goals based on a priority list. Inexperienced clinicians in a new situation sometimes try to do everything the first year. This is not only impossible but also unwise even to attempt. The result may be spreading oneself too thin and not accomplishing anything satisfactorily. For example, the clinician may have to decide whether a teacher in-service program or a parent in-service program is more important during the first year. The clinician may then rationalize that the teachers are more readily available and need to understand the program more immediately than do the parents, so the in-service program for teachers would take precedence. During the following year, however, the clinician may decide to devote more time and energy to the parent in-service program, and that program would be given top priority.

After priorities for the year are established, the long-range program goals are written. It should be pointed out that long-range goals need to be examined periodically and modified if necessary. The goals for the year should indicate the time (or times) of the year that the goals would be implemented and accomplished as well as the amount of time involved.

Goals may be written for an entire school year, or some school clinicians may prefer to write them for a semester. A combination of the two time slots may also be utilized.

Program goals should not be confused with goals that individual clinicians establish for themselves. These clinician's goals and the program goals may not necessarily be at odds, but it should be kept in mind that although clinicians may come and go, programs, it is hoped, go on forever. Setting goals for the program, with the clinicians as the implementers, will allow smooth, continuous functioning of a program despite changes in personnel. There is probably nothing more frustrating for a school clinician who is stepping into a job than to learn that the previous clinician left no records concerning what was planned, what was accomplished, when it was accomplished, how long it took, and what has yet to be done.

In addition to establishing yearly or semester program goals based on a priority list of the tasks involved in the clinician's job, other information would have to be available, including

1. Number of speech, language, and hearing clinicians on the staff
2. Number of schools to be served
3. Amount of travel time between schools
4. Enrollment figures for each school building. This would have to be further broken down into the following figures:
   a. Enrollment by grade level
   b. Enrollment of special education classes, including hearing impaired, physically impaired, mentally retarded, emotionally disturbed, learning disabled, and trainable mentally retarded
5. Number of preschool children in the school districts based on child-find figures

The school clinician uses this information to decide on the appropriate methods of delivery-of-service and scheduling systems.

Planning for the Week

In planning for the week the key word is *flexibility*. The school clinician will have to decide how much time during the week will be spent in actual therapy and in travel if more than one school is involved during any one day. Specific blocks of time can be devoted to these activities. An activity such as screening must be carried out in a block of time, and the school clinician may want to reserve blocks of time at certain times of the year or the semester for this part of the program.

Such activities as diagnosis and assessment, staffing and placement, and consultation are necessary parts of the program, and time for these activities may be set aside in daily or weekly blocks. For example, the staffing and placement team may not meet every week, so the block of time set aside weekly could be used on alternate weeks for staffing and placement and diagnosis and consultation.

Record keeping and time spent in organizing, planning, implementing, analyzing, and evaluating the program could be scheduled at times of the day when staff members are in the school but children are not present. For example, mornings before children arrive at school and afternoons after they are dismissed could be utilized for these activities. Many school systems set aside a time usually referred to as *coordination time* for tasks of this nature.

In-service training programs for classroom teachers may be part of the school's regular routine, and the speech, language, and hearing pathologist may be asked to take part in them. Certainly they are an important part of a successful program, and time should be set aside for them. Some school clinicians provide in-service programs for teachers, administrators, other school personnel, and parents.

If paraprofessionals and aides are assigned to the program, time must be planned for their in-service training programs, and time must be allowed for the supervision of such personnel.

For many of the activities mentioned, time is not planned on a regularly scheduled basis but certainly must be set aside to include these important facets of the program.

Planning for the Day

In planning time for the day the school clinician will have to know how many hours per day the children are in school. What is their arrival time and what is their dismissal time? How much time is allowed for lunch and recess?

The time that the teachers are required to be in school and the time they may leave in the afternoon is set by school policy, and school clinicians should follow the same rules that teachers are required to follow. This sometimes poses a problem for the school clinician who is scheduled in School A in the morning and School B in the afternoon, but who must return to School A for a parent conference after school is dismissed. The problem arises when the teachers in School B think the clinician is leaving school early. The problem can usually be alleviated by following the rule of always informing the principals of School A and School B of any deviation in the regular schedule.

The greatest percentage of actual therapy time will take place in the morning because the morning sessions are longer and children are available for a longer period of time. This is true in most school systems, but there will be exceptions.

The school clinician will have to decide the length of the therapy sessions. There does not have to be a uniform length, and sessions may range from 15 minutes to an hour. The length depends on a number of factors, and before determining the pattern of the sessions the clinician may want to look at the school's schedule of classes, recess, dismissal time, and so on.

Among the considerations are the number of children to be seen in total, the number in groups, and the number in individual therapy. Also, some children will be in the carry-over phase of therapy and do not require as much time as children who are just beginning. It is wise to schedule the sessions a few minutes apart to allow for children to arrive on time or to allow time for the clinician to locate a child whose teacher has forgotten to send him or her to therapy. Children often assume the responsibility of remembering when to come to therapy, and for younger children who have not yet mastered the art of telling time, a clock face drawn on a sheet of paper with the hands pointing to the time of the session will allow the child to match the clock face with the clock on the wall.

In planning the daily schedule the school clinician will need to retain as much flexibility as possible. Children change and their needs change. The child who once required 30 minutes of individual therapy per day may later need only 15 minutes twice a week. Or the child who once needed individual therapy may need the experience of a group to progress. This flexibility must also be understood by the principal and the teachers, and it is the responsibility of the clinician to interpret the rationale involved in making changes in schedules.

As a result of mainstreaming and the influx of more seriously disabled children into the public schools, the school clinician will need to allow time for working with classroom teachers of the mentally retarded, emotionally disturbed, hearing impaired, learning disabled, and multi-handicapped. In fact, any communicatively handicapped child may require direct or indirect intervention by the speech, language, and hearing pathologist in the school, and depending on the needs of the children in a specific school, the clinician will have to make allowances for the intervention in both the daily schedule and the overall scheduling of services.

Personal Time Management

The school clinician must take into consideration two factors in overall time management. The first is the need to plan time on a yearly, semester, weekly, and daily basis; the second is the need for the clinician to manage his or her own time within the larger framework. In respect to both factors, planning is an essential first step. The next important step is setting priorities and sticking with them.

The school clinician who is the sole speech, language, and hearing specialist will have much greater responsibility than a person stepping into a job where there is an ongoing program with other school clinicians already involved. In the latter situation, the new clinician fits into the program that has already been set up. In the former, the clinician may be the key planner and organizer.

Time-saving techniques are not necesarily new; most people are too busy to implement them or perhaps do not know how to implement them. One technique is to make a list of things to be done *today,* then to set priorities on that list and follow them. Another piece of advice is to keep a card file containing alphabetized names and telephone numbers of persons and agencies necessary to the work. A record of incoming and outgoing telephone calls might be recorded on a sheet and later put in a loose-leaf notebook, providing a record and synopsis of the conversations. An example of this form follows:

Telephone Calls

STAFF MEMBER: (your name)

Date	To or from	Results
2/16/89	From Billy Jones' mother, Mrs. Henry Jones	Requested results of Billy's hearing test. Letter sent 2/16/89. See file
2/17/89	To Susan Smith, prin. Findlay Jr. High	Confirmed date of talk to teachers (March 3rd)
2/18/89	To Tommy Brown's parents, M/M Jack Brown	Requested parent conference. Agreeable. Will call me back re time

Another important factor in personal time management is not to let paper work pile up. A period of time each day or each week should be devoted entirely to this task.

It is also important to look at ways that may be wasting time, for example, attending too many meetings or allowing too many interruptions. Most school clinicians would like to add an extra hour to a day now and then or think in terms of an occasional eight-day week. Because time is scarce it must be managed with maximum effectiveness. Experts in time management tell us that selecting the best task from all the possibilities available and then doing it in the best way is more important than doing efficiently whatever job happens to be around.

No matter how one looks at it, we are dealing with that precious and fleeting commodity—time. It is scarce, inelastic, does not have a two-way stretch, cannot be stored or frozen for future use, and cannot be retrieved. It can, however, be managed with effectiveness.

SUPPORTIVE PERSONNEL

Ptacek (1967) suggested the utilization of aides to expand the services of the speech-language pathologist and audiologist. The advent of PL 94-142 in 1975 presented an immediate, intense, and continuing need for increased services to handicapped children in the public schools. The use of supportive personnel is one way to provide increased services.

"Guidelines for the Employment and Utilization of Supportive Personnel" were published by the Committee on Supportive Personnel, American Speech-Language-Hearing Association (1981). The guidelines include the definition of supportive personnel, qualifications, training, roles, and supervision. The following issues formed the basis for the guidelines:

1. The legal, ethical, and moral responsibility to the client for all services provided cannot be delegated; that is, they remain the responsibility of the professional personnel.
2. Supportive personnel could be permitted to implement a variety of clinical tasks given that sufficient training, direction, and supervision were provided by the audiologist and/or speech-language pathologist responsible for those tasks.
3. Supportive personnel should receive training that is competency-based in character and specific to the job performance expectations held by the employer.
4. The supervising audiologist and/or speech-language pathologist should also be trained in the supervision of supportive personnel.
5. The supervision of supportive personnel must be periodic, comprehensive, and documented to ensure that the client receives the high-quality services that he or she needs.

A number of pilot programs utilizing communication aides have been reported in the professional speech, language, and hearing journals. One of the earliest was a pilot program undertaken by the Colorado State Department of Education. It involved ten aides working in nine school districts of metropolitan Denver for one semester. The aides observed clinicians at work for four days and worked under their assigned clinicians for two days. Instruction also covered school organization and administration; the role of the speech clinician; professional responsibilities and ethics; child growth and speech and language development; speech and hearing mechanisms; disorders of speech, language, and hearing; and identification and remediation of these disorders (Alpiner, 1970).

The majority of the aides' time was spent working with children with articulation problems; the remainder was divided between clerical duties and working with children with language disorders. The result was that these areas matched those in which the clinicians felt the aides were most helpful. In general, the communication aides were accepted by the classroom teachers, school administrators, and school nurses in the buildings in which the aides worked. Several of the clinicians had some reservations about the aides; they gave many reasons, but their major complaint was a problem in keeping the aides occupied. They also felt that the use of aides should not be mandated by the state. The majority wished to continue working with the aides but expressed a desire to interview them before employment to increase the likelihood of compatibility.

A pilot project, reported in the Montgomery County Public Schools of Maryland (Braunstein, 1972), was designed to aid in the remediation of language problems. The aides' responsibilities were as follows:

. . . to meet groups of children on a daily basis and conduct activities, to record daily progress, to record comments on students' behavior and responses, to tape-record weekly group sessions for evaluation, to confer with the clinician regularly, to participate in in-service activities designated by the clinician and approved by the principal, and to assist in the preparation of materials.

Each aides' caseload was made up of children with mild to moderate language problems in kindergarten through the second grade. Each aide worked with three groups of eight children for at least 25 minutes daily. The remaining time was allotted for conferences. All the materials used in therapy were part of a prepared programmed language-development series. The aides received 35 to 40 hours of training and analyzed 25 to 30 hours of audio and video tapes. At the outset of teaching the clinician and aide alternated the duties three times a week.

Another paraprofessional program involved language remediation for culturally different children in Price George County, Maryland, under a program called "Operation: Moving Ahead" (Lynch, 1972). Begun in 1966, it involved children in kindergarten through the third grade. Its primary objectives included the acquisition of standard English vocabulary, increased standard English familiarity, and the use and refinement of standard English.

The aides were divided into two groups: children's aides and parent helpers. The children's aides' function was to help small groups of children by reinforcing the instruction program planned and provided by the classroom teacher. These aides were supervised by the *helping teacher,* who did the diagnoses, further planning, and evaluations. The parent helpers' functions were to help parents learn about the school program, to understand the importance of language in the child's future success in school, and to suggest ways of working with the children in the home. They primarily worked in the community by visiting homes and distributing materials. They also developed a language box for stimulating language in preschool children and a folder containing ideas for making materials and equipment from inexpensive objects found in the home.

During the 1972–73 school year, the Los Angeles Unified School District established a paraprofessional/volunteer program to supplement and expand the services of the language, speech, and hearing clinicians (Scalero & Eskenazi, 1976). These supportive personnel were intended to work with the remediation of articulation and language disorders. The aides received an intensive 70 hour preservice training course; they then worked six hours five days a week. The volunteers attended a condensed form of the training course— mainly in-group sessions which emphasized practice with the programmed materials; they then worked in two-hour blocks a minimum of two days each week.

At the outset, the speech clinicians tested all potential clients. The 15 aides and 15 volunteers then used programs designed specifically for them. They each kept a log of the pupils' performance and the particular lessons completed. The clinicians then evaluated the clients' progress and determined when they were to move to the next stage; they also supervised and rated the aides through the use of checklists and rating scales. Throughout the year the supportive personnel worked with 125 articulation cases and 136 language problems. A postinstruction evaluation of the clients revealed 90 percent of the articulation problems had 80 percent or more carry-over in 15 weeks or less of therapy. These successes were independent of the age, education, or previous training of the aides but were related to their rapport with their pupils and their ability and willingness to follow directions. The children who worked with the volunteers attained the same goals as the children who worked with the aides, but in longer periods of time.

A slight variation of the paraprofessional program was attempted in Maine to meet the requirements of PL 94-142 in the isolated rural districts without speech clinicians (Pickering & Dopheide, 1976). Instead of being trained to perform supervised therapy, these aides were to screen for communication disorders. In two separate workshops, 51 people from 20 different schools were trained; the majority of these trainees were school aides, but classroom teachers and "floating" teachers were also involved. Each workshop lasted two days and had performance-based success levels.

As a result of the screening by the paraprofessionals, 11 percent more children were identified in the first testing. Voice quality was the most difficult for the trainees to evaluate and for the instructors to define. A total of 1,700 children were screened, with the aides referring 35 percent of the children tested and the teachers referring 28 percent; of these referrals one-third needed remediation. The program significantly reduced the amount of time the language, speech, and hearing clinicians had to spend in screening children.

Some school speech, language, and hearing programs utilize the services of volunteers or unpaid aides. These individuals have been used in assisting with hearing screening programs. The school clinician must train the volunteers in the specific tasks they are to perform. Often mothers of schoolchildren will serve as the volunteer aides in the screening programs.

Strong (1972) reported on a program in northern Minnesota designed to utilize supportive personnel in screening school populations for speech problems and managing direct therapy with children over eight years of age who exhibited frontal or lateral distortions of sibilant phonemes or distortion of the phoneme /r/. The program was carried on in a rural area, and the results indicated that the use of supportive personnel allowed the school clinician to devote more time to the more severe cases.

Galloway and Blue (1975) described a program in Georgia which was carried out over a period of three years. The paraprofessionals were trained to administer programmed materials to first- through fifth-grade students who had articulatory errors. The errors exhibited were in the mild to moderate range of functional articulation problems. The findings suggested that paraprofessionals using a preplanned program and materials can enhance the program carried out by the school pathologist by allowing more time for problems that require greater expertise.

A pilot program for training and utilizing communication aides in Head Start programs in Wyoming was reported by Jelinek (1976). According to Jelinek benefits other than the statistical inferences were realized from the program. The aides became skilled in the delivery of language programs and more knowledgeable in child development and behavior management. "Project staff were able to develop a liaison with Head Start staffs, parents, and other professionals in the community which might not have been possible without the development of the pilot program. Because of the success of the pilot communication aide program, this model has been expanded to include all Head Start centers in Wyoming.''

Costello and Schoen (1978) studied the effectiveness of paraprofessionals in an articulation intervention program in California using programmed instruction. The results indicated that paraprofessionals using a clearly written, previously tested programmed instruction format compared favorably with the results obtained by a fully qualified speech clinician. The use of audio- and video-tape aids ensured a standard quality program and reduced the responsibilities of the paraprofessionals. Costello and Schoen suggested that a possible future role of the speech clinician would be that of a program writer, program researcher, trainer, and supervisor of a paraprofessional staff. This would leave more time for clients with special and more complex needs, and would also enable the program to serve larger populations more effectively.

Paraprofessionals have been referred to by many titles, such as classroom aides, educational associates, teacher aides, and volunteer aides. A paraprofessional may be a paid employee or a volunteer. The background and educational levels and amount of training may vary, depending on the requirements of the school district.

Paraprofessionals in special education usually receive specialized training. The assistants in audiology and speech-lanugage, according to the guidelines of the American Speech-Language-Hearing Association (1981), may receive training provided through formal course work, workshops, observation, and/or supervised practicum under a qualified speech-language pathologist or audiologist. Appropriate areas of training may include

1. Normal processes in speech, language, and hearing
2. Disorders of speech, language, and hearing
3. Behavior management skills
4. Response discrimination skills including but not limited to the discrimination of correct and incorrect verbal responses along with the dimensions of speech sound production, voice parameters, fluency, syntax, and semantics
5. Program administration skills including stimulus presentation and consequation, data collection and reporting procedures, and utilization of programmed instructional materials
6. Equipment and materials used in the assessment and/or management of speech, language, and hearing disorders
7. Overview of professional ethics and their application to the assistant's activities

Some institutions have training programs leading to state certification of paraprofessionals.

As the goal of full educational opportunities for all special students is realized, the utilization of paraprofessionals by speech-language pathologists and audiologists will enable the professional to provide more services and allow more personal contact with more communicatively handicapped students.

COMPUTERS

The utilization of computers by the speech, language, and hearing profession in the schools, and by the profession as a whole, is rapidly becoming a reality. The school clinician has been slower to use the computer than has his or her colleagues in other settings; however, this is changing. According to Hyman (1985),

> In 1984, less than one-third of all ASHA-affiliated school personnel had ever used a computer. However, it is important to note that since 1982 the proportion of computer users in school settings more than doubled, representing the highest rate of growth in computer usage among all work settings. This may be attributed in part to the recent emphasis on computer assisted instruction (CAI), the increasing availability of powerful and inexpensive microcomputers, and the existence of more "user-friendly" software for diagnosis and treatment.

In the school speech-language pathologist's role as an administrator and manager, the computer could provide a number of advantages: saving time, conserving human energy, and increasing benefits to clients. The stumbling blocks to computer usage in the schools include lack of familiarity with computers, financial restraints, fear of learning how to use a computer system, and a dearth of speech-language professionals who understand its potential applications.

What are some of the benefits of the microcomputer (a smaller, less expensive computer) in the school? According to Krueger (1985) the memory capacity of the computer allows storage of a virtually unlimited number of items in the objective bank. In addition, items may be added to the bank for students who are not adequately described by existing statements or whose parents request additional items. Use of the computer assures that all steps necessary for compliance with due process are completed. This provides procedural consistency across clinicians so that every clinician in the school system follows the same procedure for each student, increasing the accountability of the department.

Krueger further explains that whereas in the past, therapy sessions had to be cancelled for one or two weeks to allow time for clinicians to complete yearly progress reports, computerization allows for typed documents, which are easier to read and more professional; in addition, the time saved can be used for an extension of direct therapy time. Krueger also pointed out that the use of a computer program could increase the possibility of research in the school system because of its data storage and analysis capabilities.

Accurate caseload figures, building figures, and disorder and severity data allow more efficient use of school personnel. Required reports can be compiled more quickly by the computer and more accurately. An analysis of computer data can also help identify trends, such as increases in a disorder or a population shift within the school district (Krueger, 1985).

Computers can be utilized in the generation of Individual Educational Plans (IEPs). Software programs have been developed that could save clinicians considerable time and effort in dealing with the deluge of paperwork involved in developing IEPs.

Screening programs for speech-language and audiologic problems can be facilitated with computers, as can the analysis of diagnostic data. Moreover, the potential for articulation testing and the analysis of these tests is inherent in computer usage.

The follow-up of students with hearing problems can be facilitated by computers. The hearing impaired can be helped through computer programs that utilize interactive learning and synthesized speech. The computer is also valuable to the hearing-impaired student as a means of access to information and visually oriented training and instruction.

A computer may be purchased by a school system for special education services, including speech, language, and hearing services. Before a purchase, however, there are a number of factors to consider. A major consideration is whether the computer will be used for administrative services or for direct therapy. Krueger (1985) outlined the six major steps utilized by the Great River Area Education Agency 16, Burlington, Iowa, a 13-school district area, which used computerization for reporting and administrative purposes in their speech program:

1. *Targeting the needs.* The decision was made to focus on administrative tasks rather than remediation. At this point a decision should be made regarding who will do the actual work on the computer, as it requires computer skills and a commitment of personnel time.
2. *Gaining access to equipment.* Three choices usually exist: leasing equipment from a computer vendor; using a computer service, which does all the work at set rates; or purchasing equipment.
3. *Obtaining equipment.* Before making the financial investment it is wise to visit a program with an operational system. The next steps included choosing the data format, setting up the format, programming, and preparing an item bank.
4. After the system is prepared *each step is thoroughly tested* to reveal possible shortcomings in the system.
5. When thorough testing indicates that the system will function as planned, *implementation* may begin. During the implementation period, staff training must be thorough. After the system has been tested and implemented, the system should be used "as is" through one entire cycle. If changes have to be made it is more efficient to make them simultaneously rather than one at a time.
6. The final step is a *systematic evaluation.* It was suggested that the system should be evaluated after six months, one year, two years, and five years of operation.

The school SLP contemplating the purchase of computer software (a list of instructions to tell the computer how to perform a specific task) is faced with a bewildering array of information and material. Beginning in the March 1985 issue of *Asha,* the Materials Section began publishing a review of currently available computer software. The Educational Technology Committee of ASHA (1985) developed the following review checksheet to assist in the evaluation of computer software (Table 5-2).

Today colleges and universities, continuing education programs, community education programs, professional organizations, and interested groups are offering courses, seminars, workshops, and short courses on computers. There are also some excellent books on the market that provide good basic

TABLE 5-2 Software Review Checksheet

| 1. Poor | 2. Fair | 3. Good | 4. Excellent | 5. Not Applicable |

1. Program Description
    a. Is the purpose of the program clearly defined? _____
    b. Is the manner in which the program works clearly described? _____
    c. Are the instructions for getting started with the program clearly described? _____
    d. Are the instructions for storing and retrieving data clearly described? _____
    e. Are hardware requirements clearly stated? _____

2. Program Effectiveness
    a. Is the software program logical and reasonable? _____
    b. Will the program produce consistent results in various settings under various conditions? _____
    c. Is there a reprint of an article, a technical report or other information describing the results of a study(ies) of effectiveness? _____

3. User Friendliness
    a. Is the program easy to enter, e.g., a turnkey system? _____
    b. Is the program easy to exit? _____
    c. Are the instructions displayed on the screen easy to understand and complete? _____
    d. Are the input responses to the machine familiar (such as "Y" for "yes" and "N" for "no")? _____
    e. Are program options displayed as "menus"? _____
    f. What does the program do if the user strikes a wrong key (does it give a prompt reminding him of the correct options and disregard the error)? _____
    g. Can input errors be easily corrected? _____
    h. Are data outputs easily retrieved? _____
    i. Are data outputs complete and attractively formatted? _____

4. Support/Documentation
    a. Is the documentation complete (does it tell you everything you need to know)? _____
    b. Is the documentation concise (does it tell you *more* than you want to know)? _____
    c. Is the documentation written in terms you can understand? _____
    d. Is the documentation well organized (can you find answers to specific problems by referring to an index or table of contents)? _____
    e. Does it adequately describe the hardware needed and any special instructions for its use? _____
    f. Are hardware and software options clearly explained? _____
    g. Is there a source for help (someone to call or write if you have a question)? _____
    h. Are back-up copies provided (if not, are instructions for making back-up copies included)? _____
    i. Can the program be returned if the user decides that it is not appropriate for his setting? _____
    j. Can replacement copies be obtained at a reduced rate if the originals become damaged? _____
    k. Can updated program revisions be obtained at a reduced rate? _____

SUMMARY OF RATINGS

---

1. Program Description*   _____
2. Program Effectiveness*   _____
3. User Friendliness*   _____
4. Support/Documentation*   _____
5. Overall Rating**   _____

---

*Summaries of ratings are the averages of items in each category.

**The overall rating may be different from the average of the summary ratings.

and advanced information. Perhaps you have had a course in your elementary school or your high school on the use of computers that included some "hands-on" experience. If you haven't had such a course you would be well advised to take one because, without question, computers are and will continue to be valuable tools in speech, language, and hearing programs in the schools. Not only in record keeping but also in therapy, computer usage will be limited only by the extent of human creativity and imagination.

Some universities are offering courses on microcomputer applications in speech-language pathology and audiology. Rushakoff and Lombardino (1984) outlined such a course and provided an excellent bibliography and a beginner's microcomputer glossary.

Computers won't replace competent speech-language pathologists and audiologists but they will replace people who don't know how to use computers.

DISCUSSION QUESTIONS AND PROJECTS

1. What are some yearly program goals you, as the SLP, might develop?
2. What are the advantages of written program plans and goals?
3. Is there state licensure in your state for paraprofessionals? If so, are there requirements for training, education, and supervision?
4. How could paraprofessionals be utilized in an audiometric screening program?
5. Are there training programs for paraprofessionals in your state? Where are they?
6. Check with the school SLPs in your area to find out whether or not computers are available to them in their school systems.
7. Write a report on Ruschakoff and Lombardino's (1984) article. Does your university have such a program? Do they have plans for one?
8. How would you, as the school SLP, utilize a microcomputer?

SIX
TOOLS OF THE TRADE: SPACE, FACILITIES, EQUIPMENT, AND MATERIALS

INTRODUCTION

It is important that adequate facilities and equipment are available to the school speech-language pathologists so that students are adequately served. Space, facilities, equipment, and materials may be considered the tools of the trade. Just as a carpenter needs good tools so does the SLP. In this chapter we will consider the basic needs and how they can be met.

PHYSICAL FACILITIES

There is at the present time a wide variation in the quality of work space available to school SLPs. The reasons for this are not always clear. Some schools are overcrowded, and the school clinician is in competition with other school personnel for the available space. Many school districts are financially strapped and can't provide the space. School buildings, new as well as old, have not been planned with the speech, language, and hearing services taken into account. In some cases the school administration is either unaware or apathetic about the issue of adequate working space. On the other hand, increasing numbers of school systems provide excellent facilities.

The beginning school clinician needs some sort of "yardstick" by which to evaluate and define adequate facilities. In many states minimal standards are established by the state board of education. These do not necessarily describe superior facilities, but they do provide a standard below which schools may not go. There is sometimes confusion about this issue, and the school clinician needs to be aware of exactly how the standards are worded.

The ASHA Committee on Speech and Hearing Services in the Schools (1969) published a list of recommendations for the housing of speech services in the schools. This may serve as a good checklist during both the planning stages of a program and the evaluation of an ongoing program

ROOM

Location: In a relatively quiet area near administrative unit with accessibility to classrooms, waiting area, secretarial services, and other special service personnel

Size: 150–250 square feet to be used primarily (or ideally exclusively) for the speech and hearing services

Number: One room, ideally with an adjoining office

Lighting, artificial: 60–75 foot candles

Lighting, natural: At least one window with shade, ideally with drapes

Heating: Adequate heating, ideally with thermostatic control

Ventilation: One window that can be opened, or air conditioning

Acoustical treatment: Acoustical treatment of ceiling, doors, and walls, ideally draperies and carpeted floors

Electrical power supply: One 110V double plug on each wall, ideally a rheostatic mechanism to facilitate use of audio-visual equipment

Intercom: Ideally, one intercom unit, connected to administrative offices

Chalkboard: One 3′ × 5′ (approximate) mounted on wall

Mirror(s): One 3′ × 5′ (approximate) mounted on wall at appropriate height for pupils. Should be able to be covered

FURNITURE

Desk: One office desk

Chairs, Adult: At least two chairs

Chairs, Child: Sufficient number of student chairs to accommodate pupils at various grade levels

Table: One table adjustable in height to accommodate pupils at various grade levels

Equipment stand: One stand on casters suitable for tape recorder, record player, etc.

STORAGE FACILITIES

Storage
space: Locked storage space
File case: Locked file cabinet
Bookcase: Bookcase with 4'–8' (approximate) linear space

EQUIPMENT

Audiometer: Properly calibrated portable audiometer
Auditory
training
equipment: Individual amplification units available according to need
Tape
recorder: One assigned for exclusive use of clinician
Phono-
graph: One 3-speed phonograph available in building
Telephone: One telephone, ideally a direct outside line
Typewriter: Available
Electric
clock: One
Wastebasket: One

In establishing criteria for evaluating physical facilities, the factors of
"realism" and "idealism" must be taken into account. Although it might be
ideal for the speech-language clinician to have a room used exclusively for the
speech, language, and hearing program, it may not be realistic; the speech
pathologist may be on an itinerant schedule, and the space could be utilized
by the reading teacher, for example, on the alternate days.

Another factor to consider is the existing facilities (things as they are
today) and the potential facilities (things as they might be with some modifications), particularly in setting up a new program. It is important that there
is a set of criteria which indicate that although the existing facilities may not
be satisfactory, they could and should be modified in the future. In assessing
this aspect of the program the policies of the school must be known. For example, is the supervisor of the speech, language, and hearing program involved in the planning of new facilities or the modification of existing ones?
Are staff members included in the planning? Are alternative plans considered,
such as the use of mobile units, remodeling of areas of buildings, or rental of
additional space? What are the budgetary allowances and constraints?

According to Scarvel (1977), the following questions should be asked:

1. Are the facilities of adequate size or space to permit total program flexi-
    bility? (The Key Term is Total Program Flexibility.) Can this be used by both
    Speech and Language Clinicians and Itinerant Hearing Clinicians?
2. Is the facility relatively free from extraneous noise? The Key Word is Rel-
    atively in being realistic in terms of the existing physical plant. (For example,
    one set of criteria required acoustically treated walls and acoustic tile on
    ceilings.) This is fine; however, we may find ourselves in a room not having
    this, but still free from extraneous noise because of its location.

3. Are there adequate furnishings for the type of services offered? (The Key Word is Adequate.) Ideally, maybe there should be more than those appearing on this list; but we're looking for *adequate* furnishings.
4. Are sufficient electrical outlets provided? (Key Word-Sufficient) This depends upon the type(s) of services to be delivered and/or equipment utilization necessary (rather than specifying an exact number).
5. Is the lighting adequate and the facility properly heated or cooled? (The Key Word is again Adequate.) For example, one source mentions the use of artificial light in addition to natural light; specifically, at least one window is needed.
6. Are facilities accessible to physically handicapped students? This criterion would apply only in those instances where physically handicapped students need to be serviced in a particular facility. As with the other criteria, those criteria not applicable to a program, or to the specific services provided, would not be used.

In addition to evaluating the room itself, there are other considerations in the planning stages. First, the room must be accessible to physically handicapped pupils and located in a area of the building convenient to all who use it. It should not be too far from the kindergarten and first-grade classrooms because these children sometimes have difficulty finding their way to and from the room.

Space is often at a premium in school buildings, and many buildings are old and not well planned for present-day needs. With a little imagination and resourcefulness, however, some simple remodeling and rejuvenation can transform unused space into completely adequate facilities for the school pathologist. For example, a portion of a large entry foyer may be partitioned and utilized for the speech-language and hearing program.

If a new building is being contemplated, the speech-language clinician will need to be in on the planning stages to insure adequate space allotment. School architects are not always well informed about the space and facility needs of the program, and the school pathologist can be of invaluable assistance in providing needed information.

The policies of the school in regard to space must also be known when planning physical facilities. For example, the school pathologist should know how space is assigned in a building and whether or not staff members are consulted when the assignments are made. The school pathologist should also know whether or not there are provisions for modifying the room. If space is to be shared, staff members should know the procedures for obtaining input from all the persons sharing the room.

Observation of Therapy

The school clinician may want to have parents and teachers observe the therapy sessions. One way would be to have them in the room with the pupil. This may be especially desirable with young children when the clinician wants to involve the parents in the therapy. Or in some cases it may be more desirable to have the parents or teachers observe from behind a one-way mirror. The addition of the one-way mirror, and possibly an intercom system, allows the school pathologist an opportunity to work more closely with parents and teachers by involving them in the therapy while it is taking place. Often school clinicians hear the comment from teachers, "But what do you actually *do* in a therapy session?" Having them observe would take some of the mystery out of therapy and would make vividly clear to them ways in which they could interact with the therapy process in the classroom and thereby help the child to generalize what he or she has learned.

Pleasant, Comfortable, and Functional Rooms

Most people feel better and do better in surroundings that are attractive, comfortable, and pleasant. Children are no exception. Color, adequate lighting, and comfortable furniture are conducive to good results in therapy. A child who is seated on a chair that is too big for him or her is going to be very uncomfortable. In a short time the child will begin to squirm and wriggle and will be unable to focus on whatever the therapist is presenting. The child may seem like a discipline problem to the unseeing clinician, but in reality the little boy or girl may simply be attempting to find a comfortable position.

One of the most attractive therapy rooms I have seen was in an old school building in a rural area. The whole building sparkled with cleanliness—wooden floors were polished, walls were painted in soft colors, and furniture was in good repair and arranged harmoniously. The therapy room was pleasant, with a carpeted floor and colorful draperies. A bulletin board served both a useful and decorative purpose. The obvious pride in the surroundings was reflected by the way the children treated the therapy room and its furnishings. The clinician reported that everyone in the school, including the custodian, the principal, the teachers, and the children were proud of their attractive building and worked to keep it that way.

In furnishing and equipping the therapy room the clinician should keep in mind that garish colors and busy patterns are disturbing and distracting to some of the children. Children with sensory problems, children with problems related to brain dysfunction, and children who are mentally retarded, may have difficulty functioning in a room that is too stimulating and distracting. The clinician may wish to arrange one corner of the therapy room in such a way that all potentially distracting things are out of the child's range of vision.

The room plans in Figures 6–1 and 6–2 suggest ways of utilizing space in a school for the speech, language, and hearing program.

Mobile Units

Overcrowded schools and substandard space within school buildings have prompted some pathologists to look elsewhere for the solution to the problem. Howerton (1973) described how he built a mobile unit to serve the speech and hearing program. He cited a number of advantages in using mobile units: They contain everything necessary for the program, thus eliminating gathering up and storing items every day; equipment is better cared for when it remains stationary and doesn't have to be transported in the trunk of a car; they provide quiet facilities for hearing, testing, and screening; and they represent a saving in tax dollars in comparison to the cost of building permanent facilities.

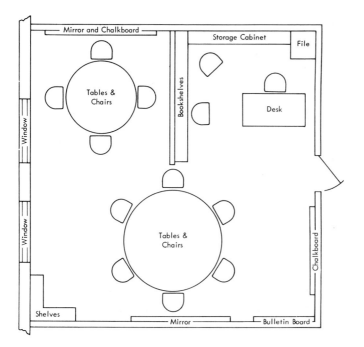

FIGURE 6-1 Room Plan

FIGURE 6-2 Room Plan

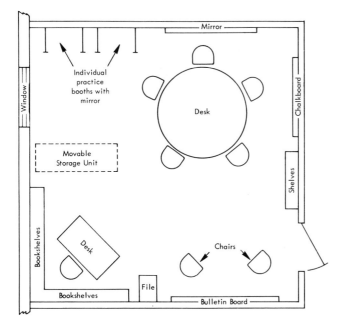

The Carteret, New Jersey, school district developed a mobile diagnostic speech, language, and hearing vehicle. The mobile unit provides for the evaluation of public and parochial (or private) schoolchildren with speech, language, and hearing problems. The program was developed through Project I.D.E.A.S. (Innovative, Developmental, Educational, Audio Speech) and was funded through a Title III E.S.E.A. Grant. The program allows communities to provide services that had been previously unavailable in a school (Nigro).

FACILITIES FOR ADOLESCENT STUDENTS

Obviously, facilities for intermediate and high-school students will be different than those for elementary and preschool students. The size and type of furniture as well as the arrangement of the classroom should facilitate group discussions and lessons. The typical classroom of rows of desks is not conducive to the type of learning that takes place in a typical situation. The use of carrels and learning centers provides the opportunity for independent work. Activity centers related to specific learning skills could incorporate vocabulary cards, work sheets, and learning games. Learning centers might include tape recorders, language masters, and microcomputers. A library center might have reading materials, books used for book reports, story wheels, and writing materials. A career education center might contain materials related to various occupations, job application requirements, and forms.

Figure 6–3 is an example of a speech-language center in a high school. A description of the high-school program in Evanston Township High School can be found in Chapter 8.

FIGURE 6-3   Speech Modification Suite, Evanston Township High School, Evanston, Illinois

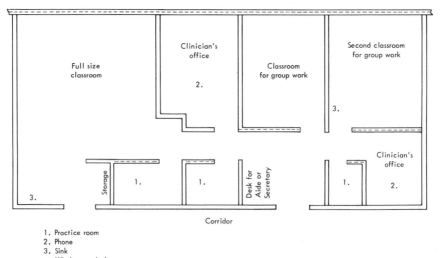

1. Practice room
2. Phone
3. Sink
— — — — — Windows and glass

SPACE ALLOCATIONS

The space allocations in schools have been improving in recent years, perhaps because SLPs now spend more time in each school and more schools have full-time or nearly full-time therapy programs. Also, school administrators are becoming more aware of the importance of speech, language, and hearing programs, and the needs of the programs are receiving more attention. Nonetheless, it is of vital importance that the school SLP assumes the responsibility of making the needs of the program known to the principal, director of special services, and superintendent. The school pathologist must be assertive and forthright in this endeavor. The student with a hearing loss, language-learning disability, fluency problem, voice disorder, or articulatory problem cannot benefit from therapy in the nurse's station, where there are constant interruptions and exposure to illnesses; in a room next door to where the band practices; or in a storage room that is inadequately lighted, ventilated, and heated or cooled.

MATERIALS AND EQUIPMENT

In addition to the therapy room, its furnishings, and the basic equipment described earlier in this chapter, other materials and supplies are needed for a successful program. In a new program the clinician should be prepared to submit a list of needed items along with the cost and the companies that manufacture or publish them. It might be well to consider the items on this list under the headings of *equipment* and *materials/supplies*. Equipment is an item that is nonexpendable; retains its original shape, appearance, and use; usually costs a substantial amount of money; and is more feasible to repair than to replace when damaged or worn out. Materials and supplies, on the other hand, are expendable, used up, usually inexpensive, and are more feasible to replace than to repair when damaged or worn out.

Sources of Materials

During recent years there has been an increase in commercial materials. Some of them are excellent and some of them are not useful for the purposes they claim to accomplish. On the other hand, there are many excellent homemade materials. These have the advantage of being inexpensive, and because many of them are designed for a specific purpose, they are useful.

Without decrying the use of materials, homemade or commercial, the clinician would do well to evaluate them from another point of view. Do they accomplish a goal in therapy for the child, or do they serve as a prop or a "security blanket" for the clinician? This letter from a staff member at Shady Trails, a camp for speech, language, and hearing handicapped children, illustrates the point:

> Before I went to camp they sent me a list of things to bring along. I didn't notice any mention of therapy materials. Should I take some along? I had been working

as a school clinician and had therapy materials of my own. What should I do? Well, if they didn't tell me to bring any, perhaps they furnished staff members with them after you got there. When I got to camp no materials in sight! What was I expected to do for therapy! I panicked.

Within a very short time we were plunged into the camp program and things moved along at a fast clip. Suddenly, in the middle of the summer, I realized I had been doing therapy for several weeks and hadn't even missed any therapy materials. How could this be! In analyzing the situation I realized we had been using the life experience situations at camp, the activities, the surroundings, the educational programs and the other people in the camp as our "materials." The therapy grew naturally out of the environment.

Perhaps we often overlook the most obvious source of materials—the school itself. If therapy in the schools is to be meaningful to the child it must be a part of the school program. The school clinician needs to know what is going on at various grade levels in the way of instruction and should then tie the therapy to the classroom activities. Looking at the books children read, talking with the teacher about the instructional program, becoming familiar with the school curriculum, and looking about the classroom itself will help the school clinician become more familiar with classroom instruction and will suggest ideas for therapy techniques and motivational devices.

In most states there are regional resource centers, which provide local school districts with resources designed to improve the quality of instruction for handicapped children. Instructional and diagnostic materials are available on a loan basis to school clinicians. The instructional resource centers provide other services with which the school clinician will want to become familiar. Visiting the resource center give the clinician an opportunity to examine a large number of tests, materials, and books before making a decision on which ones to purchase for the school. Personnel at the resource centers are also helpful in discussing the use of various items of material and equipment.

Regional, state, and national meetings of speech, language, and hearing pathologists usually include displays by commercial companies of equipment, materials, and books. Demonstrations of equipment are carried on by company representatives. This is also a good opportunity to get on the mailing lists of commercial companies. The school clinician may want to maintain a file of company brochures and current prices.

Shared purchasing of equipment   Another way to become familiar with materials and equipment is to discuss them with other clinicians in the area or with university staff members, if there is a university training program nearby. School clinicians in a geographical area may want to consider joint purchase of expensive pieces of equipment that could be shared. Or one school district may purchase one item which could be loaned to a neighboring district, while that district may purchase another item with the idea of setting up a reciprocal loan system. Time-sharing policies and insurance considerations would have to be worked out in advance.

Portability   The portability of materials should also be taken into consideration. The clinician on an itinerant schedule should keep in mind the bulk and the weight of the materials. Lugging materials and equipment in and out of buildings, not to mention up and down long flights of stairs, several times a day requires the stamina of a pack horse and has caused more than one school clinician to trim down the amount of materials used.

Activity File

Usually students enrolled in clinical practice classes start to collect their own materials and ideas. Many students have found it useful to start a file box of various therapeutic and motivational ideas. If the file is well organized it can be expanded and ideas can be added during student teaching and beyond.

The file should be organized in such a way that material can be easily retrieved and replaced. It is suggested that information be put on 5-by-8-inch cards so that an 8½-by-11-inch standard sheet of paper can be cut in half and will then fit the card.

Some students have found it convenient to color code the file, whereas others have preferred to alphabetize the information under headings such as *consonants, vowels, expressive language, receptive language, stuttering, voice, hearing,* and others.

Here are some suggestions for the ingredients of a file for therapy and motivational ideas:

1. Various ways to teach a child to produce a consonant or a vowel
2. Lists of words containing sounds in initial, medial, and final positions (If the student already owns a book such as Fairbanks, 1960, *Voice and Articulation Drillbook* or Schoolfield, 1937, *Better Speech and Better Reading,* it would not be necessary to make lists of words, but rather, to give the source of the lists.)
3. Sentences loaded with specific sounds
4. Ideas for auditory discrimination
5. Ideas for tactile and kinesthetic production of sounds
6. Poems, riddles, and finger plays
7. Flannel board ideas
8. Worksheets for home practice
9. Exercises for tongue and lip mobility
10. Ideas for teaching-unit topics (for example, astronauts, early American Indians, baseball, good nutrition)
11. Role-playing ideas
12. Relaxation techniques
13. Ideas for language and speech stimulation techniques that could be done at home by parents
14. Progress sheets or charting methods
15. Bulletin board ideas (These could be related to seasons or holidays or be of general interest.)
16. Word lists and pictures related to holidays
17. Utilizing puppets in therapy
18. Laminated picture cards illustrating nouns or verbs

19. List of records and books for children
20. Lists of dos and don'ts for parents
21. Ideas of movement activities that could be tied to therapy
22. Ideas for speech development and speech-improvement lessons in the classroom

The card file can serve a number of useful purposes. It can be an inventory of available materials and publications; it can aid in lesson planning; and the cards can be easily removed from the file and used during the sessions. In addition, it can serve as an aid when consulting with classroom teachers in speech and language development and improvement and serve as a source of ideas when working with parents. Plus, it is concise, easy to construct, convenient to use, and inexpensive.

Evaluation

At the present time there are numerous language programs on the market, but unfortunately many of them are untested. The clinician who purchases them may have no information concerning their effectiveness, validity, or reliability. Connell et al. (1977) have suggested that clinicians should not obtain language programs unless the information necessary to evaluate their usefulness is available from the company publishing them. They recommend that the information should minimally include (1) experimental analysis of mean or median trials to criterion and variance for each program step, (2) percentage of clients who complete each program step, (3) precise description of all the clients who were used in obtaining data, and (4) experimental analysis of the generalization of trained language behaviors.

The same cautions should be applied to the anticipated purchase of testing materials. New tests in particular should be evaluated carefully before they are purchased. Advertising brochures should not be the only criterion for selection, and the clinician should seek the pertinent information by querying the publishing company directly.

Expendable Materials

Supplies, such as paper, crayons, chalk, and some materials that can be used only one time, are usually supplied by the school; however, it does not necessarily follow that the school clinician has access to an unlimited supply. These items may be rationed or budgeted to the clinician on a yearly or semester basis. The clinician should be aware of the school's policy in regard to supplies. It should also be pointed out that because clinicians may function in several different schools within the same system, each school may have its own policy in regard to the availability of supplies.

Sometimes budget allowances are made on the basis of pupil enrollment. Both money and supplies may be determined in accordance with the total number of children enrolled or the number enrolled at any given time. Because budgets must be made out in advance, the figures may be dependent on last year's enrollment or on the estimated enrollment for the next year.

Budgeting for Materials

Materials, supplies, and equipment are purchased by the schools. In some schools the clinician is given a fixed sum of money each year to spend for these items. In considering the purchase of equipment, it should be kept in mind that although the initial expenditure may be great, it may not have to be replaced for many years. There is, however, the matter of repair, maintenance, and general upkeep to be considered. For example, an audiometer needs yearly calibration. This should be taken into account before the purchase of the audiometer and discussed with the company representative.

Commercial therapy materials are subject to wear and tear if they are used frequently and may have to be budgeted for periodically. Considerations in the purchase of therapy materials might be whether or not they can be adapted for a variety of uses and occasions and whether or not they serve the purpose for which they are being purchased. They must be appropriate to the age, maturity, and interest of the children.

Another matter to be considered is insurance on audiometers, computers, language masters, and other items of electronic equipment—a figure that should be in the budget. Also, if equipment is to be rented, the rental costs will have to be included in the budget.

The storage of equipment during the months when school is not in session, or equipment is not in use, is a matter to be determined by the SLP and the administration.

Budgeting for professional materials and activities   Professional books may also be considered part of the school clinician's equipment and therefore would be justifiable budget items. The clinician may want to add to his or her own library of professional books, and these, of course, would not be a part of the school budget. The same is true for dues for professional organizations.

Budgeting for travel   Some school systems allow travel money and expenses for personnel who attend professional meetings. It is wise for the new clinician to check the policy in regard to this matter.

If a clinician must travel between schools as part of the job, a travel allowance is available. Some school clinicians are paid a flat amount for a specified period of time, whereas others are paid by the mile. Some school systems make up for this difference by paying the clinician a higher salary that the person whose job does not entail travel between schools during the working day, for example, the classroom teacher.

DISCUSSION QUESTIONS AND PROJECTS

1. Visit several school speech-language programs and rate their facilities according to the ASHA guidelines.
2. Are mobile units used in your state? What are their advantages and disadvantages? Under what conditions would you use one?
3. You are the school clinician. The principal has assigned you to a small former storage room with no windows but a convenient location. You

are not satisfied with the room. Would you try to have another room assigned or would you modify the assigned room? Outline the steps you would follow, using either alternative.

4. Collect five advertisements from publishing companies of speech, language, and hearing materials and equipment. They can be brochures or advertisements in professional journals. Analyze the advertisements by using the Connell et al. (1977) evaluation system.

5. Start an activity file. Justify the method you have chosen to organize it.

6. Interview a SLP to find out how he or she budgets for equipment and materials and how the materials are procured through the school system. How are maintenance and insurance handled?

7. Draw a plan for your ideal therapy room (1) for an elementary school and (2) for a high school.

SEVEN
CASE FINDING,
CASE SELECTION,
AND CASELOAD

INTRODUCTION

One of the most challenging areas for the school speech-language pathologist is decision making in caseload, case-finding, and case-selection procedures. The ultimate task of the SLP is to identify and treat the student whose communication problem interferes with his or her educational achievement. The SLP makes decisions about how students are to be identified, how they are to be assessed, and which children should be placed in therapy. These processes are the cornerstone of accountability.

School SLPs are expected to comply with federal and state standards in screening, diagnosis, case selection, caseload, and delivery of service. At the same time they are accountable to the state standards and the local education agency requirements as well as the professional code of ethics. Sometimes these requirements are in conflict. The information in this chapter is presented to help the school SLP formulate the many decisions that must be made in these areas.

DEFINING THE PROCESS

Case finding (or case identification) refers to locating the communicatively handicapped student in the public school system as well as the preschool child who is at risk. Where it is not in conflict with state law and practices and court order, case finding would also include those aged 18 to 21. Case finding in schools is accomplished by referrals and screening programs.

Case selection refers to the process of determining which students are eligible for speech, language, or hearing services. Not all students referred nor all students who fail screening criteria may necessarily be candidates. Those with communication problems are determined through the following steps:

1. *Obtaining appropriate background information,* that is, a case history, including onset, past development, present status and other relevant information from parents and teachers
2. *Appraising* the problem by observing, interviewing, describing, and testing when appropriate
3. *Diagnosing,* which includes making a tentative identification of the problem and determining probable causes

It should be pointed out that the SLP must use judgment in determining how rigorously these steps are followed.

For example, the third-grader who exhibits what appears to be a serious voice problem may be suffering from a cold and sore throat. That information would preclude interviewing parents or obtaining a case history.

Caseload and composition refer to the size of the caseload, or the number of students comprising it, and the range of communication problems represented in it. Caseload sizes are often mandated by state and local education agencies to serve inordinately high numbers of students. In addition, there is little or no agreement at this writing among state and local education agencies concerning what is an appropriate caseload size.

Let us now look at each of these issues in greater detail and in the chronological order in which these procedures would be carried out by the school SLP.

CASE FINDING

Case finding is usually accomplished by utilizing two procedures, either singly or in combination—*referral* and *screening.* The purpose of both referral and screening is the identification of the student with the communication problem. In many school systems referral is becoming widely used because of its perceived efficiency and effectiveness. In some situations, however, it may be more efficient to utilize screening, for example, on the kindergarten or first-grade level.

Referral

Let us look first at the process of referral. The school clinician needs to be aware that a particular child might have a communication problem. The clinician, in the final analysis, is the one who is responsible for determining if such a problem exists; however, referrals can be made by anyone who has the child's welfare in mind and suspects a problem. This would include the child's parents, teachers, family doctor, school nurse, school counselor, principal, or the child.

Referrals should not be discouraged even though the clinician may sometimes feel that the classroom teachers overrefer or refer children who have problems other than those in speech, language, and hearing. The door should always be kept open for referrals. Teachers should be encouraged to refer any child they feel might have a problem, and the procedures and opportunities for referral should be presented to the teachers periodically. The school clinician will soon learn which teachers in a school are able to identify the communicatively handicapped child with a high degree of accuracy.

Teacher referrals for speech problems   Diehl and Stinnett (1959), in a study regarding the efficiency of teacher referrals in a school testing program, found that elementary teachers with no orientation in speech disorders were able to locate speech-defective children with less that 60 percent accuracy. They could be expected to fail to identity two of every five children who would be located in a regular school-screening program. They were able, however, to locate with 80 percent accuracy children with severe articulation problems. Teachers had the least skill in identifying second-graders with voice disorders.

Prahl and Cooper (1964) reported on a study in which 30 teachers in schools that had never had speech-therapy programs were given a statement describing and defining speech problems. The teachers then referred children in their rooms whom they judged to have a speech problem. Each child in the classroom was later tested by an experienced speech clinician. The classroom teachers were able to identify approximately two out of five children with speech problems. The percentage of accurate referrals tended to rise as the severity of the disorder increased. Teachers were able to detect stuttering problems more readily that articulatory disorders and were least efficient in referring children with voice disorders.

Roe et al. (1961) have indicated that school clinicians frequently use teacher referrals as a method of case finding. Almost as frequent was the use of surveys by the clinician.

These and other studies indicate that the school clinician cannot rely solely on teacher referrals and other referrals if all the communicatively handicapped children in a school system are to be located. Teacher referrals are, however, an important adjunct in locating the speech- and language-handicapped children.

Referrals on the high-school level   In the elementary school, teacher referrals can be utilized along with a screening program. Because of the difficulties encountered in arranging a screening in the middle school or the high school, it may be necessary for the school clinician to rely more heavily on the referral from specific teachers who have the greatest opportunity to hear the child speak. For example, the high-school English teacher might be a good referral source. The same might be said of the physical education teacher or the school counselor, both of whom have an opportunity to hear the child talk in a more informal situation.

On the high-school level, self-referrals or parental referrals are often good sources of identifying individuals with communication problems. High-school students who have a speech, language, or hearing problem will have to know about the services offered if they are to refer themselves. This means that the clinician will have to find ways of letting students know the services are available, as well as make it easy for them to refer themselves.

Helping teachers make referrals   If teachers are to be used effectively as referral sources, they will need to know several things, including what is meant by an articulation, stuttering, voice, language, and hearing problem. The clinician will have to be able to define and describe the various types of communication problems as well as demonstrate them. As a prospective clinician, are you able to imitate or simulate various kinds of problems? A library of tapes of various types of problems would be helpful for demonstration. Regional resource centers may have tapes, films and filmstrips available to school clinicians for teacher in-service programs. These can be borrowed from the center.

Teachers will need to have information on how children are referred and the criteria used in selecting children for therapeutic intervention. For example, why are some children included and some not? Also, why would it be better not to include a particular child with a stuttering problem in the therapy sessions until after some parental counseling has taken place?

Many colleges and universities have a course in speech, language, and hearing problems that is required of all education majors. It would be helpful to the school clinician if all teachers were to have such a course, but this is not always the case. The school clinician may want to consider teaching an in-service course to teachers. For many years in Youngstown, Ohio, clinicians would not service a building until its teachers completed and in-service course in speech, language, and hearing problems.

Although teachers and parents are probably the most prolific referral sources, others are also important. Other school personnel, such as the principal, school psychologist, and school nurse, are excellent referral sources. Outside the school, the welfare agencies within the community, physicians, health care specialists, and voluntary agencies such as United Cerebral Palsy, the Society for Crippled Children and Adults, and others may all be considered valuable referral agencies.

Referrals can be initiated in person, by telephone, or in writing. The school clinician will also need to know and comply with the school system's policy regarding referrals. Usually a written referral form must be filled out by the referring agent.

Following the initial referral, and depending on the information about the child gathered from the referring agent, the speech, language, and hearing clinician will have to make a decision about whether the student is to receive a battery of screening tests or a more complete assessment. In addition, parental permission must be obtained.

Screening

The clinician must decide when and where the screening will take place and which children will be screened. There are some general factors to be considered before making these decisions. According to Conlon et al. (1973) the following questions will have to be resolved if the school clinician is to make the best possible use of the screening time: What are the goals of the total speech, language, and hearing program in the school system? Is the program new to the school? Is the school clinician new to the community? Is the school's population a mobile one, is there significant turnover in the population each year, and is the population increasing or decreasing each year? How long has 60 percent of the staff been at the school?

When the answers to these questions have been obtained, the goals of the screening program can be established. It is important that these goals are not only established, but also in writing and made available to the school administration. When the goals are established, the procedures for carrying out the screening program can be made. The procedures should also be in writing and should be available to the superintendent, the director of special education, the elementary and secondary supervisors, the principals of each school, and the teachers in each of the schools to be screened.

It is inefficient and it creates ill will to collect data through screenings in schools and classrooms where the SLP does not expect to conduct therapy. Screening on the kindergarten and first-grade levels of schools to be serviced, however, may be the best way to identify children in need of further evaluation. This method is almost always combined with teacher referrals on these levels as well as parental input.

The purpose of screening is to determine (1) if a problem exists, (2) if further evaluation is needed, and (3) if referral to other professionals is needed.

The first step would be a screening process that would serve to identify children with communication handicaps. A second screening would be made of those children identified by the first screening or by referral as having possible communication problems. The second screening would be somewhat more extensive and would help the clinician pick out those children who are candidates for therapy. The third step would be complete diagnostic evaluation for children who need therapeutic intervention and/or referral to other professionals.

A procedure used successfully by many clinicians is to take three children at a time. While one is being tested the other two can observe and will know what to do when their turn comes without the clinician having to explain. As each child is finished he or she goes back to the room and gets the next child in the row. There is no interruption of the teacher's schedule, and the classroom activities go on as usual. A class of 25 children can be screened in approximately 30 to 40 minutes.

The same general screening procedures may be applied to small groups of children. The clinician takes a group of six to eight children to the therapy room where the screening is carried out, returns the group, and gets the next group. If aides are available, they may take the children to and from the classroom.

In many school systems a team approach is used in the preschool screening program. The team members often include the school nurse, psychologist, speech pathologist, audiologist, and other specialists who test vision, hearing, speech and language, motor coordination, dentition, general health, and physical well-being. Paraprofessionals or volunteer aides also assist in this type of screening program.

General considerations   Because the purpose of the rapid screening is detection, not diagnosis, the clinician will have to resist the temptation to spend more time that is needed with a child who obviously has a problem. Also, the clinician will have to tactfully discourage a talkative child from telling a lengthy, complicated story.

The results of the screening task should be recorded immediately after each individual is seen. All absentees should be noted, and arrangements should be made to screen them later.

Screening tests   Instruments for assessing communicative abilities during a screening program differ according to the ages of the children. The instruments should be easily administered and should identify quickly those children needing further testing. In a school screening, whether one clinician or several are involved, the screening devices should be the same, and the standard for judging the results should be consistent from one tester to another. The screening procedures should also take into account differences in ethnic and socioeconomic backgrounds of the children being tested. The examiners need to keep in mind that they are attempting to detect differences in speech, language, voice quality, fluency, or any other problems in communication that might be potentially handicapping to the child's ability to learn in school or function as a useful member of society.

Let us look at the rapid or first screening procedure. Several models can be utilized and some general principles can be applied for the rapid screening for speech, language, and hearing problems. The major purpose is to determine whether or not a problem exists. Ideally, all children enrolled in the school are screened. The screening must be done quickly and accurately; that is, it must be done with a maximum degree of professional expertise and with a minimum expenditure of time, money, and professional energy. Planning is absolutely essential. In addition to a general plan, there must also be a plan to encompass all the details of the screening.

Much of the screening is carried on during the first few weeks of school, but it may be done at any time of the year. Many clinicians prefer to screen the upper elementary classes early in the school year and the kindergarten and primary grades later. This allows the classroom teachers to become better acquainted with the children, and the very young child to become more accustomed to school. In some schools preacademic children are screened during a preschool roundup in May or August, just before enrolling in school.

Federal regulations do not require written permission of the parents prior to a group screening program; however, some states and some school districts do require that parents be notified.

Screening programs can be carried out by one clinician, by a team of clinicians, or by a team composed of clinicians and trained aides. If the school system is small and employs few clinicians on its staff, those individuals may want to team up with clinicians in adjacent towns or counties to accomplish the screening in both school districts more quickly. If more than one person is involved in a screening program, the procedures should be clearly understood by all to insure uniform administration and greater reliability.

Class survey method of screening for speech and language   The class survey method of screening can be used with any grade level and can be carried out by one clinician or by a team of clinicians. It is done within the classroom or just outside, preferably as close as possible to the classroom. The clinician makes arrangements through the principal and arranges a time schedule so that teachers know when to expect the screening to take place. The clinician explains the procedure to the teacher and also prepares the children by giving them an explanation at their level of understanding. Young children are sometimes fearful and may not be as cooperative as the clinician would hope unless they are prepared.

The class survey can be carried out so there is little interruption of the classroom routine. The teacher supplies the clinician with a roster of the children and indicates which ones are absent that day so the clinician can screen them later. If the roster is in the form of a seating chart, the clinician can take the children in order of their seating. In this way the clinician will not take up too much time trying to figure out the identity of very small children who have difficulty saying (or remembering!) their last names.

A comprehensive screening battery carried out by the speech-language specialist or as a part of a comprehensive screening program could include the following:

1. Hearing evaluation
2. Articulation appraisal
3. Intelligibility appraisal
4. Voice appraisal
5. Fluency appraisal
6. Language appraisal (receptive and expressive) on the
   a. Semantic level
   b. Syntatic level
   c. Phonological level

Screening procedures on any age or grade level are subject to the same degree of error. Some children will slip by undetected, and others may not be identified correctly. School clinicians and classroom teachers must work together to recognize any of these children.

Screening for articulation disorders in primary grades   According to studies, children in kindergarten, first grade, and second grade exhibit many phonetic errors. Some of these children will overcome their errors through the process of getting a little older and being exposed to the school environment; however, there are children in this group who will not improve without a therapy program. Differentiating between these two groups creates a dilemma for the school clinician. Obviously, because of the large numbers, all these children cannot be included in the therapy program. Through prognostic testing at the screening level school clinicians will be able to sort these children into two general groups: those who need therapeutic intervention and those who would benefit from a general speech-language improvement program.

The Predictive Screening Test of Articulation (PSTA) was developed by Van Riper and Erickson (1973) to identify among primary-school children who have functional misarticulations at the first-grade level, those who will and those who will not have acquired normal mature articulation by the time they reach the third-grade level. The PSTA has of 47 items, requires no special testing equipment, and is available from the Continuing Education Office, Western Michigan University, Kalamazoo, Michigan, 49001. The PSTA assesses the child's degree of stimulability—the ability to to repeat sounds, nonsense syllables, words, and a sentence; the ability to move the tongue independently of the lower jaw; the ability to detect errors in the examiner's speech; and the ability to follow the examiner in a handclapping rhythm.

In a study by Barrett and Welsh (1975), the PSTA was found to be a valuable speech-adequacy screening device for a first-grade population. The test was able objectively to substantiate, with approximately 90 percent accuracy, the opinion of the speech clinician that a child's speech is normal.

Other prognostic factors related to articulatory errors have been explored. One is the rate of change toward correction of kindergarten children. Steer and Drexler (1960) reported that the most effective and reliable predictive variables appear to be the total number of errors in all positions within words, errors in the final position, errors of omission in the final position, and errors on the *f* and *l* consonant groups.

Another factor related to the predictability of the correction of functional articulation problems is the inconsistency of errors. It has been generally accepted that the more inconsistent the child's articulatory errors, the more possibility there is that he or she will outgrow them. The rationale is that the child may be able to produce the sound correctly sometimes but has not learned the appropriate times to produce it. Children exhibiting this type of error should be further tested with an instrument that provides more comprehensive and systematic testing on the way sounds are presented in all possible phonetic contexts. For example, the McDonald (1964) Deep Test would yield helpful information.

Teacher interview screening   A method that combines screening and teacher referral was developed by Finn and Gardner (1984) at Heartland Area Education Agency 11, Ankeny, Iowa. Known as the Teacher Interview Screening, it is comprised of two processes: mandatory teacher in-service programs and the teacher interview. It was developed to utilize the teachers' expertise in observing communicative behavior. According to Finn and Gardner,

> The speech and language clinicians were required to inservice, as a minimum, all second grade teachers, but preferably all of the teachers in their assigned schools in order to improve the quality of all referrals. Second grade was targeted to screen as it was felt that this would eliminate most developmental articulation

errors (Heartland). To facilitate the inservice, a Communication Competency Screening scale (Figure 7–2) which describes communication skills was developed and light-hearted overheads made available.

The teacher inservice was held in the fall so that the teachers had a semester to observe their students' speech and language skills prior to the teacher interview in January or February. During the teacher interview, each second grade teacher was asked the following questions for each member of the class. "Considering the skills outlined on the communication competency scale, do you feel this child's communication skills are adequate when compared to his/her classmates?" The teacher and clinician then had three options available to them. (Refer to the flow chart, Figure 7–1.)

They could pass the child who had adequate skills, fail the child who obviously

FIGURE 7-1

Teacher Interview Screening Method

Flow Chart

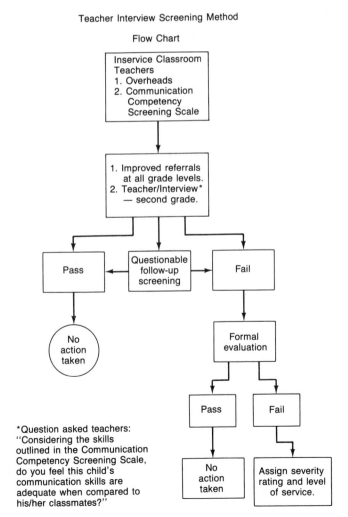

*Question asked teachers: "Considering the skills outlined in the Communication Competency Screening Scale, do you feel this child's communication skills are adequate when compared to his/her classmates?"

FIGURE 7-2 Communication Competency Screening

	POOR	POOR	ADEQUATE	SUPERIOR	SUPERIOR
Skill in communication	limited awareness of listeners; speaks with little effort to evoke understanding from others; pace of words and inflection of voice not adjusted to listeners				adjusts pace and inflection to listener; is aware of need to make self understood and can adjust content to listener's needs and responses
Organization, purpose and control	rambles; limited sense of order or of getting to the point; rattles on without purpose; cannot tell a story in proper sequence				plans what is said; gets to the point; controls language, can tell a story in proper sequence; speaks fluently
Wealth of ideas/amount of language	seldom expresses an idea; appears dull and unimaginative; doesn't originate suggestions or plans during play periods; seldom talks; rarely initiates; needs to be prompted to talk				expresses ideas on different topics; makes suggestions on what to do and how to carry out class plans; shows imagination and creativity in play; talks freely, frequently and easily
Vocabulary	uses a meager vocabulary, far below that of most children this age; uses ambiguous words				uses a rich variety of words, has an exceptionally large and growing vocabulary
Quality of listening	demonstrates poor comprehension of spoken language; inattentive; easily distracted				superior understanding of spoken language; attentive

Quality of sentence structure	omissions of structural elements, including word endings; uses only simple active, declarative sentences; word order difficulties in question formations				includes all structural elements; mature sentence patterns; maintains constant tense reference within a paragraph or story; mature use of phrases and clauses and conjunctions
Articulation	child is difficult to understand due to speech sound errors; speech draws attention to itself				all speech sounds are produced appropriately
Voice	distracts listener from meaning of the message; denasal or nasal quality; frequent loss of voice; recurrent hoarseness				voice is pleasing to the listener; does not draw attention to itself
Fluency	frequently repeats parts of words and whole words; demonstrates long periods of silence while attempting speech; demonstrates' struggle behavior				speaks smoothly

Adapted by: Heartland Education Agency from LOBAN'S ORAL LANGUAGE SCALE had inadequate skills or for those children whose skills were questionable, the clinician conducted a followup screening. The followup screening consisted of a classroom observation or a more traditional one-on-one screening depending upon the areas of concern (Figure 7–3).

In order to evaluate the effectiveness of the teacher interview, results were compared to the traditional method in terms of cost, reliability and compatability with current philosophies.

In terms of the cost comparison, a two year study was conducted. During 1980–81, data was gathered on the cost of using the traditional screening method with 4645 first graders. The following year data was gathered on 7292 students using the teacher interview method of screening. The results indicate the total time spent by the staff doing the new screening method was 100 hours and 42 minutes or approximately 13 working days. The traditional screening method took 897 hours or approximately 120 working days. At a perdiem salary of $90.00, this amounts to a significant savings. Reliability was examined by selecting one second grade classroom from one-half of the Area Education Agency's clinical speech services staff. Each clinician was trained in the use of a traditional screening tool. This was specifically designed to delineate the same skills as the Communication Competency Screening scale used by the teachers. Each child who failed either the traditional screening or Teacher Interview Screening was evaluated and the results were compared (Table 7–1).

Interpretation of the data shows 84% agreement between the teacher interview and traditional methods of screening. There was a 63% rate of false failures using the teacher interview method of screening compared to a 72% rate of false failures using the traditional method.

Even though both groups had a high rate of false failures the teacher interview method did a better job that the traditional method. It should be noted that there were no disordered students, those having a severity of 4, that were missed by either group. Also in the group missed by the teacher interview method, there were no students with a severity of 3, while there were 2 in the group missed by the traditional method.

Finally, compatibility with current pragmatic philosophies, which demand that communication be observed in a meaningful environment, has been met.

With the completion of this project it was felt that there is a better way to screen students for speech and language impairments. Using a well developed teacher interview procedure screening can:

a.   be efficient,
b.   sample a student's communication skills in his natural environment, and
c.   utilize the skill teachers have or can develop to identify students in need of our services.

Screening for articulatory disorders in older elementary children   In older elementary children, speech and language screening can be accomplished by having them give their name, address, and telephone number, by counting to 25, by naming the days of the week or months of the year, or by responding to pictures of objects designed to test sounds. The best screening test is spontaneous speech because it is most likely to yield a sample of the child's habitual speech and language. If the child is asked to read words, sentences, or paragraphs, the clinician must be sure that the material is within his or her reading ability.

COMMUNICATION COMPETENCY SCREENING

School: _____ Grade: _____

Teacher: _____ Inservice Dates: _____

Clinician: _____ Screening Dates: _____

Student	Pass	Fail	Conversational Skills	Sentence Structure	Articulation	Voice	Fluency	Comments

CC: White — Teacher
Pink — Clinician
Yellow — Office

FIGURE 7-3 Communication Competency Screening.

TABLE 7-1

Total Screened	– 812
Traditional/Teacher Interview Agreement	– 684 (84.0%)
Passed by Traditional/Teacher Interview	– 636 (78.3%)

	Failed by both	Teacher Interview Pass Traditional Fail	Traditional Pass Teacher Interview Fail
Total	48 (6.0%)	74 (9.1%)	46 (5.7%)

Evaluation Results:

Pass	1	53	29
*Severity of 1	4	3	4
Severity of 2	29	18	11
Severity of 3	14	—	2

*NOTE: Severity of problem was determined by use of the Iowa Severity Rating Scale (Freilinger, J. J., et al.) in which a rating of "1" is a developmental problem, "2" or "3" is deviant, and "4" is disordered.

A number of picture articulation tests can be used for screening. For example, the Templin-Darley Screening Test (Templin and Darley, 1969) contains 50 of the most common consonants and blends in the English language. The Photo Articulation Test (Pendergast et al., 1966) can be used in a developmental articulation test. The Picture Articulation and Language Screening Test (PALST) (Rodgers, 1976) is designed to be used in the classroom. It is easy to administer and score, and the clinician may also make note of any anomalies such as dental deviations, tongue thrust, or characteristics of hearing. The Goldman-Fristoe Test of Articulation (1969) tests phonemic proficiency in words and sentences. Spontaneous speech samples will yield information on the overall intelligibility of the child.

Screening for language disorders The identification of language disorders in the preschool and school-age child is a complicated, difficult, and often frustrating task. A thorough knowledge of speech and language development is required of the examiner as well as an appreciation of the fact that both the identification and the assessment of language disorders is a continuous process shared by the persons who are best able to observe the child in many situations. These persons are the parents and the teachers as well as the speech-language pathologist.

The amount of information on language is overwhelming, while at the same time, much of it is inconclusive. Professional speech, language, and hearing journals contain many reports of studies comparing language tests and measurements, which simply means that more is being added to the body of knowledge.

In the schools many behaviors are dependent on language abilities: reading, spelling, speech, writing, mathematics, problem solving, creative thinking, comprehension, and others. An intact language system is important in the learning process. The SLP plays a necessary role in the identification, assessment, and treatment of the student with a language disorder.

Keeping in mind that screening is an identification process, we therefore need to *identify* the student with the language disorder. The facets of language are reception (decoding) and expression (encoding). The components of language are phonology, morphology, syntax, semantics, and pragmatics. A complete language evaluation should include all of these aspects. On the screening level it is important to ascertain whether or not the language behavior is adequate and commensurate with the age of the student. The in-depth diagnosis would follow after the individual has been identified.

Language screening may include the following tests but need not be limited to them:

1. Zimmerman, Steiner, Evatt, *Preschool Language Scale.* Assesses skills in auditory comprehension, verbal ability, and articulation. (45 min.)
2. Stephens, *Oral Language Screening Test.* Identifies children in need of more detailed evaluation. (10 min.)
3. Carrow, *Screening Test for Auditory Comprehension of Language* (STACL). Identifies children in need of more detailed evaluation. (10 min.)
4. Rodgers, *Picture Articulation and Language Screening Test* (PALST). Designed to be used in the classroom. (5 min.)
5. *Bankson Language Screening Test.* Based on expressive modality but can be used to test receptive verification. (40 min.)
6. Mecham et al., *Utah Test of Language Development.* User may find it necessary to develop regional norms. Screening items include nursery rhymes, colors, sentences, forms, and pictures. (2½ min.)
7. Fluharty, *Preschool Language Screening Test.* Ages 2–6. Standardized from four racial or ethnic groups, three socioeconomic classes, and varied geographical areas. Assesses vocabulary, articulation, and receptive and expressive language. (6 min.)

It will be necessary for the school SLP to (1) become familiar with the various language tests; (2) find out what the test *purports* to measure and what it *actually* measures; (3) utilize the most appropriate test or tests for the particular situation and the students tested; (4) check the reliability, norms, and standardization of the test; (5) know the difference between "norm-referenced" tests and "criterion-referenced" tests; and (6) utilize clinical judgment and expertise in synthesizing the information from the tests. These issues need to be applied not just to language-screening tests but to all tests.

Screening on the secondary-school level Case finding on the high-school level is carried out more often by teacher referral than by screening (Neal, 1976). School clinicians, while recognizing the need of improved case-finding procedures at this level, point out the difficulties of a screening program because of the inflexibility of high-school class schedules and the greater mobility of high-school students, who are changing classes.

Another factor that would hinder both a screening program and a teacher referral program on the secondary level was pointed out by Phillips (1976). The study indicated that the higher the grade taught, the less aware the teachers were of speech disorders. She suggested that this might be a result of the fact that an increasing number of universities are requiring a basic remedial speech course of elementary-education majors but not of secondary-education majors.

One method of screening secondary students was described by Sommers (1969). In this program all the testing was done on succeeding Mondays because this was the day during which there was a minimum of interruptions. It was done in the English classes because each student in the school was enrolled in those classes. The English teachers were made aware of the screening program in advance. The clinician was seated in the back of the classroom and each student was called individually to read a short screening passage. A brief phonetic analysis was completed for those students with speech problems.

If a sufficient number of clinicians were available, the task of screening the English classes on the junior-high and high-school levels could be accomplished in a short period of time.

O'Connor and Eldredge (1981) suggested that screening English classes is one way to present the program to a large number of students. Another alternative is to screen the physical education classes; however, this might involve working in the corner of a noisy gym or standing on a windy field. Another alternative is to screen with the school nurse during the hearing and vision screening because there will usually be a small private room available.

Screening devices for adolescents often include reading short passages, answering questions posed by the examiner, and recounting events. Voice quality can be noted at the same time. Spontaneous speech can be elicited by asking questions, which will give the examiner some information about expressive language. A short test of auditory discrimination might yield important information as well.

The examiner needs to be aware of the possibility of fluency disorders during the screening. Verification would have to be made by consultation with the teachers who would be most likely to have heard the student in an informal speaking situation. These teachers might include the physical education teacher, the English teacher, and the guidance counselor.

Few screening tests for adolescents have been developed at this writing. One is the Screening Test of Adolescent Language (STAL) by Prather et al. (1981). The STAL is a screening instrument designed to measure receptive and expressive language skills through vocabulary comprehension and use, auditory memory span, language processing, and, explanation of proverbs. The test is appropriate for junior and senior high-school students, and the administration time is six to eight minutes.

COMPARING SCREENING AND REFERRAL METHODS

Matthews et al. (1984) described a study conducted in the Phoenix, Arizona, Union High School District. The purpose of the study, which was started in 1974, was to compare screening to teacher-referral methods on the ninth-grade level. The school district has eight high schools comprised of grades 9 through 12, a vocational center, several alternative schools, and a school for the train-

TABLE 7-2   Phoenix Union High School System

RESULTS OF SPEECH THERAPY SCREENING OF NINTH GRADE STUDENTS
1980–81

SCHOOL	GOOD SPEECH	RECHECKS-POSSIBLE SPEECH DEFECT	ABSENT	TOTAL TESTED
Alhambra	621	54	79	675
Trevor Browne	494	63	66	557
Camelback	509	44	40	553
Central	397	51	28	448
East	309	16	43	325
Carl Hayden	342	39	59	381
Maryvale	650	66	96	716
North	119	12	20	131
Phoenix Union	169	27	89	196
South Mountain	321	29	152	350
West	258	35	31	293
Desert Valley	4	37	6	41
District Total	4193	473	709	4666

SOURCE: Elizabeth C. Matthews, Kathleen A. Moore, and Amy Harris, "Comparison of Screening versus Teacher Referral in the Secondary Schools," Phoenix Union High School District, Arizona. Presentation at the American Speech-Language-Hearing Association Convention, San Francisco, 1984.

able mentally handicapped. The students come from 13 separate elementary districts and represent a cross-section of socioeconomic classes: 54.2 percent white, 28.2 percent Hispanic, 12.8 percent black, 3.1 percent native American, and 1.7 percent oriental.

During the five years of district-wide screening, between 5,000 and 6,000 freshmen were screened each year. Of those screened, approximately 5 percent were found each year to have speech-language defects. During the two years of the teacher-referral procedure only .7 percent of the freshmen in the district were referred each year for testing.

According to Matthews et al., a comparison of the results of the screening versus the referral process revealed

1. There was a significant decrease in the number of students identified with speech-language problems since the teacher-referral process was initiated.
2. Fewer students with voice or fluency disorders were identified because they were not being referred.
3. There was a decrease in the number of mainstreamed students identified with speech-language problems. Referrals were primarily special education students.
4. The referrals received from teachers were not always appropriate.

The results also revealed that the teachers on the high-school level preferred the screening process and did not feel qualified or comfortable in identifying speech-language problems.

In a telephone conversation with Matthews on January 10, 1985, she

```
                                              Phoenix Union High School System
                                                 2526 West Osborn Road
Memorandum                                       Phoenix, Arizona 85017

Date:      October 13, 1986

To:        Principals

From:      Dan Mangelsdorf, Director
           Liz Wallace, Speech Therapy Coordinator

Subject:   Speech Screening of 9th Grade Students


           Between September 6 and September 21, 1985, the district Speech Pathologists
           screened the 9th grade students at all eleven high schools.  Of the 6,053
           students tested, 675 were identified as having speech significantly deviant
           from the norm to warrant more detailed testing.  This testing will take
           approximately one week per school.  After this testing, the pathologists
           will be able to schedule students into therapy on a regular basis.

           On seven campuses we also screened upper class transfer students on the
           same day that we screened the freshman students.  Of the 371 transfer
           students tested, 45 students will require more detailed testing.

           The speech screening went very smoothly this year.  We found the English and
           Reading Departments to be very cooperative and pleasant on all campuses.

           I would like to thank all Exceptional Student Programs Chairpersons.  Having
           an on-campus chairperson to "clear our roadblocks" is extremely helpful.
           Attached is a summary of the district-wide speech screening totals.


           LW:db

           cc:  Chairpersons of Exceptional Student Programs
                Sheila Breecher
                Kathleen Moore
                Liz Prather
                Cindy Smith
                Lee Stafford

           att.
```

FIGURE 7-4

FIGURE 7-5   Speech Screening. (Instructions to Class)

1. Fill out the top part of this form with your name and student ID number, age, the name of this school and today's date.

2. You are going to have your speech evaluated; it's a very short and easy evaluation.

3. All of the freshman students in this school are receiving the same evaluation.

4. You will be asked to read a sentence aloud; it contains all of the sounds that are in the English language.

5. You'll also be asked a question or two.

6. We must have complete quiet in the room during the testing.

1. What's your name?

2. Read this sentence out loud, please. "After school today, I would like to get in the car, drive to the lake, jump in the water and swim from the shore to an island where I can catch some fish and think pleasant thoughts."

3. Have you ever had any speech therapy in the past? (Ask for details)

4. Do you ever have trouble with stuttering?

5. (If a dialect) Do you speak any language other than English?

6. (If language difficulty) Conversational speech: Where have you lived besides Phoenix? Do you have any brothers or sisters?

FIGURE 7-6   Speech Screening (Instructions to Student)

indicated that although screening on the high-school level does not save time it does yield better information about the students and seems to be a more accurate method of identification. Referrals from teachers are always encouraged, but high-school teachers are less likely to refer than elementary teachers. The speech-language pathologists in the Phoenix system felt that under the referral system students with voice, fluency, and language problems were often missed. Matthews also said that although STAL was not a part of the screening process, it was administered to students when it seemed to be indicated.

FIGURE 7-7

Memorandum

Central High School
4525 North Central Avenue
Phoenix, Arizona 85012

Date: Tues., Aug. 29, 1986

To:

From: Liz Wallace, Speech Pathologist

Subject: Speech screening of freshman students

Six speech pathologists will be at Central on Friday, Sept. 15, to screen all ninth grade students. We will do the testing in the English classes, English CRT classes, and Reading MRT classes. Please make a notation on your calendar. I'll contact you personally before then.

Thanks!

Liz

Phoenix Union High School System
2526 West Osborn Road
Phoenix, Arizona 85017

Speech Therapy Screening Form

Name _____   School _____

Student # _____   Date _____

Past Speech Therapy:

Articulation _____   Fluency _____

Voice _____   Language _____

Recommendation: Pass ____
                    Recheck ____   _____
                                          Speech Pathologist

Recheck Information

Date _____

_____ 1. No speech, language, voice or stuttering problems observed during reading or conversation.

_____ 2. Very slight problem; does not warrant therapy at this time.

_____ 3. Slight problem; possible enrollment if therapy slots become available.

_____ 4. Voice quality attributed to _____ . Recheck in _____.

_____ 5. Problem appears to be related to dental structure _____ tongue thrust pattern _____ , other _____ .

_____ 6. Recommend placement in therapy.
       a. Referral and Placement Form sent ____
       b. Referral and Placement Form received ____
       c. Enrolled in therapy____
       d. Refused therapy____

Comments:

_____
Speech Pathologist

FIGURE 7–8

Memorandum

Phoenix Union High School District, No. 210
2526 West Osborn Road
Phoenix, Arizona 85017

Date: June 25, 1987

To: Principals, ESP Chairs, English Dept. Chairs, Reading Dept. Chairs

From: Kathleen Moore - Speech Pathologist; John Miller

Subject: Speech screening

The Speech Pathologists have again planned a Districe-wide screening
program for our incoming freshmen. This screening will take place
between September 3, 1987, and September 18, 1987.

Below is the tentative screening schedule for ninth grade students
during English and, at some schools, Reading classes.

Please make a note of this date. We would like to avoid any conflicts
with school assemblies or district testing. You will be contacted the
first week of school by your school's speech pathologist. At that time
this schedule will be finalized or changed, if necessary

Wed.	September 3	West
Thurs.	September 4	Carl Hayden
Mon.	September 8	Trevor Brown
Tues.	September 9	East and North
Wed.	September 10	Alhambra
Thurs.	September 11	Camelback
Mon.	September 15	Central
Tues.	September 16	Maryvale
Wed.	September 17	South Mountain
Thurs.	September 18	Phoenix Union

Speech - At the high school level, various types of speech problems
are found. Following is a description of the major categories:

____ S1 Articulation defect: These students produce speech sounds
         incorrectly. One example is the "lisper" who produces the
         "s" speech sound incorrectly. ("I want thum thoup for lunch.")

____ S2 Stuttering: These students repeat sounds or words or "get stuck"
         when talking. The severity of this disorder can range from very
         mild to very severe.

____ S3 Voice defect: These are students whose voices are hoarse,
         nasal, breathy, harsh, too high, too low, too loud, too
         soft. They may have cleft palates, vocal nodules (growths
         on the vocal cords), or other medical involvements.

____ S4 Language defect: These students may have difficulty handling
         language related tasks such as speaking, reading, and writing.
         They may have trouble understanding and following directions
         and/or stating their ideas clearly.

FIGURE 7-9

FIGURE 7-9   (continued)

```
Frequently these students don't volunteer to speak in the classroom.
In fact they often are adept at avoiding speaking situations.  Stutterers
in particular develop strategies to avoid the embarrassment of speaking.
If you observe a student in your class who doesn't speak very often,
talk with him individually.  Here is a sentence we have found useful
because it contains all of the English Speech sounds.  You may wish to
ask a student to read this sentence aloud if you have not had an
opportunity to hear him speak.

After School today, I would like to get in a car, drive to the lake,

jump in the water, and swim from the shore to an island where I can catch

fish and think pleasant thoughts.
```

CASE FINDING: THE HEARING-IMPAIRED CHILD

The early identification of the hard-of-hearing child, whether the hearing loss is mild, moderate, or profound, is of concern to the educational community. Educationally, children with even mild and intermittent losses can have difficulties in the classroom. These children may seem only mildly inattentive and will be able to follow most fact-to-face conversations; however, they may suffer from one to two years of educational retardation as a result of bilateral chronic otitis media (McCandless, 1975). Furthermore, these children may fail to develop their first words until over two years of age and may maintain a delay throughout the early years if the condition persists.

According to McCandless, several factors may influence the degree of educational retardation caused by mild hearing loss:

1. If the otitis media is sporadic and involves only one ear, the effects will be minimal or hardly noticed.
2. If it is bilateral and chronic, the effects are much greater depending on the child's intellectual ability.
   a. Superior intellects are usually able to compensate in the home and classroom and will appear only occasionally inattentive. They will progress at about the level of the average child, although they could be superior students and excel academically.
   b. Average or slower students are more seriously affected. Aside from appearing to be generally unresponsive and inattentive, they may be as much as one-third educationally delayed. They are difficult to motivate and tend to give up easily because they have to work so much harder to hear.
   c. The most devastating effects will be on the children who are educationally marginal.

Who carries out the program of identifying children with hearing deficits in the schools? In a survey by Wall et al. (1985) of audiometric practices and procedures, it was found that the threshold testing part of the program was done by technicians (12.89 percent), nurses (46.47 percent), speech-language pathologists (25.89 percent), or audiologists (19.78 percent).

Public Law 94-142 requires the completion of an Individualized Education Plan (IEP) for all children with special needs, and this, of course, includes the hearing-handicapped child. The Wall et al. survey (1985), "The American Speech-Language-Hearing Association Guidelines for Identification Audiometry" (1985), and the "Audiological Services in the Schools Position Paper" (1983), strongly recommend that the identification and management programs for hearing-impaired children in the schools be carried out by audiologists; however, in many school systems educational audiologists are not available, nor do the school systems have access to audiological services in the community. In some states school and public health nurses are licensed to conduct screenings in the schools. In many school systems the screenings are carried out by SLPs, nurses, or the cooperative efforts of both, often augmented by volunteers and aides.

Teacher referrals for hearing problems   In regard to identifying children with hearing loss in an elementary school, limited research has been done. Curry (1950) reported that teachers were able to identify correctly one out of four children with hearing loss. Kodman (1950), by comparing audiometric findings and teacher identifications, found that teachers were able to identify correctly one out of six children with hearing loss.

Nodar (1978) conducted a study in which teachers of 2,231 elementary schoolchildren were asked to identify those with suspected or known hearing losses. An audiometric screening was then carried out; it was found that the teachers identified 5 percent of the children as being hearing impaired, whereas the screening identified only 3 percent. Following the teacher interviews, rescreening and tympanometry were conducted, and the results showed that the teacher screening and tympanometry were in agreement on 50 percent of the hearing-loss group. Nodar concluded that the observations and suspicions of classroom teachers can play an important part in identifying children with hearing loss in the elementary school. He recommended that teachers be included as part of the screening team and that their observations be given serious consideration.

The role of the SLP in regard to the hard-of-hearing child is to aid in screening programs and provide remediation. Where there are no audiological services available the SLP may have to assume the responsibility of the hearing-conservation program, including the screening program. Other options include contracting for audiological services or sharing service providers with nearby school districts.

The Model Regulations of ASHA (Jones & Healey, 1973) provide for identification audiometry as follows:

   a.   The hearing screening program shall be based on audiometric testing of individuals or groups of pupils. Individual tests shall be administered to prekindergarten through third-grade pupils, except in those cases where the

(Department) approves computerized or other appropriate procedures. Individual or group tests may be used with pupils above the third-grade level.

b. Screening audiometers shall be calibrated to American National Standards Institute (ANSI) specifications initially, and recalibrated as needed, and at least (annually). Daily listening checks shall be performed to determine that audiometers are grossly in calibration and that no defects exist in major components.

c. The ambient noise level in any space used for audiometric screening shall not exceed 51 dB.

d. Identification audiometry programs shall be conducted or supervised by a qualified audiologist or speech pathologist with appropriate training in audiology. Support personnel may administer hearing screening tests under the supervision of a qualified speech pathologist or audiologist, after appropriate training. Control measures shall be included to validate and, where necessary, correct testing procedures.

e. Screening procedures shall be administered uniformly by all examiners, with specified test frequencies, screening level and criteria for failure. Minimum procedures shall include: screening at 20 dB HTL at 1000 Hz and 2000 Hz and at 25 dB HTL at 4000 Hz; failure to hear at the recommended screening level at any frequency is the criterion for failure.

f. Rescreening of failures shall be provided within a reasonable period after the initial testing, preferably within one week.

g. Comprehensive audiological evaluation shall be secured for failures on rescreening and be administered by qualified audiologists.

h. Pupils shown to have hearing loss as a result of comprehensive audiological assessment shall be referred for otologic examination to a licensed physician.

The typical hearing screening test utilized by school clinicians has been the pure tone audiometric test in which the frequencies 500 to 4000 Hz have been presented at 20 or 25 dB HL to each ear of the child being tested. Children failing to respond at any of these frequencies were then referred for further evaluation.

Impedance Audiometry

Berg (1976) stated that a comprehensive program of identification audiometry should be conducted in each school system on a continuing basis. He recommends that the program include conventional and/or impedance audiometry to identify ear pathologies and hearing loss among children.

Navarro and Klodd (1978) feel that impedance audiometry is superior to pure-tone screening because it is capable of detecting middle-ear pathologies with greater reliability; middle-ear problems are often associated with less severe conductive hearing losses, which may not be detected if the ambient noise level in the testing facility is not adequate. In addition, Navarro and Klodd feel that impedance audiometry would be an advantage to the school clinician because it does not rely heavily on the cooperation of the child, enabling very young children to be tested with more reliability. Impedance audiometry is not influenced by the high levels of noise present in schools.

A possible disadvantage to impedance audiometry at the present time is the high initial cost of the equipment. This problem may be lessened as more units are sold and the cost becomes lower. The cost factor may also be somewhat alleviated if several school systems purchase the equipment cooperatively and share the use.

Cody (1976) stated that in his opinion impedance audiometry used in conjunction with pure-tone screening audiometry is the best possible means available to identifying children with ear problems. He further feels that the cost of this equipment is insignificant when compared to its ability to detect and thus allow early treatment and correction of ear problems that have proven to be educationally handicapping in young school-age children.

Importance of Screening Special Populations

Many children who have been labeled as learning disabled, mentally retarded, cerebral palsied, and emotionally disturbed may also have hearing impairments, which may go undetected because the other handicapping conditions are more obvious. In some instances these children may have been misdiagnosed. It is important for the school clinician to be aware of these children and apply the appropriate screening and diagnostic evaluations.

It is also possible that many children who were thought to be retarded, schizophrenic, or brain damaged were hearing impaired instead. A child who cannot hear speech or sounds in the environment will have great difficulty learning both in the schoolroom and in the preschool years.

The screening and assessment of special education children and children being considered for placement in special education classes should be included in the general testing program. When the facilities for further evaluation of these children are not available in the school, they should be referred for audiological services to a university clinic, hearing and speech center, hospital clinic, or wherever they may receive the appropriate services.

The Pediatric-Otologic Diagnostic (P.O.D.) Clinic in Ohio serves as a referral facility for school clinicians. These clinics are a function of the Ohio Department of Health in cooperation with personnel from local health departments; university speech pathologists and audiologists; medical personnel; and school speech, language, and hearing pathologists. The P.O.D. clinics are held periodically, usually monthly, in 47 geographical areas of the state. Preschool and school-age children are referred to the clinic by nurses, doctors, and school clinicians, and are accompanied to the clinic by the parents and often the school clinicians. The staff is composed of a pediatrician, otolaryngologist, audiologist, speech-language pathologist, and nurses in the local health department. There is no charge to the parents for the examination of the child by each of the specialists. The follow-up of the referrrals is accomplished by the nurses.

Preschool Screening

According to Bergman (1964), with some individual exceptions, children from ages three to five years are ready for the application of monaural low-intensity screening tests.

A recent unpublished study of over 3,800 preschool children in New York City Day Care Centers demonstrated that the simple handraising responses to the test tones, as employed with older children, is a quick, efficient method for large-scale testing of children from three to five years. A key aspect of such screen testing of three-year-olds is the instruction and preparation of the children in groups. Ideally this is accomplished by the regular nursery teacher, who has been instructed by the test supervisor. In this way the test becomes a familiar game for all the children. The preparation involves group hand-raising responses to soft chirp sounds produced by the teacher, followed by individual children (first the more confident ones, then the more timid), each demonstrating to the rest of the children how well and how quickly he can raise his hand in response to the sound. On the day the tester arrives one, two, or three screening audiometers and testers are installed in one room of the nursery. The children come to the audiometers in groups of three for each instrument, are briefly reinstructed and two sit quietly by as one is rapidly screened. Each child, therefore, has had the benefit of previous instruction, reinstruction and observation while two of his peers performed the test task. With such preparation, from 85 to 95 percent of three-year-olds can be successfully tested on each ear with the simple pure tone screening audiometer. Approximately 96 percent of four-year-olds and 99 percent of five-year-olds can be thus screened in a nursery or similar group situation even with less preparation.

For children below three years of age the screening techniques described thus far do not apply. This not to say that it is not important to detect and assess the hearing of very young children; it is extremely vital. There are today, however, guidelines and techniques that audiologists have found useful and effective in the testing of newborns and infants.

Hearing Testing Facilities

School clinicians encounter a number of problems in screening programs. One major problem is the lack of a room sufficiently quiet to produce reliable test results. It would be extremely unusual to find a space with an ambient noise level below 51 dB, as recommended by the Model Regulations (Jones & Healey, 1973). Testing in unsuitable rooms results in a large number of rescreenings, and eventually, in overreferrals. This can be translated into time wasted by the clinician and both time and money wasted by parents.

In order to overcome noisy testing conditions, the tester may compensate by raising the dB HL level above 20 or 25. As shown by Melnick et al. (1964), this may result in serious limitations in identifying children with slight conductive hearing losses. Middle-ear problems are often associated with slight conductive losses, so it is a possibility that many children with middle-ear pathologies will not be detected if there is not strict compliance with recommended screening procedures.

The school clinician should insist on good testing facilities in the school. Sometimes this means demonstrating to the principal and administration what is meant by a quiet room by actually measuring the ambient noise and comparing it to the recommended standards for testing.

Mobile testing units When good testing facilities are not available within the school buildings, some schools and communities have attempted to solve the dilemma by taking the service to the client. Mobile testing units have been used with success in many parts of the United States and Canada. These vehicles are often custom designed. They are self-contained units with their own water supply systems, heating and cooling systems, electrical power generators, and other necessities needed in such laboratories. The vehicles are fitted with soundproof rooms; noise-reduction barriers in the walls; clinic areas with desks, tables, and chairs; storage space for records; testing equipment; electronic calibrating equipment; and space for therapy equipment supplies and other materials needed.

Mobile hearing and speech units are often joint cost-sharing projects of local school systems, local health departments, voluntary civic organizations, and universities. Many areas are served by these units, which test preschool children and are also used in the testing of adults and in industrial hearing conservation programs.

Further readings You, as a potential school SLP, need to become familiar with two articles published in *Asha,* both of which provide detailed information on audiological practices in educational settings: "Audiological Services in the Schools Position Statement," May 1983, and "Guidelines for Identification Audiometry," May 1985. The latter article contains information on screening children three years old through the third grade.

Further references on this topic are

BERG, FREDERICK S. *Educational Audiology: Hearing and Speech Management.* New York: Grune & Stratton, Inc., 1976

CLARK, JOHN GREER. *Audiology for the School Speech-Language Clinician.* Springfield, Ill.: Charles C Thomas, Publisher, 1980.

ROSS, MARK, with DIANE BRACKETT and ANTONIA MAXON. *Hard of Hearing Children in Regular Schools.* Englewood Cliffs, N.J.: Prentice-Hall, Inc., 1982

CASE SELECTION

Priority System of Caseload Selection

Zemmol (1977) reported on a priority system of caseload selection developed by the Department of Speech and Language Services, School District of the City of Ferndale, Michigan. The priority system was used by the school SLPs to organize the delivery-of-service systems according to pupils' needs. It provides a rationale for time allocations, supports accountability, and is adaptable to various scheduling models.

According to Zemmol,

The priority system of case-load selection is based on a continuum of need and is comprehensive inasmuch as it encompasses the full range of speech and language services within a case load. All pupils with communication problems are reviewed as they progress along a continuum of need for first priority, second priority, third priority, consultative, and reevaluation services at a given time. The amount of clinical time available is allocated so that pupils with handicapping speech and language disorders receive more clinical time and attention than those with speech deviations or developmental lags in articulation or language acquisition. Consultative services are provided to pupils who do not require regularly scheduled sessions, as well as to teachers, other school personnel, and parents. Activities oriented toward prevention are included under consultative services.

The priority system of case-load selection provides for equitable distribution of services by speech and language pathologists since school assignments are based on a weighted ratio of priority cases rather than case-load numbers or school enrollments. The system provides evidence for increasing or decreasing clinical services as specific school populations and their problems change.

The categories described within each priority grouping are not complete, mutually exclusive, or listed in order of importance. They serve to illustrate the possible problem areas within a case load. At times clinical judgment overrides priority boundaries when appropriate for individual cases.

First priority   This group encompasses pupils with severely handicapping communicative disorders for whom intensive programming is indicated.

     I.   Language
        A.   Severe delay in language acquisition
        B.   Handicapping disability in reception, integration, or expression of language.
     II.   Organically based articulatory disorders
        A.   Dysarthria, oral dyspraxia
        B.   Developmental anomalies
     III.   Articulatory disorders of unspecified etiology resulting in unintelligible speech
     IV.   Dysfluency—severe
     V.   Voice disorders, particularly at the initial stages of vocal rehabilitation
     VI.   Speech and language problems related to moderate-to-severe loss of hearing
     VII.   Hypernasality
     VIII.   Multiple speech and language problems

Second priority   Pupils with moderate speech and language handicaps or deviations are included. Scheduling is less frequent than for pupils falling within the first priority.

     I.   Language
        A.   Moderate-to-mild delay in language acquisition
        B.   Moderate-to-mild deficit in reception, integration, or expression of language
        C.   Residual problems of pupils previously enrolled under first priority
     II.   Articulation
        A.   Pupils with moderately handicapping articulatory defects—fair intelligibility
        B.   Former first priority cases who can be scheduled less intensively

   III.   Dysfluency—moderate
   IV.   Voice deviations—moderate
    V.   Speech and language problems related to mild-to-moderate loss of hearing

Third priority   Pupils with mild speech or language handicaps or deviations are scheduled in the available time, as feasible.

     I.   Pupils listed previously as first or second priority who are approaching stabilization of appropriate or optimal speech patterns
    II.   Pupils with poor motivation or for whom the likelihood of significant progress is highly questionable
   III.   Pupils previously dismissed or at the consultative level who could benefit from supportive work
   IV.   Those not previously enrolled who demonstrate developmental articulatory errors, or mild speech or language deviations

Consultative services   Scheduling allows for evaluations and consultation by appointment.

     I.   Pupils not actively enrolled in the program who require periodic reevaluation
    II.   Parents
        A.   Counseling regarding the prevention of hearing, speech, and language handicaps
        B.   Speech and language stimulation activities for preschool children
        C.   Appropriate strategies for home practice
   III.   In-service training for teachers
        A.   Reinforcement of speech and language in the classroom
        B.   Speech and language acquisition
        C.   Identification of speech and language disorders for diagnostic referral
        D.   Recognition of potential language-based learning disabilities
   IV.   Administrators
    V.   Preschool evaluations and referrals

The population served on the continuum of need in the priority system of case-load selection parallels the continuum of school-clinical services described by Healey (1973). First priority cases, those with severely handicapping speech and language disabilities, correspond to pupils in the communicative disorders component. Second priority cases, those with moderate speech or language handicaps, correspond to the communicative deviations component. Third priority cases, those with mild speech and language handicaps, correspond to the communicative development component. Consultative services are appropriate for those pupils who require periodic reevaluation or intervention.

Pupils who enter the clinical speech program at a given priority level generally move along the continuum into a priority of lesser need. As their speech and language behaviors are modified they may move to consultative services prior to dismissal. Periodic review tracks each pupil's movement through the progression of priority rankings to dismissal from the program.

The use of performance objectives aids in this evaluative process and enables the speech pathologist to chart the longitudinal progress of each pupil.

A Rating Scale for Case Selection

Iowa's Severity Rating Scales for Communication Disabilities (ISRS) (Barker et al., 1982) is based on the continuum-of-services concept (see Chapter 4). The rating scales (see Figure 7-10) assist the SLP in case selection and suggest the intensity of the service-delivery model.

FIGURE 7-10

ARTICULATION SEVERITY RATING SCALE	
RATING	CHARACTERISTICS
0	Normal
1	Inconsistent misarticulation of phonemes, whether substituted, omitted, or distorted. Sounds must be stimulable and no more than 6 months below the developmental age for the phoneme.
2	Consistent misarticulation of phonemes, but not interfering with intelligibility. Phonemes may be stimulable but due to age or other factors, self-correction is not expected.
3	Interferes with communication. Shows signs of frustration. Some phonemes may be stimulable. Distractible to a listener. Intelligibility may be affected.
4	Unintelligible all of the time. Interferes with communication. Pupil show signs of frustration and refuses to speak at times. Difficult to stimulate most sounds. Distracting to a listener.

LANGUAGE SEVERITY RATING SCALE	
RATING	CHARACTERISTICS
0	Normal
1	According to appropriate diagnostic tests used, the receptive-expressive, or combined receptive-expressive skills indicate a language difference. Inconsistent; a 0 to 6 month delay from established norms.
2	Appropriate diagnostic tests indicate a noticeable difference from the norm. Conversational speech shows definite indications of language deficit. A 6–12 month delay.
3	Appropriate diagnostic tests indicate a language problem which is interfering with communication and educational progress and is usually accompanied by a phonological deviation. A 12–18 month delay.
4	Appropriate diagnostic tests indicate a significant gap from the norm. Communication is an effort. Could range from no usable language to unintelligible communication. Educational progress is extremely difficult. Usually accompanied by a severe phonological deviation. A delay of 18 or more months.

When evaluating pupils in a regular classroom, a comparison should be made between pupils' language age scores (as determined by appropriate diagnostic instruments) and their chronological ages. Language age scores should be compared to mental age scores for pupils assigned to special education classes.

FLUENCY SEVERITY RATING SCALE

RATING	CHARACTERISTICS
0	Normal
1	Observable nonfluent speech behavior present. Pupil is not aware or concerned about the nonfluent speech. Normal speech periods are reported or observable and are predominant.
2	Observable nonfluent speech behavior is present and observable on a regular basis. Pupil is becoming aware of the problem and parents, teachers, or peers are aware and concerned.
3	Stuttering behavior is noted on a regular basis. Pupil is aware of a problem communicating. Struggle, avoidance, or other coping behaviors are observed at times.
4	All communication is an effort. Avoidances and frustrations are obvious. Struggle behavior is predominant.

VOICE SEVERITY RATING SCALE

RATING	CHARACTERISTICS
0	Normal
1	Inconsistent or slight deviation. Check periodically.
2	Voice difference is not noted by casual listener. Pupil may be aware of voice deviation.
3	Voice difference is consistent and noted by casual listener. Pupil may be aware of voice. Medical referral may be indicated.
4	There is a significant difference in the voice. Voice difference is noted by casual listener. Parents are usually aware of problem. Medical referral is indicated.

A 5-point rating scale identifies the degree of deficit in each parameter in which 0 = Normal, 1 = Developmental Delay, 2 = Deviation, 3 = Deviation, and 4 = Disorder.

For each scale in which the pupil shows a deficit, a total number quotient is obtained. This total value is then used to classify the pupil as having a communication disorder, a communication deviation, or a developmental communication delay.

A rating above 4 can be achieved if the pupil has communication problems in more than one parameter. For example, a pupil could earn a score of 4 (disorder) in the area of articulation and a score of 3 (deviation) in the area of language, making possible a total rating of 7, or a minimum score of 4.

The ISRS does not dismiss clinical judgment. For example, the speech-language clinician would need to consider the following factors:

1. The consistency of the inappropriate communication patterns
2. The pupil's ability to interact verbally with others
3. The effect of the communication problem on school performance
4. The possible impact of the communication problem on the listener

5. The ability of the pupil to communicate well enough to satisfy his or her needs
6. The status of speech and language stimulation in the home

Before a priority system can be put into use there would have to be the endorsement and support of the school administrator responsible for determining policy for the speech, language, and hearing department. The understanding of the priority system and the cooperation of the school principals would have to be enlisted for the system to function satisfactorily. The principal would be a key factor in the success of such a program. The classroom teachers would also have to be familiar with the priority system for it to work well.

It is important that in a situation where more than one clinician is employed in a school system, there is agreement on all the elements of the priority system. The system can be reviewed periodically by the entire staff of speech, language, and hearing clinicians, and any necessary changes and modifications can be made.

One of the major advantages of the priority system is that it establishes a continuum of services for children based on their individual needs. It is far superior to a service program based on unrealistic and outmoded caseload numbers or enrollments. The priority system allows for flexibility in changes in school enrollments and in the changing needs of the children.

Appraisal and Diagnosis

According to PL 94-142, all handicapped children must be assessed before placement in a special education program. This assessment cannot be racially or culturally discriminatory, must be administered in the child's native language, must be done by a valid testing instrument, and must by administered by qualified personnel. In addition, it must be administered so that a child with a sensory impairment, such as hearing loss, or a child who has difficulty using his or her hands, or a child who is unable to speak or whose speech cannot be understood will be accurately assessed and the results will honestly reflect the child's true achievement and aptitude levels.

Native language as defined by PL 94-142 means the language used by the child, not necessarily by the parents. For example, a child who uses English at school but Spanish at home could be evaluated in English. However, if it is obvious that the child is more competent in Spanish, the testing must be done in Spanish.

Public Law 94-142 indicates that each handicapped child should be assessed in more than the suspected area of deficit. According to Dublinske and Healey (1978),

> The communicative status of all school children should be assessed. However, some state and local school agencies do not require the participation of speech-language pathologists or audiologists on child assessment teams. As a consequence, the ASHA School Services Program recommends that all pupils suspected of being handicapped be screened by a speech-language pathologist and audiologist to determine the presence or absence of communicative disorders. If

the screening results suggest disorder, appropriate assessments should be completed and presented *at the child staffing by qualified personnel.*

Diagnostic-educational teams provide a comprehensive multifactored evaluation of children with potentially significant problems, including children with communication problems. Not all speech-, language-, or hearing-handicapped children necessarily require a comprehensive evaluation, but such an evaluation of children with concomitant psychosocial or learning problems can be important in determining their placement and therapeutic follow-up.

Speech, language, and hearing clinicians' responsibility in diagnoses
The speech, language, and hearing specialist in the school system has the responsibility of providing diagnostic services for children referred by the assessment team (of which the specialist may be a member), as well as all the children picked up by the speech, language, and hearing screening program and referred by teachers, nurses, parents, and others.

A minimal diagnostic appraisal would include an assessment of the pupil's articulation abilities and language competencies, fluency, voice quality, and hearing acuity and perception. There should also be an examination of the peripheral speech mechanism. In many cases it may be important to have additional information, which can be obtained through a case history. Such information would include developmental history, family status and social history, medical history, and educational history. A physical examination may be needed as well as a psychological and educational evaluation.

Parental permission is required in most states for the diagnostic procedures. The permission should be in writing, and usually a form is utilized for this purpose.

In some cases the school system may not be able to provide some of the diagnostic procedures because of lack of specialized personnel. In this event the school system may arrange to have these procedures carried out by a qualified agency with qualified personnel in the immediate community or nearby. It is the responsibility of the school system to see that the required procedures are carried out. Such referrals are made only after written permission is obtained from parents.

It should be kept in mind that the purpose of the appraisal and diagnostic procedures is to select children who may be placed in the speech, language, and hearing programs in the school. The school clinician must be prepared to describe how the pupil's disability will interfere with his or her ability to profit from classroom instruction.

Steps in diagnosis   To obtain a clear picture of the child's communication problems, the first procedure is to gather as much pertinent information as possible through a case history and an interview with the parents, the teachers, and if possible, the child. Each informant contributes information vital to the whole picture. The parents can give background information on the development of the child, the teachers may provide needed information on the present status of the child, and the child may be able to contribute information which may be of great value to the clinician.

After the background information is obtained, the clinician needs to add to it by describing the problem. This is done by observing the child using appropriate tests that measure the degree of the problem and suggest associated aspects. The clinician must be an astute observer and must be able to record information objectively and without bias. In other words, the clinician must be a good "reporter."

After all the information has been gathered, the clinician makes a diagnosis of the communication problem (or problems). A diagnosis, or an identification of the problem, is in reality a tentative diagnosis because as a human being grows and changes, the problem changes. A diagnosis is much more than putting a label on a person. It is convenient for professional persons to use diagnostic labels when communicating with one another if all parties concerned understand that the label is not the diagnosis. A diagnosis involves weighing all the evidence, discarding some of it as not being pertinent, and keeping that which merits further investigation.

On the basis of the gathered information, the testing, and the tentative diagnosis, the clinician then determines the prognosis and sets up a long-range plan for the remedial procedures. The long-range plan includes therapy appropriate to the communication problem as well as other strategies and treatment. The school clinician is involved in an interdisciplinary team approach with others who are interested in the child's welfare, and these individuals work as a team in establishing an IEP. The school clinician is responsible for the appraisal and diagnosis of the communication problem, but the clinician is a team member in the overall appraisal, diagnosis, and treatment of the child.

The clinician uses professional judgment about whether or not to utilize a long case history form or a short one. The clinician should have available forms appropriate for specific problems, including assessment of language and speech, voice, fluency, articulation, and hearing. A form for the oral peripheral mechanism examination should also be available.

The Placement Team

The appropriate placement of the handicapped child must always be made by a placement team involving, in addition to the child's parents (or surrogate parents), those individuals knowledgeable about the child. The federal law also specifies that the team should include a representative of the local educational agency, the teacher, and if appropriate, the child. Although the law does not state that other individuals are required to be present, good educational practice would suggest that other team members also attend. This list would include those persons who by virtue of their professional backgrounds and the child's unique needs would reasonably be expected to be involved. It might include the principal, psychologist, reading teacher, occupational therapist, physical therapist, vision consultant, and speech, language and hearing clinician.

The parent need not be the natural parent of the child as long as he or she meets the legal qualifications of the parent surrogate.

The child may be included *whenever appropriate*. Schools may develop their own criteria in regard to appropriateness.

The results of the evaluation and the possible placement options should be available when the placement team meets.

Coordinator of the placement team   The representative of the local educational agency usually is the *team captain* and coordinator, and as such arranges for the meeting, presides over the meeting, determines that all necessary persons are present, and acts as spokesperson for the school system. The chairperson presents the necessary information and data or calls on the person responsible for presenting it. The chairperson also has the responsibility of informing the parents of their rights. Setting the tone of the meeting and seeing that all the basic ingredients of the individualized education program are present, and that the procedures are carried out according to state and local guidelines, are also within the responsibilities of the chairperson (Sherr, 1977).

The teacher as a team member   The teacher is the person most responsible for implementing the child's program. The teacher in the case of the communicatively handicapped child may be the speech-language and hearing clinician or the classroom teacher. The teacher's responsibilities as a team member at the meeting include explaining to the parents various techniques used to meet the annual goals. The teacher will also explain to parents why one particular strategy was used instead of another. In addition, the teacher will answer questions parents might have about events that occur within the classroom. In effect, the teacher is the main emissary between the school and the parents (Sherr, 1977).

Speech-language pathologist's role on the team   The role of the speech-language clinician on the placement team may vary according to the guidelines and practices of the local education agency. If the child in question has a communication problem, the person providing the language, speech, and hearing services in the school needs to participate in the placement process. Although the placement team has the responsibility of developing an educational program for each pupil, the school clinician will need to provide input into the process of establishing goals, objectives, and intervention strategies. The school clinician will also be responsible for reporting to the placement team the results of any diagnostic and assessment testing and may recommend further testing.

Parents as team members   Making parents team members whenever possible gives both parents and speech-language pathologists, as well as other members of the team, an opportunity to observe each other's interaction with the student. Under PL 94-142 the parents may be team members in the actual diagnosis, treatment, and carrying out of the IEP. Furthermore, the more the parents are included in these processes, the smoother and the more consistent is the delivery of instruction to the child.

Both parents and SLPs gain from the insights of the other, and both will be able to use each other as a source for added ideas. Also, parents and SLPs will be able to keep each other informed about the progress of the child.

Reports to parents, both oral and written, should be in clear, understandable language and not in professional terminology. Clear explanations of the diagnosis should be made to parents. The SLP should make it plain to parents that diagnosis is an ongoing process and that, as the child changes and progresses, the assessment of his or her condition will change.

Speech-language pathologists should avoid labels as much as possible when talking with parents. If labels have to be used, it should be made clear to parents that they are merely a device for communicating.

The placement team's purpose　The ultimate result of the placement meeting is to develop an IEP for the child and to achieve agreement to that plan by the parents and professionals. The plan must be a written document, filed and distributed according to the policies of the state and local education agencies. Policies also regulate who shall have access to the report and how these copies shall be made available. A copy of the report is made available to the parents. All placement team members sign the report.

In most cases the speech-language pathologist is a member of the team if the child displays communication difficulties. If the clinician is not on the team (an unlikely but not impossible situation), a copy of the document should be made available to the clinician.

INDIVIDUALIZED EDUCATION PLAN

A sample IEP form is found in Table 7–3 (Dublinske, 1978).

> The components included on the sample IEP form conform to the IEP require-
> ments contained in Public Law 94-142. Many alternatives exist to develop the
> IEP and comply with the law. The suggested format is designed to provide speech-
> language pathologists and audiologists with decision-making information that
> can be used, if necessary, to improve program and case management procedures.
> The content included in the sample IEP shows how the information would ap-
> pear on an IEP. Many IEPs will be more complex and detailed than the sample
> IEP.
>
> I. *Identification/Development Information*
> This section contains demographic information related to the child and in-
> formation on IEP development and implementation activities. Components in-
> cluded in this section may vary depending on information required by the local
> education agency.
>
> The "case coordinator" could be a staff person assigned to coordinate case
> assignments within the agency, or the person with primary responsibility for im-
> plementing the IEP.
>
> If the IEP has to be approved by an immediate supervisor, this person can
> sign off in the "approved by" space.

TABLE 7-3   Individualized Education Plan (IEP)

I.   IDENTIFICATION/DEVELOPMENT INFORMATION

NAME: Bret I. Valip   D.O.B.   5/3/73

Case Coordinator: Mr. SLP   Approved by: Ms. S. E., Director

Service Year: 197X–7X   Date IEP Developed: 9/15/7X

IEP Entry Date: 10/1/7X   IEP Exit Date: 10/1/7X

Follow-up/Review Dates: 12/1/7X, 5/1/7X, 9/25/7X

Persons Developing IEP	*Person(s) Implementing IEP*
Mr. SLP	Mr. SLP
R. C. Teacher	
Mrs. I. Valip	

II.   ASSESSMENT INFORMATION

ASSESSMENT PROCEDURES	DATE	RESULTS	EXAMINER
LEA Spatial Relations test	8/28/7X	20% accuracy for spatial relations *in, on, under, behind, above*	R. C. Teacher
Carrow Test of Auditory Comprehension of Language	8/30/7X	Obtained age equilvalent score of 3.6. Analysis of preposition items found child identified 90% incorrectly	SLP
Spontaneous Language Sample	9/5/7X	Analysis of a 50-item sample found 10% correct use of prepositions	SLP

III.   SPECIAL EDUCATION AND RELATED SERVICES NEEDED

SPECIAL EDUCATION AND RELATED SERVICES	TIME	PARTICIPATION IN REGULAR EDUCATION PROGRAMS	TIME
1. Enroll in the language teaching resource program one hour per day	33%	1. Enrolled in regular kindergarten class two hours per day	66%
2. Refer to the University Medical Center for otologic and neurologic assessments			

(continued)

TABLE 7-3   (continued)

IV.   PLACEMENT JUSTIFICATION

Analysis of the assessment information finds the child to have a communicative disorder with a severity rating of seven. The recommended frequency of service for this type and severity of communicative disorder is intensive continuous. The child initially will be enrolled in a special language teaching resource program for one hour per day of individual and small group instruction. With daily instruction, the child's prognosis for acquiring the language skills needed for academic success appears positive. For the remaining half day, the child will be enrolled in the regular kindergarten class.

V.   PRESENT LEVELS OF PERFORMANCE

Language: Uses/identifies spatial relations (prepositions) *in, on behind,* and *above* with only 10% accuracy

Speech:

Hearing:

VI.   NEED STATEMENTS

---

1. There is a need to increase correct use of prepositions

VII.   ANNUAL GOALS

---

1. By June 12, 197X the child will use prepositions *in, on, behind,* and *above* with 80% accuracy.

_____
Signature (parent or guardian)

        VIII.   Instructional Objectives
          IX.   Recommendations
            X.   Status Report

STATUS CODE	PARTIALLY COMPLETED CODE
A – According to schedule	1 – 0–19%
B – Not Begun	2 – 20–39%
C – Completed	3 – 40–59%
D – Delayed	4 – 60–79%
E – Eliminated	5 – 80–99%
R – Revised	
PC – Partially Completed	

TABLE 7–3   (continued)

PERFOR-MANCE AREA	VIII. INSTRUCTIONAL OBJECTIVES	IX. RECOMMENDATIONS	X. STATUS REPORT A B C D E PC R
Language	By December 1, 197X the child will be able to use the preposi-tions *in* and *on* with 80% accuracy in a conversational sample consisting of at least 10 *in / on* prepositions used in sentences. The speech-language pathologist will pro-vide instruction and record correct/ incorrect responses.	Use the LEA Preposition Teaching Program. Com-plete two lessons per day until program criterion is met for each preposition.	

REVISION OR COMMENTS

The "IEP entry date" indicates the date services will be initiated. The "IEP exit date" indicates the date services included in the IEP will end. Since IEPs have to be reviewed on an annual basis, the duration of services indicated between the entry and exit date is typically one year.

The time between the entry and exit dates constitutes the "service year." Space is provided to indicate the "follow-up/review dates." The IEP can be reviewed as often as necessary but must be reviewed at least annually. The review can take place anytime during the service year.

The "persons developing the IEP" must include as a minimum the parent, teacher, and person qualified to provide or supervise special education and re-lated services.

II. *Assessment Information*

Informal and formal "assessment procedures" used to determine the child's eligibility for special education should be included. No child can be placed in special education based on a single assessment procedure. "Results" of the as-sessments should be described and interpreted in a manner that facilitates un-derstanding by other persons viewing the IEP. Complete names of assessment instruments should be used. The "date" of assessment and the name and title of the "examiner" also should be included.

III. *Special Education and Related Services Needed*

This section must indicate all of the special education and related services the child needs to receive an appropriate education. Statements should include in-formation on the specific placement alternative the child needs and the frequency service will be provided.

The percentage of time the child will spend in each special education and related service program and regular education program must be indicated. The percentage can be computed by determining the total number of educational hours available during the year and dividing the number into the number of hours spent in the various special and regular education programs.

IV. *Placement Justification*

If the IEP is used as a placement document, the parents' signatures must be secured to indicate they approve of the child's special education placement. As a placement document, the IEP should include a summary statement indicating the placement recommended and the rationale for the placement.

V. *Present Levels of Performance*

From the assessment information collected, data-based statements of performance must be developed. These statements indicate the performance level for specific tasks or behaviors. Preferably, each statement will include a numerical reference to the child's performance level. Performance levels can be indicated for such areas as language, speech, hearing, or any other breakdown appropriate for the child or the informational needs of the LEA.

VI. *Need Statements*

Need statements show the direction of change that is to occur as the present level of performance is modified. Need statements indicate that a behavior is going to increase or decrease.

VII. *Annual Goals*

Goals indicate the projected level of performance for the child as a result of receiving the special education and related services indicated in the IEP. Goals should include the components when, what, and criterion and should be numbered, 1, 2, 3. . . .

VIII. *Instructional Objectives*

"Area" refers to the specific performance area to which the instructional objective relates, for example, language or articulation.

"Goal number" refers to the number of the annual goal included in Section VII. By including the goal number, IEP viewers will know which objectives relate to which goals.

"Instructional Objectives" indicate the specific behaviors that will be acquired as the child moves toward accomplishment of the annual goal. Each annual goal may have a number of instructional objectives depending on the intermediate steps needed to accomplish the goal. Each objective should include the components when, who, to whom, what, criterion, and evaluation.

IX. *Recommendations*

Primary or unique methods and materials that are needed to complete the instructional objectives are included under "recommendations." Recommendations should include the following components: what, how many, and how often.

X. *Status Report*

The "status report" section provides a method for reporting progress made in accomplishing objectives. On the date the instructional objective is to be accomplished, or on any other regularly scheduled review date, the evaluation component in the instructional objective can be executed. Progress the child has made in completing the objective can be indicated by using the status code. The "partially completed" code allows staff to indicate the amount of progress made by the child in those instances when 100% of the indicated criterion has not been met. Under "PC" in the status column, the PC code number 1–5 can be listed. Under "C" in the status column the date the objective is completed can be indicated.

"Revision" made in any objective or "comments" on why the objective was not completed should be included to provide information that can be used in developing future IEPs.

CASELOAD SIZE

A system of caseload selection and caseload size based on the ASHA continuum-of-services concept was developed by the Committee on Language, Speech, and Hearing Services in the Schools (1984). This system provides information on four service-delivery programs: (1) consultation, (2) itinerant, (3) resource room, and (4) self-contained. The committee noted that if the service-delivery programs are combined, the caseload sizes are not additive. For example, if the school clinician uses both the consultation program and the itinerant program this does not imply a caseload size of 40 to 80.

Other issues that affect the program are travel time between schools and the many additional responsibilities of the school-based clinician, such as conferences, paperwork, and school duties.

Table 7–4 indicates the appropriate caseload size in the schools recommended by the committee. The recommendations are intended to give direction to SLPs and school administrators when considering what is the reasonable caseload size for a particular setting.

Caseload sizes are often mandated by state and local education agencies, and more often than not, the numbers of students the SLP is expected to serve are extremely high. This impedes the quality of service and slows down the progress of individual children. With cooperation between SLPs and school administrators the result will be realistic caseload rules and regulations that will facilitate high-quality services.

A PHILOSOPHY: THE BASIS ON WHICH TO BUILD

Knowing who and what you are and where you fit in will provide the basis from which to make many decisions and plans for the program.

Traditionally, the concept of categorical labeling, whereby handicapped children were diagnosed, tested, and labeled according to the functional area of the handicap, has been the approach to dealing with handicapped children in a classroom. This psychological-medical orientation failed to provide information on the degree of educational handicapping for individual children. To provide better services for the communicatively handicapped child in the school it is necessary to describe the problem in terms of the educational deficits it is imposing on the child. Furthermore, it is important that the classroom teacher as well as the parents understand the connection between the communication handicap and the child's ability to profit from the instruction in the classroom. For example, it is not enough to label a child *hearing impaired* and let it go at that. In the school it is necessary to describe how the hearing loss affects the child's ability to hear the teacher's and other children's voices;

TABLE 7-4 Recommended Caseload Size for Speech-Language Services in the Schools

	8 CONSULTATION PROGRAM (Indirect Service)	9 ITINERANT PROGRAM (Intermittent Direct Service)	10 RESOURCE ROOM PROGRAM (Intensive Direct Service)	11 SELF-CONTAINED PROGRAM (Academically Integrated Direct Service)
1 CASES SERVED	12 —All communicative disorders —All severities (mild to severe)	19 —All communicative disorders —All severities (mild to severe)	26 —All communicative disorders particularly language and articulation —All severities	33 —Primary handicap: communication —Severe/multiple disorders particularly langauge and articulation
2 SERVICES PROVIDED	13 —Program development, management, coordination —Indirect services	20 —Program development, management, coordination, evaluation —Direct services —Coordination w/educators	27 —Program development, management, coordination, evaluation —Direct service/self-study/aide —Coordination w/teacher(s) —Teacher has academic responsibilities	34 —Program development, management, coordination, evaluation —Direct services plus academic instruction
3 GROUP SIZE	14 —Individual or Group (Indirect service)	21 —Individual or small group (up to 3 students/ session)	28 —Individual or small group (Up to 5 students/session)	35 —Up to 10 students/speech-language pathologist —Up to 15/speech-language pathologist w/supportive personnel

	15	22	20	36
4 TIME PER DAY	—Variable: Possible range —½ hr. (mild) to 3–4 hrs/day	—½ to 1 hour/day	—1 to 3 hours/day	—Full school day
	16	**23**	**30**	**37**
5 TIMES PER WEEK	—1 to 5 times/week	—2 to 5 times/week	—4 to 5 times/week	—Full time placement
	17	**24**	**31**	**38**
6 RATIONALE FOR CASE-LOAD SIZE	—Time necessary by organization —Variable needs	—Complex cases demand lower caseloads —Approximates national average	—Cases require intensive services —Consistent w/regulations	—Consistent w/regulations —Provides for intensive services
	18	**25**	**32**	**39**
7 CASELOAD* MAXIMUMS	—Up to 15–40 students	—Up to 25–40 students	—Up to 15–25 students	—Up to 15 students w/aide —Up to 10 students w/out aide

Draft prepared by the Committee on Language, Speech, and Hearing Services in the Schools August 1981. Final revision July 1983.

*NOTE: Maximums are not additive across programs and do not account for travel time.

to monitor his or her own speech, language, and voice; to discriminate among sounds of the language; and to receive information. The effect of the hearing loss on the child's self-image should also be explained.

Speech, language, and hearing clinicians work in many settings. The clinician who chooses to work in an educational setting has the responsibility of removing or alleviating communication barriers that may hinder the child from receiving the instruction offered in the school. The clinician who works in the schools also has the responsibility of evaluating the communication problem and assessing its impact on the learning process. Another responsibility of the school clinician is to serve as a resource person for the classroom teachers and specialized teachers who have the communicatively handicapped children in their classrooms.

Perhaps it is the term *special education* that has led our thinking astray. It is in reality education for children with special problems. The education of handicapped children is not something distinct and set apart from education; it is a part of the total school program.

DISCUSSION QUESTIONS AND PROJECTS

1. How would you introduce yourself to a first-grade class you were about to screen for speech-language? How would you explain to them what you were going to do? Role-play this situation in your class.
2. The third-grade teacher sends not only the students who have articulation problems but also all the "problem" readers as well, when you ask for referrals. How would you handle this situation?
3. How would you generate self-referrals on the high-school level?
4. Compose a memorandum to the teachers of Kenwood School in which you explain the procedures of the speech-language screening you will be conducting there.
5. Is it legal to screen only selected grades when PL 94-142 says all handicapped children must be served?
6. Interview a school SLP to find out what speech-language screening tests he or she uses.
7. Survey several SLPs in the schools to find out how they identify hearing-impaired students.
8. Invite an educational audiologist to speak to your class on his or her roles and responsibilities.
9. Find out what is required in your state in regard to diagnostic procedures for speech-, language-, and hearing-handicapped children.
10. Find out how preschool speech-, language-, and hearing-impaired children are identified in your area.
11. Collect samples of IEP forms used in various school systems.
12. Look in Chapter 4 at the continuum-of-services model. Now look at Table 7-4, the Recommended Caseload Size model. How would you, as the school SLP, utilize these two models in planning a program in your school system?

EIGHT
SCHEDULING
AND IMPLEMENTING
THERAPY

INTRODUCTION

This chapter might well be called the "nuts and bolts" of speech-language programming in the schools. In it we will look at what the school speech-language pathologist does before, during, and after the actual therapy session. We will consider different ways of scheduling and the scheduling of different age groups. We will also look at special populations with communication disorders, deviations, and differences and the school SLP's responsibilities to them in providing services.

Many of the topics in this chapter have been vigorously debated by speech, language, and hearing professionals, and there is not always agreement on what is the right way or the wrong way to approach and solve these problems. But fortunately, the discussions continue, often generating more research, and eventually common ground is reached. (Read Iglesias, 1985, "The 'Different' Elephant," on how a position paper was developed.)

USING THE PRIORITY SYSTEM OF SCHEDULING

In Chapter 7 priority systems for case selection were discussed (Barker, 1982; Zemmol, 1977). One aspect dealt with the identification and further diagnosis of individual children who were possible candidates for intervention. Let us now turn our attention to the scheduling of children on a priority list basis.

In implementing the system based on the continuum-of-services concept the SLP would allocate his or her time so that the children in the highest priority category would receive the most attention. As the children progress, their priority ratings change, and they move along the continuum-of-services until they reach maximum potential and are dismissed from therapy.

This system is based on the needs of the child and meets the letter and the spirit of PL 94-142. Rather than servicing "schools" the SLP is servicing children. Too often administrators expect the SLP's time to be divided equally among schools without regard to the needs of the children. This puts at risk the reputation of the program and may result in lack of support and fewer referrals from teachers, principals, and eventually parents.

ASHA has provided guidelines for the establishment of a case selection priority system through its delivery-of-service model described in Chapter 4. The guidelines are flexible and can be adapted to large, small, or medium-sized school systems. They can also be applied to pupils from preschool through high school.

The children falling in the first priority grouping will be those with severely handicapping communication problems in language, voice, fluency, articulation, and hearing. This group would also include children with multiple problems as well as problems associated with irreversible conditions and unspecified etiologies. They would require direct and intensive remediation.

The second priority group would be children with mild to moderate developmental or nonmaturational deviation. This group would include children with mild to moderate delays in language acquisition as well as mild to moderate problems in expression, reception, or integration of language. This articulatory category might include children whose speech is fairly intelligible but contains some articulatory errors. These children would require direct or indirect clinical management. The category also includes children with moderate fluency problems, voice problems, and speech and language problems related to moderate hearing loss.

The children in the first and second priority levels would also require assessment and evaluation services from the school clinician. It is also possible that a child might "graduate" from the first priority level to the second.

The third priority level would include children with developmental problems. These children need not be enrolled in direct therapy programs but would be served through speech- and language-development programs in the classroom. Reinforcement of the classroom teacher's services can take place through demonstration lessons by the school clinician. Parental guidance and in-service training of parents would also be appropriate for this group. The focus of service for these children would be the prevention of communication problems.

The children in special education classes and learning disability classrooms might also be served through strategies in this level.

Also on the third level priority list are preschool children in need of speech and language stimulation; children who had previously been enrolled in therapy but who need periodic evaluation; and children previously enrolled on the first and second priority levels who need to stabilize and generalize appropriate speech, language, fluency, and voice patterns.

There are a number of options open for the delivery of services in the schools, and it should be understood that it is not necessary to choose and utilize only one. A plan of possible alternatives was described in *Standards and Guidelines for Comprehensive Language, Speech and Hearing Programs in Schools* (Healey, 1973) and was discussed in Chapter 3. The options can be used in combination, and the combinations of options may be dependent on a number of factors. One of the primary factors is the availability of staff. In a school system employing only one speech, language, and hearing clinician, the options may be considerably smaller than in a large school system employing many clinicians.

Other factors include the following:

1. The geographic location of the schools, the clinician's "home" office, and the distance and travel time between these locations
2. The availability of working space in each of the schools
3. The type and severity of the communication problems within the schools
4. The number and population of the schools (Would some schools warrant a full-time clinician?)
5. Time allotted for coordination activities, including in-service training; supervision of paraprofessionals or aides; record keeping; parent conferences; placement team conferences; consulting with classroom teachers, special education personnel, and administrators; administration of diagnostic tests; and so on
6. School policies affecting the transporting of students from school to school to place them in locations where they may receive the appropriate services
7. The level of the school (It is entirely probable that the junior high schools and the senior high schools may have smaller populations of communicatively handicapped students than elementary schools.)

THE ITINERANT MODEL

Many of the children with severe communication disorders, as well as those with mild to moderate deviations, will be in regular classrooms with speech, language, and hearing services provided by the school clinician on an itinerant basis. The itinerant model has been used from the time it was suggested in 1910 by Ella Flagg Young, who felt that it protected the young teacher from "depression of spirit and low physical conditions resulting from confinement in one room for several successive hours while working with abnormal conditions." Not until recent years, with the advent of mandatory legislation, more sophisticated tools of identification, evaluation and program management, larger numbers of children needing services, and the recognized need for an interdisciplinary approach, have other systems of scheduling been developed.

This is not to say that the itinerant model is not a good one, but it should not be considered the only one.

The itinerant model may be effective in situations where schools are within a few miles of each other or where school populations and caseloads are low. It may also provide continuous therapy for children who need more frequent intervention over a longer period of time, such as children with fluency problems, hearing problems, and problems resulting from such conditions as cleft palate and cerebral palsy.

The itinerant (or traditional) model may take several forms. The school clinician may serve one, two, or three schools, working with a small group of children (two to five) or individual children on an intermittent basis of twice a week. An example of this schedule follows:

	MONDAY	TUESDAY	WEDNESDAY	THURSDAY	FRIDAY
AM	School A	School C	Coordination and Consultation Day	School A	School C
PM	School B	School C		School B	School C

Intermittent therapy may also be provided by a clinician based in a single building. This would be appropriate for a school with a large population and a large number of pupils with communication problems.

Another possible option in a school system with two or more SLPs would be to assign the clinicians on the basis of their areas of specialization. In a variation of this model in a large school system, part of the staff might be on an intinerant schedule while several clinicians would serve as "specialists," matching their strengths to the students' needs.

INTENSIVE CYCLE SCHEDULING

Another model of scheduling services is the intensive cycle, sometimes called the block system. In this model the child is seen four or five times a week for a concentrated block of time, usually four to six weeks.

MacLearie and Gross (1966) reported on an experimental program in intensive cycle scheduling in the Ohio communities of Brecksville, Cleveland, Dayton, and East Cleveland city schools and the Crawford County schools. The research was carried on over a period of four years, and the results were reported both subjectively and objectively. The Ohio study indicated the following advantages of the plan:

1. A greater number of children could be enrolled during the school year.
2. A larger percentage of children were dismissed from therapy as having obtained maximum improvement.
3. The length of time children with articulatory problems were enrolled in speech therapy was reduced.
4. Although not statistically significant, the Brecksville study gave some indications that a greater carryover of improvement occurred.

5. Closer relationships between the therapist and school personnel and parents was noted because of the greater acceptance of the therapist as a specific part of a particular school's staff.
6. Students appeared to sustain interest in therapy over a longer period of time.
7. Less time was needed in reviewing a lesson since daily therapy sessions occurred.

Participants in the study made the following suggestions concerning the length and nature of intensive cycle scheduling:

1. The first block scheduled should be longer to account for screening and program organization.
2. Sessions should be a minimum of four weeks in duration.
3. A minimum of two cycles, and preferably three to four each year, are needed for best results.

Problems related to intensive cycle scheduling follow:

1. Some problems of a psychogenic nature may need more frequent contacts on a regularly scheduled basis.
2. Administrative problems and reactions to students leaving a classroom on a daily basis may be a problem if the intensive cycle program is not carefully explained to the school staff.
3. Monopolization of a shared room for therapy services may cause scheduling problems.

One of the anticipated problems was the reaction of the classroom teachers to having children leave their classroom on a daily basis. In the Brecksville study, it was reported that of the 35 teachers responding, 30 felt that the intensive cycle method fitted better with other aspects of their daily program. Two stated they had no opinion, and three preferred the itinerant method.

Results of the study in Cleveland (MacLearie & Gross, 1966) indicated that regardless of the scheduling method used, the group receiving the intensive program first had a greater average gain than the group receiving therapy on an intermittent basis first. The implication seemed to be that an optimum program may be therapy on an intensive basis first and on an intermittent basis next as the child's communication improves.

Objective Evaluation

a. A breakdown of the articulation caseload by grades indicated that best results were obtained in grades four, five, and six in terms of number and percent of pupils corrected
b. The groups which responded least were made up of seventh and eighth graders
c. Intensive cycle scheduling seemed to be less effective with problems involving organic impairments such as cerebral palsy, cleft palate, and brain injury
d. Intensive scheduling provided the opportunity for a greater number to receive speech therapy and for a greater percent of improvement

e. Experimentation with length of blocks revealed that the ten eight-week blocks enrolled more pupils than did the eighteen-week blocks. However, the ten eight-week block schools were first-year schools. The previous study showed that first-year schools enrolled more pupils than did those using intensive therapy for the second time. The correction rate of total caseloads was similar in each school

f. The limitation of four buildings per therapist was thought to
1) Provide an on-going program of once a week therapy for selected children between blocks on the intensive cycle plan
2) Permit scheduling of selected children as needed.

Subjective Evaluation

The project directors felt that intensive cycle scheduling tended to:

a. Provide better integration of speech therapy with the total school program
b. Result in more consistent oral practice at home and more sustained interest
c. Permit more frequent contacts between therapists and school personnel
d. Minimize the effect of pupil absence on speech progress
e. Shorten time allotted to speech screening
f. Result in fewer problems in scheduling therapy classes for upper elementary children as they could be seen at times which best suited their program
g. Stimulate more frequent conferences with parents and teachers
h. Permit the enrollment of a larger number of children with speech problems without detracting from the quality of the work accomplished
i. Provide a higher rate of correction.

THE COMBINATION OF MODELS FOR SCHEDULING

Another option in the delivery of services would be a combination of models, for example, a combination of the itinerant model with the intensive cycle scheduling system. In this option an intensive program (with children receiving therapy on a daily basis) might be followed by a scheduling model of intermittent therapy. This plan would insure compliance with PL 94-142 in that children needing therapy over a longer period of time would not be dropped because the intensive cycle terminated. Obviously, this would be easier to arrange if there were more than one SLP on the staff, if communication aides were available, if the program were carefully coordinated, and if the clinicians and the school administrators all agreed on the program.

OTHER SCHEDULING OPTIONS

Other delivery of service options outlined in Chapter 4 include diagnostic center placement, special classroom placement, home and/or hospital services, parent/infant instruction services, and residential placement. In most of these models the SLP and the audiologist provide a related service. The SLP may also provide services to children in a resource room. The resource room is a part-time class (less than half-time) for children with severe language, speech, or hearing problems. The services provided by the SLP for children with severe language disorders often utilize the resource room model.

The school clinician may provide related services to the pupils in transition or integration classes. As the name implies, these children are beginning integration into regular or special classes, where they spend the remainder of the day.

School SLPs have not fully exploited these options. The pupils in most of these classes often have moderate to severe language disorders and should have more attention by the school SLP than they are presently getting. School clinicians are often aware of this situation, but it takes the full support of the school administration with the cooperation of the SLP to effect these changes.

SCHEDULING IN JUNIOR AND SENIOR HIGH SCHOOLS

Some special considerations need to be taken into account in scheduling junior and senior high-school students. Because of the inflexibility of the classes and the study programs on those levels, the Task Force on Traditional Scheduling Procedures in Schools (1973) recommended these alternatives: (1) the clinician discuss scheduling periods with the school principal before the beginning of the school year, (2) consideration be given to regularly scheduled speech and language classes with credit as part of the academic curriculum for those pupils in need of such services, (3) a rotation system be developed so students do not miss the same class each time, (4) scheduling during the regular academic year be omitted completely and intensive services be provided during the six-week summer period, or (5) additional staff be employed to serve only these students.

Two examples of programs on the high-school level are in DeKalb County, Georgia, and Evanston Township High School, Illinois.

DeKalb County Program

The communication disorders program for adolescents and adults in DeKalb County provides service to secondary students partly through a central clinic and partly through itinerant services to the high schools in the county. Also served are college students and the adult residents in the district. Case finding is accomplished through a continuation of services from the elementary program and through referrals from counselors, teachers, students, parents, physicians, and specialists. Because of difficulties associated with carrying out a screening program on the secondary level, a teacher education program is carried out by the staff (Hosea, 1977).

The caseload is composed of individuals with problems in articulation, fluency, voice, and language, as well as speech and language difficulties associated with hearing impairment, cleft palate, cerebral palsy, cerebral vascular accidents, and laryngectomy.

The models of delivery of services include (1) diagnostic evaluations and individual and small-group therapy at the clinic; (2) consultative services at the clinic or in the schools that aid students with mild communication differences who do not require direct therapy, and students who have been dismissed but may need occasional contact; (3) itinerant services that include diagnostic evaluations and therapy scheduled in the schools, therapy administered by a trained aid, and structured home programs provided and monitored by the speech therapist; (4) resources offered to teachers and students in special classes.

The system used in DeKalb County has significant features and advantages (Beall, 1977):

1. Therapists who work four extended days provide services after school and work hours.
2. Delivery models are flexible; the servicing model is dependent on individual needs and circumstances.
3. Staff was redirected and reassigned at no cost to the school system.
4. Problems associated with work space, scheduling conflicts, and interference with extracurricular activities were minimized and absenteeism was reduced.
5. With students seen in the high schools the referring counselor or teacher is responsible for securing work space and arranging the schedule.
6. Cooperation of counselors and their awareness of special needs and programs were significantly increased.
7. Services were centralized, allowing for a more efficient and prompt referral system and improved instruction and evaluation.
8. Motivation and interest of students enrolled for therapy appeared significantly improved.
9. Program procedures and development of new, effective delivery systems are the responsibility of the staff; the flexibility of the present administration has facilitated the establishment of this nontraditional approach.

Two full-time clinicians, two part-time clinicians, and one teacher-assistant comprise the staff. The teacher-assistant provides secretarial help in addition to administering structured programs to high-school students and adults. Also, student aides, identified by counselors, are trained to work with their peers in the high schools.

The staff serves 24 secondary schools, grades eight through 12, with approximately 34,000 students. It also serves a community college and a continuing education program having approximately 34,000 students.

Evanston Township High School Program

The Evanston Township program in Illinois has been functioning continuously since the late 1930s. Started as an outgrowth of the Northwestern University Speech and Hearing Clinic, it is now a division of the Special Education Department of Evanston Township Schools and has been guided by Helen Sullivan Knight and Marjorie Burkland.[1]

In addition to the continuity of the program, there are some unique features. The Speech Modification Program is part of the regular curriculum of the high school. Students receive grades and high-school credit for enrolling and attending. The credit is one-quarter as much as a regular school course, and therapy may be repeated for credit. The grades are on a scale of A, B, C, D, and N.C. (no credit).

According to Burkland, the students are graded on the following criteria:

1. They must attend and they must be on time.
2. They must carry out semiweekly assignments.
3. There must be participation in the therapy process. In other words, all students in a therapy group must participate in the activities planned for that session. The participation may consist of critical listening or carrying out a specific task, but there is no just sitting back and being present.
4. There must be some personal improvement. A student may get an A even though he or she may not have perfect speech.

Perhaps the single most significant feature in the delivery of remedial speech and language service at Evanston Township High School, according to Burkland, is that all scheduling is done by computer in the scheduling office along with academic scheduling during the spring quarter preceding enrollment. The clinician provides the scheduling office with appropriate times for such courses as articulation improvement, fluency, and individual lessons, and these appear as requested on the students' respective schedules. In this way ability grouping (in overall academic functioning) as well as disability grouping (related to a given communication problem) can be provided. An additional advantage is that students begin the year with the speech modification elective clearly *a part of* rather than added to their programs. Basically the clinician provides therapy four days a week (with most lessons being semiweekly) and surveys and diagnoses one day a week, thereby developing a prospective caseload for the ensuing year. A speech aide assists as a critical listener in carrying out lessons prescribed by the clinician and devises materials geared to accomplish listening, language formulation, articulation goals, and so on, agreed on in conference with the clinician.

Ideally, motivation for enrolling in a remedial course comes from a student's inherent interest in enhancing personal adequacy, but very real motivation is provided by Evanston Township High School because speech modification courses are listed in the *Program Planning Handbook* and carry elective credit. Also, grades are given and attendance kept, thereby making this elective like all others in the curriculum.

There are minimal scheduling conflicts, according to Burkland, because the course appears on the school's regular schedule of courses. The course

[1]Marjorie Burkland, speech-language pathologist, Evanston Township Schools, Illinois. (Personal correspondence with the author.)

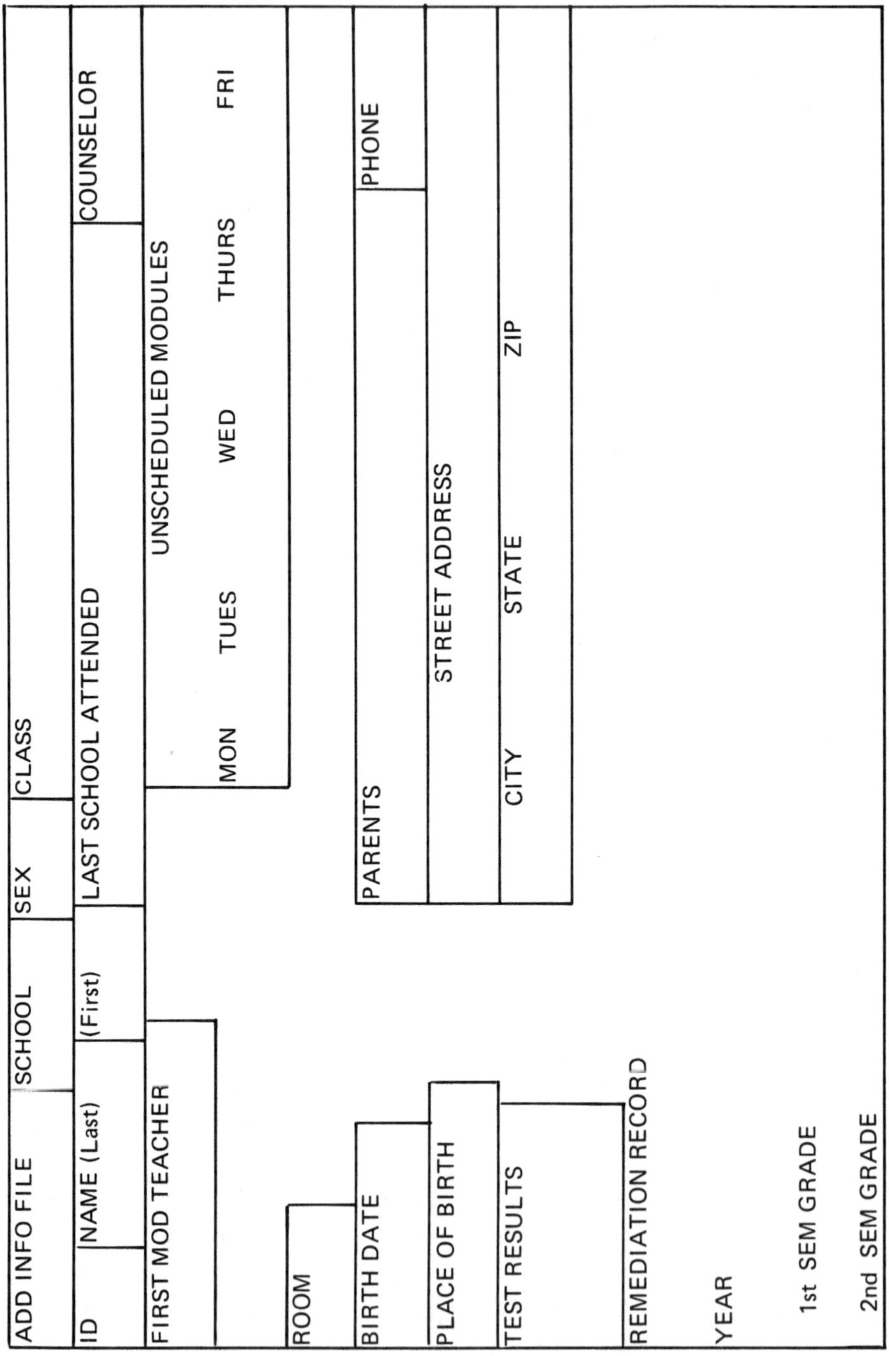

ADD INFO FILE | SCHOOL | SEX | CLASS

ID | NAME (Last) (First) | LAST SCHOOL ATTENDED | COUNSELOR

FIRST MOD TEACHER

UNSCHEDULED MODULES

MON TUES WED THURS FRI

ROOM

BIRTH DATE

PLACE OF BIRTH

PARENTS

STREET ADDRESS

PHONE

CITY STATE ZIP

TEST RESULTS

REMEDIATION RECORD

YEAR

1st SEM GRADE

2nd SEM GRADE

FIGURE 8-1

meets on a Monday-Wednesday or Tuesday-Thursday pattern, with Friday used for screening, testing, conferences with teachers, and seeing students for extra sessions. The screening is done through students' homerooms, and all freshmen are screened. Screening takes place during September, October, and November. Reevaluations continue during December, January, and February. In March and April the students are scheduled for the speech-modification course, which appears on their programs the following September. Generally students are not enrolled after the course starts, but emergency enrollments do occur throughout the year. Students are scheduled for the course for a year but may be dismissed earlier if they meet the proficiency standards set by the clinician. A specially designed therapy room is located in the high school.

Figure 8-1 shows the card used to keep a speech record of every student in school. Information is IBM printed each September for the entire class. Color coding of card is used to indicate class level of student. For example: green is used for class of 1979; yellow for class of 1980; pink for class of 1981; and white for class of 1982.

FLEXIBILITY IN SCHEDULING

The therapy program has many facets, many ramifications, and requires much from the school SLP. Decisions must be made, and they will not always be the right decisions. Speech-language pathologists are conscientious and intelligent people, but they are not infallible. They usually learn from their mistakes and often from the mistakes of others. The beginning clinician might be wise to avoid getting locked into a course of action that later, because of circumstances, might not be the best one. This can occur on the therapeutic level and on the organizational and management level. For example, if the clinician determines that the client is not responding to a particular approach in therapy, the clinician changes the procedures. On the organizational level if the SLP has "sold" the school administration on the idea that the itinerant delivery-of-service model is the only feasible one, the SLP may have difficulty if it becomes apparent in the future that other delivery-of-service models should be utilized. Allowing for some flexibility will enable the school clinician to maintain a viable program.

NONSCHEDULED SERVICE TIME: COORDINATION TIME

In addition to the time spent in conducting therapy sessions and diagnostic activities, the clinician has many other duties to perform. Some time must be set aside during the week to carry out activities necessary to the overall program. In some states this is referred to as *coordination time*. It may be a half day or a full day. Usually it is a block of time set aside on a regular basis in the week's schedule. Some school clinicians set aside a block of time during each day for this purpose.

Some of the activities carried on during coordination time are parent conferences; staffing of cases; staff conferences; in-service training; correspondence; maintaining records and reports; classroom demonstration lessons for speech and language development and improvement programs; consulting with the school nurse, psychologist, guidance counselor, reading teacher, and others; and other activities important to conducting an effective program. In some geographical areas school clinicians employed in different school systems get together for professional meetings and to assist each other in screening, in-service training programs, and other professional matters. This can be especially effective where there may be only one clinician in a school district or where the opportunity for getting together may be limited by distance and time.

Because of the myriad of activities carried on during coordination time, it is highly desirable for the clinician to keep the school administrators informed of what is done during this time. Some clinicians use a monthly report form on which they record their activities during the nonscheduled service time. Periodically they send the reports to the school administrators.

Sometimes misunderstandings arise between the classroom teacher and the school clinician when the teacher sees the clinician leave the building during coordination day to carry out duties elsewhere. If the SLP informs the teachers and the principal of his or her activities during that time, criticism and skepticism are allayed and there is a better understanding of the program.

THERAPEUTIC INTERVENTION

The school clinician spends most of the working day involved in actually performing therapy. The type of intervention used will be the decision of the clinician and will be appropriate to the age of the child as well as the type of problem. It is not necessary at this time, nor would there be space in this chapter, to discuss the various therapeutic approaches and philosophies. Suffice it to say that the school clinician should not only be well versed in the remediation approaches used in the past but also aware of current developments in therapeutic approaches. There are a number of approaches available to the clinician, and the choice will depend on what best serves the child. Beginning school clinicians will reflect on what they learned in academic courses as well as in practicum courses. They will gain additional information and practice during student teaching.

Motivation

Much has been written about motivation, and probably much more has been said. Everyone seems to be in agreement that motivation is necessary to produce good and lasting results in therapy. It is not uncommon to hear clinicians express the wish that they could motivate their client. This would imply that motivating is something one does to another person.

However, motivation is something that is within the person, driving him or her from inside. It is not realistic to think that clinicians are able to motivate clients. Rather, the recipients of our services will make a change in communication behavior only if personal values and attitudes impel them to do so.

The use of games, precision therapy, negative reinforcement, positive reinforcement, rewards, punishment, shaping behavior, and so on provides incentives, inducements, and spurs, which may bring about changes in behavior. If the inner drive, or the motivation, is absent, however, there may be regression or lack of what is commonly referred to as *carryover* or *generalization;* or there may be no change in behavior.

Although the clinician is highly anxious to change the child's speech behavior, it does not necessarily follow that the child will share that feeling. In some cases the child may be highly motivated to hang onto an immature speech and language pattern because it may be a way of coping with other members of the family. Or a child may enjoy the attention of the therapist so much that the child does not wish to improve and end the therapy sessions.

What are the implications for the clinician in regard to motivation in students? Raph (1960) suggested that there must be a shift of focus from a teacher-centered orientation of motivation to an understanding of the attitudes and values present in the child's motivation for learning. She has suggested that it would be desirable for the clinician to have some background in developmental psychology, some sensitivity to the nuances of the therapeutic relationship, and a willingness to learn as much as possible about an individual child's emotional functioning. She also suggested that understanding the feelings of the child may be as important as any diagnostic information that is gathered.

Length and Frequency of Therapy Sessions

In considering the length and frequency of therapy sessions, the most basic consideration would be the best possible use of the time allotted. This is not much help to the beginning clinician, however, who must decide whether to schedule children for 15-minute sessions or 30-minute sessions. Perhaps the best approach is to take a careful look at the schedule of classes in the school and then have the therapy schedule coincide with the class schedule. This does not necessarily mean that therapy sessions should be the same length as classes, but it would be helpful to both teachers and students if there were some coordination between the two.

Nor does it mean that all the sessions should be planned for the same amount of time. Some sessions may be ten minutes in length, and some may be 45 minutes. The decision about the amount of time should be made by the clinician on the basis of the child's needs. More time may be needed for group sessions. The child in the carryover stages of therapy may require ten or 15 minutes several times a week. In an intensive cycle scheduling system, when children are seen more frequently during the week, less time per session may be sufficient. High-school students who may be able to assume more responsibility for themselves may need only one one-hour session per week.

The amount of time needed for each child may change as the child progresses in therapy. Classroom teachers should be informed of the fact that change will occur during the year and that their input would be valuable in considering any changes in the time.

The key word in planning the amount of time per therapy session is *flexibility* and the criterion is *what is in the best interests of the child.* The responsibility for making good use of the time is the clinician's.

Therapy Planning

Therapy planning begins with the IEP. Section 121.a 346 of PL 94-142 regulations specifies the following content in the IEP:

1. A statement of the child's present levels of educational performance
2. A statement of annual goals, including short-term and related services to be provided to the child and long-term instructional objectives
3. A statement of the specific special education and the extent to which the child will be able to participate in regular educational programs
4. The projected dates for initiation of services and the anticipated duration of the services
5. Appropriate objective criteria and evaluation procedures for determining, on at least an annual basis, whether the short-term instructional objectives are being achieved

The IEP must also be specific for each child who receives either special education or related services or both. A single IEP is written for a child enrolled in special education and receiving both special education and related services. The related service may be in speech, language, or audiology. Presumably, the SLP and/or the audiologist is present at the planning meeting and contributes to the planning. When the SLP or audiologist provides the related service and the child is not enrolled in any other special education program, the IEP is written by that professional, with appropriate input from parents, teachers, or administrators.

When out-of-school services are purchased by the local board of education for a specific child, the IEP is written by the school personnel involved and contains the information regarding the nature of the service provided. The out-of-school professional is often asked to contribute to the preparation of the IEP.

The Lesson Plan

There are considerations the school SLP needs to consider when planning instructional objectives for individual lessons plans. First to be considered are the goals for that particular lesson. What does the clinician hope to have the student accomplish? Are the clinician's aims reasonable? Is the student aware of the goals for that lesson? Has he or she helped formulate them? Do the clinician and student agree on the goals? Will these goals bring them closer to the final goal?

Along with the specific goals for each therapy session, the clinician and student must be in agreement on the general, or long-range, goals. In other words, what is to be finally accomplished in the way of improvement of communication? In formulating the long-range goals, the physical, emotional, intellectual, and sociological limitations of the student must be taken into consideration. The vague goal or the unrealistic and unattainable goal must be avoided as they produce only frustration and disappointment for both the clinician and the student.

The next thing needed in the lesson plan is the list of materials. If the list contains stories or poems, the author, title of the book, and the publisher should be listed. The list should be so complete that a person unfamiliar with the session would be able to assemble the materials from the list. A complete listing of materials will provide a ready future source of reference not only for the beginning clinician but for the experienced therapist as well.

Following the list of materials, the lesson plan would then go on to the steps or the procedures in the lesson. These can be listed in order of use and include the estimated time for each. This would be particularly helpful to the beginning clinician, who has not yet been able to judge accurately the amount of time needed for each step. It is a common occurrence for the novice to complete all the activities of the lesson in half the time allotted or else to complete only the first few steps in the entire amount of time. It should be a comfort to the beginning clinician to know that with continued experience comes a more accurate judgment of the passage of time during a therapy session.

The steps in the lesson should be based on the child's needs, the general and specific goals of therapy, and the evaluated results of the previous lesson. The clinician may wish to consult with the parents concerning home assignments or with the classroom teacher on carryover.

The clinician must have justification for listing the steps in a particular order; otherwise the therapy session becomes a hodgepodge of activities unrelated to the goals. On the other hand, the order of activities must not become so sacred that it cannot be changed. I recall one professor's lecture to a class in which she said, "I expect each student teacher to teach from a lesson plan, complete with goals, materials, estimated time for each activity, and the activities listed in order of presentation. But if I come into the room and find the student teacher teaching the right activity at the right time according to the clock and the lesson plan, I'll know there's something wrong with the lesson."

Her point, of course, is that any lesson plan, no matter how carefully thought out, should be abandoned or rearranged to suit the needs of the student. If Jimmy comes to speech class and proudly announces that he has a new baby sister, or if Susie wants to show off her new shoes, or if the first snow of the season has fallen during the night, all these things are much too important for the clinician to ignore and not utilize in the therapy session.

By using meaningful activities and real-life situations, generalization becomes much less of a problem, and the clinician doesn't fall into the trap of playing endless, meaningless games with the student.

Evaluation of the Lesson

Following the list of procedures there should be a place for evaluation of the lesson. What should the evaluation include? In order to decide, let us look at the goals. Did this lesson accomplish the specific goals set forth in the lesson plan? Did the techniques employed bring about the desired results, or could the same results be accomplished by simpler, more direct methods? Did the student understand why he or she was doing certain things? In other words, did this lesson make sense to the student? Did it include an opportunity for carryover? For practice? For review?

Did this lesson have any relationship to the student's specific needs? Were the techniques and materials adapted to the appropriate age level, sex, interests, level of understanding? Paradoxically, it is possible for a lesson to be well taught and interesting to the student yet still not have any bearing on the communication problem and its eventual solution!

Was the clinician able to establish good rapport with the student? Was the clinician genuinely interested in both the student and the lesson? Did the clinician talk too much, or too little? Did both clinician and student seem to feel at ease? Was the clinician in charge of the lesson or did the student take over?

All of these questions need to be answered concerning every lesson. Too often the criteria for a therapy session are based on whether or not the student enjoyed it and whether or not good rapport existed between the student and the clinician. Although both are important, there is much more to a successful lesson. Careful preparation and careful evaluation of therapy sessions, both group and individual, are essential ingredients of good therapy.

The most effective clinicians we have observed have kept a running log of therapy, usually written immediately after each session. This is in addition to the lesson plan.

Lesson plans may serve still another purpose. When progress reports, case closure summaries, periodic evaluation reports, and letters are required, the lesson plan may serve as a source of referral and an evaluation of progress of therapy, and it could facilitate the writing of letters and reports.

Group Therapy

In a sense all therapy is group therapy. A dyadic group (group of two) in speech, language, and hearing consists of the clinician and the student. Therapy groups in the schools consist of the clinician and from two to five students, or in special instances, more students. The purpose of a therapy group is to help the client in such a way that in the future he or she becomes independent of the relationship. The clinician is in a leadership role whether he or she utilizes a nondirective approach or a direct approach. The clinician is a facilitator who is aware of the feelings, values, and tensions of the participants. The clinician may play the role of an impartial judge in the event of friction. He or she keeps the group members moving toward the completion of the tasks at hand.

Although much therapy in the public schools is carried on in individual therapy sessions, a great deal of it is also done in group sessions.

Initially, the clinician is faced with the task of deciding which children should be placed in a group. The answer would depend on the needs of the child at any given stage of therapy. Some children may need an intensive approach to master some skills, and this may best be accomplished by working alone with the clinician. Later that same child may be ready to use these skills in a social situation, and a group experience would best fit this need.

The makeup of the group is an important factor in planning for optimal therapy results. Some clinicians find it more productive to work with a group of children who have similar problems, whereas for other clinicians the homogeneity of problems is not as important as grouping children of the same age level.

On the junior and senior high-school levels it may be more productive to have students with fluency problems in a group. On the other hand, some students with stuttering problems may not be ready for a group situation until after a series of individual therapy sessions.

Beasley (1951) described the advantages of structuring a group therapy session around the development of social skills. She maintained that practice and drill on speech patterns did not give children a way of using them readily in social and interpersonal situations.

Backus (1952) viewed the role of the therapist as one who creates the kind of environment in which the client becomes able to change. She maintained that a group situation provides a greater possibility for this than does a two-person relationship. She also felt that the group situation has a wider availability of "tools" (social situations) than does the one-to-one encounter.

Backus and Coffman (1953) described a program of group therapy for preschool children with cerebral palsy. The children were enrolled for two hours each morning for a period of 12 weeks each semester at the University of Alabama. The program consisted of both individual and group instruction for the children and a program of group therapy for the parents.

Good group therapy means there must be interaction among the group members. The interaction may be active or passive. In other words, while one child is actively engaged in an assigned task or is responding to the clinician, the other children could be encouraged to listen, and in some cases they may be asked to evaluate a response. Enlist the aid of all the children by telling them they are expected to listen, watch, comment, use their "good" sounds, and be members of the group in every sense of the word by participating actively. This doesn't just happen; as the group leader, the clinician must encourage the students.

There is no rule that says all therapy sessions must take place around a table. Working in front of a mirror, a flannel board, or a chalkboard will help group members to become better participants. It has been said that learning is movement. If this is true, the clinician who sits on a chair without ever moving, and the children who remain in their places during the entire session day after day, may not be making the best possible use of the therapy time.

In deciding which children should be put in a group and which group they should join, several things need to be considered. First, there are no right or wrong ways of grouping children. Groups must be flexible and must meet the needs of each child enrolled. Second, grouping is done to control the factors that enhance learning. Third, groups should not become static. As children learn and as needs change the composition of the group should change. Fourth, groups should be structured but not rigid. A structure assists learning, and if learning is not taking place there is no purpose for the existence of the group. Fifth, the size of the group should depend on its major purposes; however, a group of more than five or six students to one instructor tends to lose its tutorial effect (Stimson, 1979).

Students with speech, language, or hearing disorders should not be put in therapy groups simply to accommodate more students in the SLP's caseload. The rationale for placing a student in a group should depend on the needs of the student and the purpose of the group.

Dismissal from Therapy

In the process of selecting students for therapy, diagnosing, providing therapeutic intervention, and maintaining students in therapy, sometimes too little attention is paid to dismissal.

The question of when a pupil should be dismissed from therapy may be predicated on (1) when the pupil reaches maximum anticipated performance or (2) when the pupil's communication problem has been completely remediated.

After the pupil has been placed in a therapy program the short- and long-term performance objectives are identified and written in the IEP. The objectives are based on what is identified through testing, observation, conference with parents and teachers, and sometimes discussion with the pupil. In this way it is determined what the pupil needs to learn.

The long-term objectives are what is hoped the student is able to do at the termination of the therapy program. The short-term objectives are the steps through which the student must progress successfully to reach the long-term objectives. This, in effect, means that long-term (or terminal) objectives constitute the exit criteria, or the point at which the student is dismissed from therapy. This is part of the IEP.

Obviously, the nature of the disorder will have a direct bearing on the expected outcome of therapy. For example, a student with cerebral palsy and apraxia of the speech musculature may not be expected to attain "normal" speech patterns, depending on the extent of the involvement. This dismissal point for this pupil may be "adequate" speech. A student with an articulatory problem may be potentially able to attain a more complete mastery of the distorted sounds, and the dismissal point for this pupil would be when the student could use the sounds correctly.

The SLP must develop dismissal criteria for each student and terminate therapy when these criteria are met. This means that dismissal from therapy may occur at any time during the school year. Students who have not reached optimum improvement at the end of the school term are carried over into the following term. Students who transfer to another school are referred to the SLP in that school system. Parents should be urged to inform the new school that their child has been in therapy and they wish it to continue. In this situation, the referring clinician secures the proper release forms to transfer the student's therapy records to the new school.

Dismissals need not be absolute. No clinician is wise enough to be able to dismiss a child from therapy with the absolute certainty that the child will never again need it. When a dismissal is made, the child should be scheduled for periodic rechecks to find out if the therapy has held. In a school it is important to have the classroom teacher check this also. It will be necessary to be very specific with the teacher on what to check. The same holds true for parents. A dismissal, then, could be called a *temporary* dismissal.

Sometimes a student may be put on *clinical vacation.* This may occur when the clinician feels that the student has reached a plateau or has been in therapy for a very long time without a break. Before the point at which boredom and apathy set in, the clinician may put the child on a "vacation" from therapy for a designated amount of time. Clinicians have reported that gains in progress have been made when the student was on clinical vacation.

The conditions of a clinical vacation should be carefully explained to the student. I recall one little fellow who, when told he was going to be on clinical vacation, seemed elated. Several days later his mother called to report that he was disappointed when he found out that being on clinical vacation did *not* mean he was being sent to Disneyland!

What we are doing as clinicians is trying to make each client his or her own clinician. In other words, we try to bring students to the point where they are able to monitor their own speech, language, or auditory problem to such an extent that they no longer need us. This is sometimes painful for clinicians to do, and at times the student is reluctant to be dismissed from therapy. Both these factors must be objectively viewed by the clinician, and when the optimum levels of performance have been reached by the student, as stated in the long-range goals, the student is ready to be dismissed. The criteria for dismissal are unique to each child and must be carefully established, evaluated, and reevaluated during the course of therapy. If necessary, they must be adjusted or modified in the light of more knowledge about the student.

Other Facets of a Successful Therapy Program

Letter and report writing   The ability to express ideas on paper as well as verbally is essential for the speech-language clinician. Some persons seem to be born with this knack, whereas others have to learn it. In any event, the techniques of writing professional reports and letters can be learned.

Often, professional letter and report writing is highly stylized and follows a definite pattern. In addition, the basic essentials of good writing must be observed. First, the writing must be clear and concise. Simpler terms are much better than complex ones, and the simplest and easiest way of saying something is usually the best. The professional vocabulary must be adequate and the terminology must be appropriate.

The beginner who is learning the skill of professional writing should keep in mind the person to whom the report is being written. This person may be another clinician, the teacher, the family doctor, or the parents. Appropriate word choices should be made in keeping with the understanding of the potential reader of the report. Avoid professional jargon when writing to parents and do not assume they know the meanings of technical words. Remember that you are one human being writing to another human being; try not to sound like an institution writing to a human being. Put yourself in place of a parent who receives a letter from the school clinician stating, "Periodically during therapeutic intervention the speech-language pathologist will attempt to assess Billy's receptive language abilities by the administration of norm-referenced and criterion-referenced tests to determine his linguistic status in relation to his peers." Why not say, "During the time Billy is enrolled in therapy I will give him several tests to help us find out how well he is progressing."

Following are several different types of reports that the school SLP may write during a professional career:

The daily log   The daily log is written for the clinician's own information. It may be nothing more than a simple jotting down of notes following each therapy session. These notes may indicate the child's reaction to the therapy, any progress made on that particular day, and suggestions and ideas the clinician may want to include in the next therapy session.

The progress report   The progress report covers a span of time, for example, a period of one month, two months, six weeks, six months, or a year. It may be written for the clinician's own information or at the request of the person responsible for the management of the students in that particular setting. The progress report could include such information as the specific dates of the therapy, the number of therapy sessions, the name of the clinician, an evaluation of the progress, a listing of the therapy goals and a statement concerning whether or not they are accomplished, the methods of therapy, and the overall results of the treatment to date. In a school the progress report may be written for the teacher's use and should be specific about what was done in therapy and what would be recommended for the teacher to follow up on. Progress reports are usually filed in the child's cumulative folder, and if the child moves from one school to another the reports may follow to the new school. Progress reports may also be sent to parents. The clinician must be sure the terminology is geared to the parents' understanding.

Final reports   Final reports or closure reports may follow a checklist format or narrative style or a combination of the two. The factual information included in the closure summary may include name, date of birth, type of problem, date of the latest service, name of the clinician and the supervisor, date when student was first seen, starting date of the therapy, and the date of recheck and results of recheck. Information about the therapy and the number of sessions may also be included, as well as whether the therapy was in group or individual sessions. A rating of the progress during the time covered by the report could also be included. The rating may be on a continuum, such as "no progress, very slight, slight, moderate, good, excellent." Clarification of these categories should also be included.

Under the mandate of PL 94-142, final progress summaries are required, and in some school systems both progress summaries and final reports are required. The reports would contain information to help determine whether or not the student had achieved the short-term instructional objectives. The contents of the final reports are shared with the parents and, in some cases, with the student. The reports must be as accurate as humanly possible and written so that they will not be misconstrued.

If other services were utilized during this time it would be necessary to include a reference to them and, if available, a summary. Such services would include psychological, social, remedial reading, medical, vocational, educational, and psychiatric. In some cases it might be necessary to attach a copy of the report. The report should indicate whether the service was obtained within the school system or in a community agency.

General information   In writing professional reports the school clinician should keep in mind that opinions, rationalizations, hunches, and unsubstantiated ideas should not be included unless they are labeled as such. They may be included under *clinical impressions* or a similar category. As long as they are labeled it is permissible to include them.

Report writing, as the name implies, means a reporting of the facts without any editorializing by the writer. The reader of the report must be allowed to draw his or her own conclusions from the facts submitted.

COUNSELING

Counseling is an important factor in a holistic approach to therapy. The SLP in the school system counsels both students and parents in communication problems. Some of the counseling is geared toward the prevention of problems. For example, the SLP may give a talk to the PTA on the nature of speech, language, and hearing problems or the development of speech and language in infants and children. Or the counseling may be directly with the student, entailing self-perception, acceptance of the problem, understanding of the problem, relationship to peers, information about the specific disorder, reluctance to talk, and feelings about the problem.

The school clinician should be alert to any signs that would indicate that the student may require psychological or psychiatric treatment. Even the faintest doubt about seeking further professional help should be pursued.

Many school clinicians have found that fears and apprehensions surrounding many types of speech disorders are based on misinformation or no information. Much of the anxiety for both students and their parents can be alleviated by factual and general information.

The student's negative feelings about the problem may also be allayed by the attitude of the clinician, who says, not only by words but also by actions, "I'm here to help you; we can work on this together."

Although SLPs are not trained as counselors, there is no question about their knowledge of their professional field and the fact that they have been doing counseling. Without counseling, therapy alone would be ineffective. Recognizing that there are some children whose emotional problems may go beyond the communication problem, the school SLP seeks consultation and possible referrals of such children to other agencies and services specifically designed to deal with them.

One of the most helpful books for those seeking more information on counseling for speech, language, and hearing problems is *Understand Those Feelings* by Eugene McDonald (Pittsburg: Stanwix House, 1962).

SUMMER PROGRAMS

One way in which many school clinicians have extended their services is to offer a summer program. There may be several reasons for carrying out a summer program: to provide more intensive therapy for children who need it, to provide services of an intensive nature to children with such problems as stuttering or communication problems associated with cleft palate, and to offer a preventive program of therapy along with a parental guidance program.

School clinicians have provided summer programs for a number of years. Some of the programs have been financed by the local education system, and some have been underwritten by such organizations as Crippled Children's Society or a local service club. In some cases, the program has been a joint effort of both the school system and a voluntary organization. In this sort of program, usually the building, facilities, supplies, and so on have been furnished by the school, whereas the clinician's salary has been paid by the community group.

The clinician in charge of the program will need to establish criteria for accepting children and will need to carry out the necessary diagnostic procedures. Often only a limited number of children can be accepted, depending on the number of staff members available.

Summer programs are usually well received in a community, and once started are often repeated during subsequent summers.

VOCATIONAL HIGH SCHOOL AND SECONDARY TRANSITIONAL PROGRAMS

The interest in preparing adolescents in high schools and vocational high schools for jobs in the outside world provides a unique challenge to SLPs and audiologists. It is not known at this time how many school SLPs serve in vocational schools but the number is probably quite small. By the same token, it is not known how many speech, language, and hearing handicapped adolescents are in vocational schools.

A vocational high school is usually jointly operated by a group of existing school districts. In some cases, if the school district is a large one both in numbers and in size, the vocational high school may serve only one school district. Students often retain membership in the "home" school district but may attend classes at the vocational school for all or part of the school day.

The curriculum of the vocational high school may include basic academic classes such as English, American history, and government. It would also contain classes related to the students' vocational choices and laboratory classes during which the theory and training are applied to actual job projects. The students upon graduation receive a diploma from the home school and a vocational certificate from the vocational school.

Because the purpose of a vocational school is to prepare a student for a specific vocation, the needs and the motivations of students in this kind of setting differ from those of students in the normal high school.

Awareness of the psychology of this age group is important to the school clinician. A strong desire to be accepted by peers and not to be different from them sometimes underlies a resistance to therapy. A good working relationship with the vocational instructor can do much to encourage students enrolled in therapy to maintain good attendance.

Penta County Vocational High-School Program

The speech, language, and hearing program at Penta County Vocational High School, Perrysburg, Ohio, is an example of a vocational high-school program. Madaras and Wozniak (1978), in a description of the program, have indicated that regardless of how severe the communication deficit may be, it is of secondary importance to the student at this age level. The intervention program is based on the student's personal and vocational vocabulary. Remedial sessions are developed around such topics as hairdressing, automobiles, getting a job, and other subjects of interest.

In addition to a remedial program, a speech-improvement program may fulfill the needs of many of the students. In one such experimental program initiated with senior dental students at Penta County Vocational High School, the students preparing for their rotation assignments as assistants to area dentists were reintroduced to the following topics: (1) selecting correct word choices, (2) eliminating slang, (3) speaking clearly with the appropriate volume and rate, and (4) eliminating syntactical errors.

> The vocational instructor worked closely with the clinician on noting common errors and providing the vocational vocabulary. A pre-test was designed to disclose other areas of weaknesses. The clinician instructed the entire class for one forty-five minute period per week for eight weeks. The results of the post-test showed that each student received a much higher score on the post-test than on the initial test. Furthermore, the students seemed to be more aware of their overall speaking habits (Madaras & Wozniak).

The Penta County Vocational High School program also includes in-service training programs for both students and staff members. Topics for vocational instructors include information on speech, language, and hearing problems and the recognition of them. In-service topics for students include speech, language, and hearing behavior in the young child for the students enrolled in the child-care program as well as the effects of prolonged and sudden loud noise on students working in shop areas, such as auto mechanics, industrial, carpentry, and agricultural shop areas.

In the Penta County program the clinician initiated a hearing-conservation program. Staff members and students involved in noisy laboratory and shop classes were made aware of the various ramifications of noise pollution and the effects on the hearing of the persons involved. The clinician arranged for decibel readings to be conducted in the suspected loud-noise areas. Measures were then taken to make ear protectors available in the school supply store for students and instructors.

High schools may also have transitional programs. In this type of program the student moves from school to the work force, with activities focused on exploring employment opportunities, assessing vocational potentials, vocational training, and job placement. For students in the secondary transitional programs who have communication handicaps or limited communication skills, the services of the SLP and/or audiologist are utilized. The programs are carried out by the school staff, often with the cooperation of potential employers.

PROGRAMS FOR SPECIAL POPULATIONS

Since the early 1970s the role of the SLP in the schools has moved into new areas. Much of the terminology has changed, research has added new dimensions, and delivery-of-service methods are becoming more flexible and diverse. In the early days programs known as "speech improvement" were designed to help preschool and early primary children improve speaking and listening "habits." These programs also focused on pupils learning English as a second language and the eradication of substandard usage of the English language.

Interestingly enough, programs for special populations today have their roots in the concerns of the early practitioners. The prevention of speech, language, and hearing problems in infants and preschool children; the communication difficulties of bilingual and nonstandard speakers of English; and language disorders in children and adolescents all constitute areas of interest and concern for today's clinician.

There are many options for the delivery of educational services, which may include self-contained special classrooms, part-time resource rooms, or full-time integrated classes with monitoring or support services. The individual needs of the children determine the amount and type of supplemental services required. The speech-language clinician may be working with teachers of the mentally retarded, emotionally disturbed, hearing impaired, and learning disabled. The children in these modules may also require the help of the reading teacher, academic tutor, psychologist, and others. This means that the school clinician will be working not only with the child's classroom teacher but also with other specialists as well as with the parents of the child.

In working with personnel in the other specialized fields, it is important to keep in mind that the instruction should be child-oriented. The specialists involved work as a team, and each team member has specific responsibilities that are known to themselves and other team members.

For example, in a program described by Parker (1972) in which the speech-language clinician was on a learning center team, the other full-time members included a teacher of the educable mentally retarded, a reading specialist, and a special learning disabilities teacher. Part-time members included a psychologist, a social worker, a hearing consultant, two tutors, a vocational rehabilitation counselor, and a school counselor. According to Parker, the team members did not teach content area subjects, but they did assist classroom teachers in developing and acquiring more diversified methods and materials. The team identified those students requiring team services; diagnosed the students' learning strengths and weaknesses; prescribed behavioral goals according to the students' needs; prescribed plans to carry out these goals; managed the prescribed plans; and evaluated the students' progress, prescribed plans, and methods.

The Prevention of Communication Problems In Very Young Children

The Committee on the Prevention of Speech, Language, and Hearing Problems of ASHA (June 1982), views the responsibility of the profession to include not only the treatment but also the prevention of communicative disorders. Included in one of the areas of prevention is the early detection and treatment of young children. Public Law 94-142 mandates the inclusion of handicapped children, ages three to five, unless the mandate is in conflict with state law. High-risk infants (zero to three years) likewise are not included in the mandate if it is in conflict with state law.

What does this mean to the school SLP? Essentially, it means that if you are employed as a school clinician in a state that includes in its laws the detection and treatment of young handicapped children, the responsibility of servicing these children will be with the local education agency. Because of financial restraints very few school systems have this type of program; however, the detection and treatment of young handicapped children are often being provided by local community voluntary agencies and by private agencies.

The school SLP has a stake in encouraging and assisting these agencies in early detection and remediation. The earlier that handicapping conditions are identified, the better chance there is of remediation. And eventually fewer of these children will turn up in the caseload of the school clinician. Communication deviations that go untreated may develop into communication disorders and cause these children difficulties with the acquisition of such academic skills as reading, spelling, writing, and mathematics.

The SLP may intervene by providing information about speech and language development, environmental factors that influence development, and techniques to facilitate and stimulate speech and language development. Talks to groups of parents, early childhood educators such as day-care workers, preschool and nursery school teachers, members of the health professions, elementary school teachers and administrators, student groups, community organizations, and other professional groups, will help individuals understand how they may prevent and ameliorate speech, hearing, and language problems in children. Information may also be disseminated through newspaper articles, radio and television appearances, and other media. In a school or preschool the SLP may also provide demonstration lessons for the teachers.

Severely Handicapped Nonvocal Students

Severely handicapped nonvocal students are those who are unable to utilize speech as a primary method of communication. They are usually placed in schools other than their home school where a complete range of services are available to them: speech, language and hearing, physical therapy, occupational therapy, psychological and counseling services, and adapted physical education, as well as academic subjects in integrated classrooms.

Included in this group of students are those with neuromuscular, neurological, and physical impairments. These students may have been diagnosed as having cerebral palsy, multiple sclerosis, oral or facial deformities, or dysarthria. They may also have central processing disorders or severe expressive aphasia. They may have normal or near normal receptive language abilities and normal nonverbal intelligence.

The SLP in this setting works closely with the classroom teacher, physical and occupational therapists, psychologist, and learning disabilities teacher.

The speech and language services provided depend on the diagnosis of each child. In addition to language therapy the student may also receive treatment for fluency, voice, or articulation deficits if appropriate. The most advantageous method or methods of communication are determined and may include gestural systems if appropriate, symbol systems, and orthographic or pictorial systems. Depending on the mode of communication selected, the process may include augmentative communication devices such as communication boards, electronic devices, speech output devices, synthetic voice instruments, typewriters, and other electronic and mechanical apparatus.

The purpose of a program for nonvocal severely handicapped pupils is to provide them with the necessary habilitation programs while keeping them within the regular classroom for as much time as possible.

The Severely Handicapped Preschool Child

Zoback and Richards (1984) have described a program of transdisciplinary intervention for severely handicapped preschoolers at the Eastconn Early Childhood Center at Mansfield Center, Connecticut. The transdisciplinary approach is characterized by three important components: joint team effort, staff development, and role release. The typical team includes classroom teachers, instructional assistants, speech-language pathologists, occupational and physical therapists, nurse, and parents. Staff development emphasizes the need for team members and parents to train one another, drawing from their specific areas of expertise or information. Role release provides the mechanism whereby the program can be effectively carried out.

According to Zoback and Richards the transdisciplinary approach is facilitated by several essentials for efficient programming:

1. Location of classrooms in public schools that also serve nonhandicapped students
2. Emphasis on the organization of a curriculum around functional life skills
3. Application of applied behavior analysis technology in direct instructional activities

4. Consistent use of quantifiable data and their visual display to assess student progress on a frequent and regular basis
5. Use of the community as a training area for students
6. Use of criterion-referenced assessment of functional skills to develop IEPs
7. Provision of activities to facilitate interactions between nonhandicapped and severely handicapped students
8. Provision of small-group and necessary one-to-one instruction

Mentally Retarded Children

In mentally retarded children, the extent and degree of language delay is related to their overall development delay. They exhibit about the same characteristics of children with specific language impairments. Public Law 94-142 has mandated the provision of services to severely and profoundly handicapped children and has acknowledged that they may be educated to the extent that their limitations allow.

Speech-language pathologists, teachers, and other school personnel must evaluate each child and plan a remedial program specific to that child's needs. Some mentally retarded children do not begin to use words until the age of five or six, whereas others may learn to communicate by pointing and gesturing. The severely retarded may never learn to communicate. Early intervention and parent counseling are important factors in a program for mentally retarded children.

Freeman and Lukens (1962) reported on a program of speech and language training for educable mentally handicapped children in Oakland County, Michigan. In the program, the teachers, speech clinicians, and county consultants formulated an interdisciplinary program which could be carried on in the schools. The speech clinician was responsible for the diagnosis of the speech and language problems and for formulating a plan for improving communicative skills. The speech clinician also treated any children whose speech and language problems were not attributable to depressed intellectual function. The speech and language skills were part of the regular classroom curriculum. The classroom teachers were responsible for cooperating in the formulation and execution of the oral communication program.

Bilingual and Dialectically Different Populations

The issue of providing speech, language, and audiological services to children whose native language is not English or who speak different dialects has been a topic of intense discussion among professionals. The discussion may be academic in locations where English is the dominant language, but in areas where the non-English-speaking population is ever increasing, the issue is a practical one.

According to Freeman (1977), "Dialectal differences cannot be construed as speech or language disorders. They are deviations from Standard American English which are based on the rules of the dialect, not on the speaker's ability to understand or speak. They reflect the internalization of the language rules of a primary culture or subculture."

In discussing the bilingual population in the schools, Work (1982) stated, "To consider these children speech-language disordered would be improper. Their difficulty with English is not due to a language disorder but to a language difference. Differences may be found in the linguistic structure, the phonological system, and the inflectional use of voice. Differences also exist in the cultural background at verbal and nonverbal levels."

There is little doubt that speech, language, and hearing deviations and disorders do exist among minority populations, including Hispanics, blacks, Asians (including Pacific Islanders), and American Indians (including Alaskan natives). In identifying communication disorders and deviations in minority populations, the SLP must be careful not to confuse a dialect with a communication disorder. According to a paper drafted by the Committee on the Status of Racial Minorities (1985), "It is apparent that the assessment and remediation of many aspects of speech, language, and hearing minority language speakers require specific background and skills. This is not only logical and sound clinical practice, but it is the consensus set forth by federal mandates. . . . " The report further indicated that state regulations are being developed to acknowledge the need for specific competencies to serve minority language populations. In California, for example, school districts are being encouraged by the education agency to require resource specialists, speech-language pathologists, and school psychologists to pass a state-administered oral and written examination on Hispanic culture, the Spanish language, and assessment methodology before they conduct assessments for Spanish-speaking children with limited English proficiency.

Harris (1985) discussed the importance of the clinician's investing time and effort to learn about the cultural differences of the population that he or she serves. Harris, who is codirector of the Native American Research and Training Center, University of Arizona, stated,

> To appropriately measure and evaluate the English performance of minority language children on measures of speech and language, the examiner must be familiar with the behavioral characteristics of that group as they relate to language learning and language use. The level to which the particular child employs the traditional linguistic/cultural practices of his ethnic/minority group must be determined in order to assess his performance in an appropriate manner.

For example, requesting an Apache child to answer incessant questions, especially to answer in English, may put the child into a cultural conflict in which his or her resulting behavior (silence) may not be indicative of potential or knowledge but rather of cultural integrity.

This is not to say that school SLPs should not evaluate and provide services to children who have limited English proficiency and who have speech, language, or hearing handicaps. Interim strategies may be employed, such as utilizing interpreters or translators; establishing interdisciplinary teams, including a bilingual professional (for example, special education teacher or psychologist); or establishing cooperatives among school districts to hire an itinerant or consultant bilingual SLP or audiologist (Committee on the Status of Racial Minorities, 1983).

In regard to social dialects (black English, standard English, Appalachian English, southern English, New York dialect, Spanish-influenced English), it is the position of the American Speech-Language-Hearing Association (1983) that

> . . . no dialectal variety of English is a disorder or a pathological form of speech or language . . . (however) it is indeed possible for dialect speakers to have linguistic disorders within the dialect. An essential step toward making accurate assessments of communicative disorders is to distinguish between those aspects of linguistic variation that represent the diversity of the English language from those that represent speech, language and hearing disorders.

Public Law 94-142 does not permit federal funds to be designated for services that are elective or for children who are not handicapped.

A SAMPLING OF PROGRAMS

Students-in-training have often expressed interest in how school SLPs organize and manage programs. To obtain information on the various aspects of the programs, a questionnaire was sent to school clinicians located in various geographical areas of the United States. The purpose of the questionnaire was to obtain a sample of the programs in different parts of the country. No attempt was made to query representative programs or to quantify the information received or even to draw any conclusions from the comments returned. Rather, it was felt that the information these individuals provided would be helpful to prospective school speech, language, and hearing clinicians.

It might be added that all respondents at the time the questionnaire was returned in 1980 were actively engaged in school programs, and all were holders of the Certificate of Clinical Competence in Speech Pathology from the American Speech-Language-Hearing Association. The school pathologists are (1) Barbara DeWeese, (2) William Freitag, (3) Ruth Terry, and (4) Polly Young. The school systems represented are located in Arizona, Ohio, Delaware, and California.

The questionnaire contained the following questions:

A. Under which of the delivery-of-service models does your program fit?
B. How and by whom are children referred?
C. In regard to evaluation, what testing instruments are used? Who does the evaluating and what is the procedure?
D. Could you describe the class, the classroom, the equipment and furnishings, and the scheduling procedures?
E. What is the rationale of your program?
F. What about reevaluations?
G. If it is part of your program, how do you foster return to the regular class?
H. What are the advantages and disadvantages of your program?

The answers to these questions are not given in the order of the names as listed. However, the order given here is consistent throughout the series of answers (that is, number 1 is the same pathologist each time).

A. UNDER WHICH OF THE DELIVERY-OF-SERVICE MODELS DOES YOUR PROGRAM FIT?

1. A full-time special class for children with severe language disorders and aphasia.
2. Contractual and, or, cooperative series. I have been employed by the County Special Services Cooperative for the past two years and worked in 2-3 different school districts.
3. The itinerant model combined with the consultant model.
4. This program falls within the itinerant diagnostic-educational team concept for its delivery of services.

B. HOW AND BY WHOM ARE CHILDREN REFERRED?

1. Referrals may be initiated from numerous sources—preschool screening specialists, district psychologists, speech and language clinicians, pediatricians, private schools or nursery schools, parents, etc. Each student must be referred from the contracting school district of residence. That school district supplies referral letter, doctor's report, and a parent questionnaire to the county severe language disorders/aphasia program and the referral is then dealt with in the closest severe language disorders and aphasia office (SLD/A) to the contracting district.

    Children from three to six years of age, as soon as can be managed, are placed in a preschool diagnostic class which involves diagnostic teaching to determine the child's learning style and an appropriate instructional plan. The child is in the class approximately six to eight weeks. School-age pupils are seen by the diagnostic team which consists of a consultant, psychologist, language program specialist, principal, language teacher specialist, and is assisted by consulting physician, school nurse, audiologist, and other specialists.

2. Children can be referred by anyone such as a classroom teacher, principal, coordinator, psychologist, nurse, aide, parent. The largest number of referrals come from classroom teachers. In one instance, a child referred himself.

    Referrals have been received verbally or in writing and include information such as name, grade, teacher, and a brief description of the problem. Usually the children referred have been seen at least once by the speech-language pathologist because the entire school district population has been screened.

3. A brief referral form is usually used by teachers, nurses, psychologists, social workers, guidance counselors, principals or other administrators. Parents, other concerned adults, and the individual himself make verbal referrals. The completed form or referral message is sent to a SLH person.

4. Children with speech and language handicaps are identified through routine speech surveys conducted by the speech and language pathologists and supplemented by teacher and parent referrals. Referrals are also received from the county nurses who work within the system, and from the otolaryngol-

ogists in the area as well as from the orthodontists for myofunctional therapy when these children have concomitant speech problems in addition to the myofunctional problems.

We also utilize the "Strategies in Early Childhood Education" program which we implemented in 1976. Dr. Robert Wendt was one of the facilitators and original authors of the program which was developed in Wisconsin. This program is administered to kindergarten children in the fall and hopefully we will move it into first and second grade in the near future. This program assesses the visual and auditory perceptual language development and physical coordination of each child to compare his ability levels with his peer group so that we can descriptively provide educational programs at the kindergarten level for these children. Children who do not perform well in the language areas of the Strategies Program are referred to us for further testing.

C. IN REGARD TO EVALUATION, WHAT TESTING INSTRUMENTS ARE USED? WHO DOES THE EVALUATING, AND WHAT IS THE PROCEDURE?

1. Children three to six years of age are placed in the preschool diagnostic class as previously mentioned. A language teacher specialist does informal assessment and takes a 50 to 100 utterance language sample. The language program specialist does formal testing which usually consists of the *Illinois Test of Psycholinguistic Abilities, Assessment of Children's Language Comprehension, Peabody Picture Vocabulary Test, Northwestern Syntax Screening Test,* or any other test that may prove informative. The school psychologist does intellectual testing utilizing a performance test such as the Leiter performance part of the *Wechsler Intelligence Scale for Children.* The nurse does vision and hearing screening. If a child fails the hearing screening, an audiologist will do further testing. For children of school age the same testing procedure is used, but there is no placement in a diagnostic class, and the psychologist does academic as well as intellectual testing. An admittance and dismissal committee meeting is held when all assessment has been completed and a decision is made whether to admit the child into the SLD/A program. Members of the committee are the diagnostic team as mentioned above in question B and the child's parents.

   A child is admitted into the program according to the state's Administrative Code, Title V Regulations. The child has a severe language disorder which is not due to deafness, mental retardation, or autism.

2. Each evaluation includes receptive and expressive aspects of the language. Additional testing is done when warranted such as in cases of severe language development problems.

   Articulation is tested with an informal picture test, a reading sample, or the *Goldman-Fristoe Articulation Test.* Other commercial tests used include: *Auditory Test for Language Comprehension, Northwestern Syntax Screening Test, Illinois Test of Psycholinguistic Abilities, Peabody Picture Vocabulary Test, Goldman-Fristoe-Woodcock Test of Auditory Discrimination, Houston Test of Language Development, Wepman Auditory Discrimination Test.* Informal tests are used for verbal absurdities, syntax, auditory memory and blending, and expressive language usage.

   I do the speech and language evaluations in entirety but frequently check the results of Title I Reading testing and those of psychologists when they are involved with a particular child.

The procedure used (after obtaining parental permission and conferring with parents when requested) is to "test" the child by himself. The evaluation includes: articulation; imitation of word series and sentences; auditory discrimination; oral examination; informal voice assessment; hearing test; receptive vocabulary; basic information such as name and address; descriptive speech noting parts of speech used; informal assessment of fluency; absurd sentences; sound blending; similarities and differences.

A summary of the evaluation is written in duplicate or triplicate. The results are submitted to the classroom teacher, the coordinator, and sometimes the psychologist. A conference is held with the parent unless the parent waives such a requirement. Those persons who must be consulted with and notified of such a conference are the principal, coordinator, teacher, parent, special education teacher, and other persons involved with the child.

Primary language (if other than English) has to be considered among much of our school population. The primary language of the home and the child has to be documented. Some testing, such as articulation, is done in English and the child's primary language to determine whether there are articulation errors in both languages.

3. SLH person does evaluating. Initially the following tests might be used: *Predictive Screening Test of Articulation, A Screening Deep Test of Articulation, Developmental Articulation Test.* Further testing might include: (1) *Auditory Discrimination Test,* (2) *Preschool Language Scale,* (3) *Peabody Picture Vocabulary Test,* (4) for particular problems: certain sub-tests of *Illinois Test of Psycholinguistic Abilities,* (5) audiometric testing.

4. Children who are not identified during a screening may be referred by the teacher, a parent, the nurse, or member of the Special Services Department. The speech pathologists do all the evaluations of the children referred for suspected communicative handicaps.

The testing instruments vary. We will begin with the pure tone audiometric evaluation and/or impedance testing to determine whether or not the child has any kind of hearing acuity problems. Some of the more frequently used tests include: *Picture Articulation Test, Fisher-Logeman Test of Articulation Competency, or Goldman-Fristoe Test of Articulation.* The following tests may also be used: *Wepman Discrimination Test, Goldman-Fristoe-Woodcock Auditory Selective Attention Test, Goldman-Woodcock-Fristoe Auditory Memory Test, Goldman-Fristoe-Woodcock Sound/Symbol Test, Token Test, Boehm Test of Basic Concepts, Peabody Picture Vocabulary Test,* Auditory Subtests of the *Illinois Test of Psycholinguistic Abilities,* Carrow test for *Auditory Comprehension of Language,* and *Northwestern Syntax Screening Test.* We also use the *Assessment of Children's Language Comprehension Test, Utah Test of Language Development,* and *Wiig-Semel Test of Linguistic Concepts.*

D. COULD YOU DESCRIBE THE CLASS, THE CLASSROOM, THE EQUIPMENT AND FURNISHINGS, AND THE SCHEDULING PROCEDURES?

1. Classroom organization:
Location—space is rented from school districts

LEVELS	NO. OF STUDENTS	USUAL AGE RANGE
Preschool	6	3 – 6
Primary	6	6 – 9
Middle	8	9 – 12
Junior High	8	12 – 14
High School	8	14 – 21

Each class of six pupils has assigned to it a language teacher specialist and a full-time communication teacher aide. Ancillary staff available to the teacher are language program specialist, psychologist, nurse, audiologist, and occasionally a remedial speech therapist.

Classroom furnishings, organization, and scheduling are largely left up to the teacher. The pupils are bused to their school site and attend class five and one-half hours. The special classes are located at regular schools and at minimum allow for integration during lunch and playground. Pupils who the teacher deems ready to integrate, attend regular class for part of the day.

Teachers are responsible for meeting the total needs of the student and teach academics as well as language and speech. Junior and senior-high classes are career education oriented and some students at the senior-high level spend part of their school time in a job situation.

A remedial physical education teacher serves preschool, primary, and middle grade students approximately one half-hour per day.

Instruction is largely individualized, and geared to reach each pupil's unique needs. Cross-age tutors from the regular classes are often used as well as the teacher and aide.

2. Since my services are itinerant, I have many classes usually one-half hour in length twice weekly. Many of the children are seen in groups of three to four, but some are seen individually because of their communication problems and ages. The "classroom" facilities vary from school to school. Usually these are classrooms or conference rooms with oversize tables and chairs. Filing facilities are in the school office. No storage areas can be located in the rooms used for therapy.

Almost all equipment for therapy is obtained from the cooperative office. Such equipment is kept in a school office or at my home when not in use. Quite an extensive amount is available including tests, therapy materials, audiometers. Much of what I use is my own, such as teaching materials and a tape recorder. We have been fortunate in that equipment we have requested has either been available or has been ordered for us through the cooperative office.

Scheduling is done by me and is a hassle! Since I innovated the practice here of conducting therapy twice weekly in each school building, I have found it necessary to compromise and change groupings of children a number of times. The times to be avoided in scheduling include Title I Reading and Resource Room sessions. It has been necessary to schedule some students during physical education, music, and crafts. Generally the teachers have been cooperative.

Each building has been serviced twice weekly except for some students in the kindergartens and junior high school. The buildings having the greater number of students in need receive the longer half of the school day (morning). Usually grouping is based upon the nature of the child's problem, particular grade, and age.

3. The class is made up of four or less students who are the same age or grade placement. Some individual work is done. Size of group is often determined by size of room. The room itself is usually a storage closet, empty regular classroom, library, or whatever isn't in daily use by other persons in the school. Chairs and tables of appropriate size are usually available. Each SLH person has a tape recorder.

    In regard to scheduling, the children to receive therapy are listed in groups as the SLH person would like to see them. Then the SLH person talks with teachers and attempts to work out a mutually agreeable schedule. Usually this plan works.

4. We look at each child individually and try to provide as much therapy as is needed. We use a combination of the itinerant and the intensive cycle scheduling. For example, I am scheduled at Jones Elementary School on Monday morning, Thursday morning, and Tuesday and Wednesday afternoons. This allows me to see a child on Monday, Tuesday, Wednesday, and Thursday if it is needed. As the child shows progress, I can drop him or her to three times a week, two times a week, and eventually visits can be phased out completely.

    Furnishings meet state standards; we exceed any maximum standards for equipment. We have a Language Master, with both long and short cards; three pure tone, one pure tone bone and one impedance. We have an auditory trainer for working with children who have hearing probems and for children who need to work on discrimination. We also have tape recorders and a cassette library on some of our students. Through the Media Center we have access to video taping equipment which we may use with voice or stuttering cases and with the preschool language program. We also have a very extensive professional library and materials center to go along with our different tests.

    We have tried to correlate most of the tests with available remedial materials for the classroom teacher's use.

    The scheduling, whether individual or group, is determined by the needs of the children.

E. WHAT IS THE RATIONALE OF YOUR PROGRAM?

1. The County SLD/A program provides special day classes for students who exhibit severe language disorders as outlined in the state's Administrative Code, Title V Regulations.
2. This is governed largely by both a state mandate which went into operation for the 1976–77 school year, and now a federal mandate. It requires special services for all school children identified as handicapped with emphasis upon individual rights, due process, primary language, and cultural background. Primary throughout is the requirement for staffing with school personnel and parents involved. The least restrictive environment for the child is stressed. A great deal depends upon parental permission and cooperation.

    The rationale is to provide a program which meets the needs of those students identified as having communication problems. It also involves consultant and informative kinds of service, such as conferring with school personnel and parents and providing some in-service training for staff members.

3. The program exists to identify, evaluate, and provide therapy for children with SLH problems in district schools K-12 including children in a school for the TMR. The therapy is directed toward teaching children to attain a standard of speech-language skills that enables them to function satisfactorily in other areas of their school life.
4. Our philosophy is to accept each individual child as he or she is and to provide opportunities to learn effective communication skills so as to insure his or her rightful place in society. In keeping with this philosophy, our program is designed to give the most communicatively handicapped child the highest priority, scheduling him or her intensively, and reducing the caseload as needed to assure the most effective program of remediation.

F. WHAT ABOUT REEVALUATIONS?

1. Each student in the SLD/A program is brought before an admission and dismissal committee meeting at the close of every school year. The following guidelines apply to all students:
    (1) Students must have performance intelligence measures within the past three years. Those who do not have a qualifying performance test within the normal range when admitted to the program will be recommended for a performance test. (2) Students must have formal language testing within the past two years. Previous language tests with scores falling below two standard deviations will be recommended for retesting. Reading and math test results below the normal range will be recommended for retesting. (3) Students must have reading, or math measures. (4) All students whom teachers consider at this time to be possible candidates for dismissal at the end of the year will be recommended for complete testing. (5) Teachers make any other recommendations that they may have and may suggest additional testing.
2. The mandate requires reevaluation every three years of children enrolled in special education programs. Reevaluation procedures are the same as those used for evaluation.
    Also required are reviews once each semester or whenever required by the parents. The results are to be submitted to the parents. Such reviews amount to informal assessments of therapy—what has been accomplished and what remains to be done.
3. There is continuous evaluation in therapy. Reevaluation is done: (a) when in the course of therapy it seems advisable, (b) always at the end of the year, (c) at the beginning of the next school term after the summer therapy break, (d) periodically, for children not active in the program who are being watched.
4. We reevaluate the child the year following dismissal from therapy and usually one more evaluation is made six months later. Thus a child is followed after dismissal for about a year and a half before we deactivate the folder.

G. IF IT IS PART OF YOUR PROGRAM, HOW DO YOU FOSTER RETURN TO THE REGULAR CLASS?

1. Since the SLD/A classes are located at regular elementary schools, integration of SLD/A pupils is widely encouraged in any activity in which the teacher feels they could succeed. When an SLD/A student is returned to the district

into a regular class, that student is assigned to an itinerant aphasia teacher specialist who works with the pupil several hours each week at the student's neighborhood school upgrading language skills as well as aiding the pupil's academic achievement.

2. This is not an integral part of the therapy program. If a student has progressed to the point of dismissal from therapy, he or she is checked periodically during several school years following dismissal. As a student has made progress, he or she may then be seen for therapy fewer times per week or perhaps once every two weeks.

3. Does not apply to this program.

4. This is not applicable.

H. WHAT ARE THE ADVANTAGES AND DISADVANTAGES OF YOUR PROGRAM?

1. *Advantages:* Our program is fairly well-funded and ample equipment and supplies are available for use by teachers. The county has written a special education curriculum to use as a guide in dealing with Special Education students. The communication aide is a full-time employee and works a six-hour day. The class size is especially advantageous and aids in individualizing instruction. The preschool diagnostic class serves well to ready youngsters for testing and test results are usually deemed reliable. Various ancillary staff are made available to assist teachers when the need arises.

    Disadvantages: Classes are located at various sites—two to four classes to a site and twenty to twenty-five classes are under a principal. The sites and classes are spread apart geographically and sometimes communication channels are not clear and open. Teachers must deal not only with their own SLD/A principal but also with the principal of the building in which they are located. Since the program falls within a large county government and the state is now requiring so much accountability, there is a huge amount of paperwork required of the teachers and this seems to take time away from reaching the students.

2. *Advantages:* (a) Working out a cooperative offers the opportunity to share and become informed about other special services programs within the county, such as physical therapy, the hearing-impaired, and psychological services. (b) Without guidelines or an effective program previously, it has been possible to set up the program the way I want it except for the restrictions of the mandates and the limitations of number of days contracted by each school district for such services. One example is that of scheduling students twice a week instead of the previous schedule of once a week or once every two weeks. (c) Among the Special Education staff, there is a sharing of information and concern about the children served. Each of the staff members is respected for the expertise he or she can provide. There is a strong team approach particularly in regard to children with multiple handicaps.

    Disadvantages: (a) The mandates generate a great amount of paperwork. A considerable portion of time is spent on that instead of on providing therapy. (b) Because of the use of Spanish and Indian tongues by parents, it is difficult to explain the program to them and gain their cooperation. (c) The mandates make the same requirements of Speech and Language Therapy as of every other area of Special Education without consideration for the nature of the program, the number of students involved, and the role of the speech-language pathologist in diagnosing, consulting, and providing treatment. (d) There are no state guidelines for Speech and Language Therapy programs regarding caseload, frequency of therapy sessions, limits on populations served, and facilities. (e) State funding is based upon the number enrolled in the therapy program; thus, administrators can use this to pressure the therapist into providing services for larger numbers of students than would otherwise be considered practical.

3. *Advantages:* (a) We deliver service to a large number of children who need it. Many of them would not otherwise get the service. (b) Language gains are great with use of conversational experiences/language stimulation with urban children who don't get it at home. (c) Teachers often report that certain children are able to do better work in reading after having had speech therapy.

   Disadvantages: (a) Lack of adequate working space on a continuing basis. (b) Lack of adequate furnishings such as locked storage cabinet. Often the room is piled with junk. (c) SLH person is classified as a teacher, not a specialist (such as social worker, psychologist) yet is often expected to play role of specialist. (d) It is often difficult for SLH person to communicate the nature of his or her responsibility to school personnel—particularly administrators. (e) Lack of opportunity to take advantage of many continuing education programs that are offered during the school year.

4. *Advantages:* Probably the most important asset we have is the diversity of interest within the staff itself. By this, I mean each member has a particular area in which he or she excels, and we each recognize each other's strengths. When we are involved in the diagnostic evaluation, and we find that we have a child who is exhibiting a problem that falls within the expertise of a colleague, we do not hesitate to call that individual to our school, and ask that person to help in the evaluation. We can then consult and hold a staffing. When we have in-service meetings, members of the staff attend workshops and come back and report findings. I feel that we have a dynamic program because we have a dynamic staff. Members of our staff participate actively in national and local professional organizations. We have become involved in research and we have published our research findings. We have an early childhood strategies program in our kindergartens which is an adjunct to our identification program. A diagnostic-educational team concept is utilized and we consult with the classroom teacher, the school psychologist, the parents, and, in many cases, the children. We have received over $60,000 in the last seven or eight years for research and development. We have a language program for the communicatively handicapped preschool child which includes a parent guidance program.

   Disadvantages: One of the difficulties we face is the amount of time required to comply with the federal mandates. In the long run I think this will be beneficial, but the short-term effect is very constraining. Another disadvantage that results from, perhaps, a lack of emphasis and training at the university level, is that we find ourselves being asked to play the role of a reading consultant. The lack of training and the lack of information about some of the new testing instruments places us at a disadvantage when we consult with the classroom teacher. I am just barely holding my own in this area. Fortunately, there is a member of the staff who has specialized in this area and this has helped all of us. I see us playing a "catch-up" game in the area of helping the classroom teacher with reading and spelling problems.

DISCUSSION QUESTIONS AND PROJECTS

1. Using an itinerant scheduling model, schedule the following children in School A, School B, and School C:

   School A, 8:30 A.M.–3:00 P.M., 19 students
   Kindergarten: 3 language/articulation
   Grade 1: 2 articulation, 1 primary stutterer
   Grade 2: 1 voice, 1 foreign language, 2 articulation
   Grade 3: 2 voice, 1 stutterer, 2 articulation
   Grade 4: 1 aural rehabilitation
   Grade 5: 1 voice
   Grade 6: 1 articulation, 1 stutterer

   School B, 8:15 A.M.–2:30 P.M., 30 students
   Grade 1: 3 language, 1 severe articulation, 1 hearing impaired
   Grade 2: 3 articulation
   Grade 3: 3 voice, 1 cleft palate, 3 articulation
   Grade 4: 4 articulation, 1 stutterer
   Grade 5: 2 hearing impaired, 1 stutterer, 1 voice
   Grade 6: 2 articulation, 1 voice, 3 language

   School C, 8:30 A.M.–3:15 P.M., 28 students
   Kindergarten: 4 language/articulation
   Grade 1: 3 severe articulation, 5 articulation
   Grade 2: 2 articulation, 1 language
   Grade 3: 1 foreign language, 1 voice, 1 stutterer
   Grade 4: 1 cerebral palsy, 1 hearing impaired, 1 articulation
   Grade 5: 1 foreign language, 1 stutterer, 2 articulation
   Grade 6: 1 foreign language, 2 hearing impaired

2. Interview a school SLP about the type of scheduling models being used.
3. Would you schedule children during recess? Art Class? Physical education? Reading? Social studies? Explain.
4. Does the severity of the problem have any influence on the time of day you would schedule a student?
5. Plan a therapy program based on a fourth-grade social studies unit. There are four students in the group with multiple articulation problems.
6. How would you handle the dismissal of a malingerer in therapy? What conditions might encourage malingering?
7. What behavioral signs would alert you to the possibility that a child may need psychological or psychiatric treatment?
8. What information would you give parents of very young children on speech and language development and how they could enhance development? How would parents' expectations affect their role in helping children attain adequate communication skills?
9. You are the school SLP. The principal asks you to work with children with Hispanic accents, children who speak limited English and whose

parents are Vietnamese, and children with black dialects. One child of Hispanic parentage has a suspected hearing loss. A second-grade child who speaks with a black dialect is having difficulty in the classroom with reading and has a fluency problem. Would you include any or all these children in your caseload? How would you justify your decisions to the principal? Role-play the situation.

10. You are on a cross-country plane trip and discover that your seatmate is the president of the American Speech-Language-Hearing Association. You have just graduated from the university with a degree in communications disorders and hope to work as a school SLP. What pertinent questions might you ask this individual?

NINE
WORKING WITH OTHERS: THE SCHOOL SPEECH-LANGUAGE PATHOLOGIST AS A CONSULTANT

INTRODUCTION

In Chapter 3 we looked at the structure of the school system. What we need to look at now is how the roles and responsibilities of the school administrators and teaching personnel interact directly with the functions of the school speech-language pathologist. In other words, what can we expect from various educational personnel and what can they expect from us?

The school SLP works not only with school-based personnel but also with health and rehabilitation facilities and their staffs. Public Law 94-142 allows for the utilization of nonpublic schools and community agencies, and in some cases, for the purchase of services if they are not available in the local education agency. This means that the SLP must be familiar with the community agencies and the roles and functions of the various community health and rehabilitation professionals.

Public Law 94-142 has mandated the inclusion of parents and/or guardians in the planning of speech, language, and hearing services for their children. Although this is not a new role for the school pathologist, its importance cannot be emphasized enough.

The school speech-language pathologist is also a consultant to the community and a source of information on speech, language and hearing services. The roles of the director of special education, elementary and secondary supervisors, superintendent, assistant superintendents, and board of education have already been discussed in Chapter 3. In this chapter we will examine the working relationships with professionals most closely involved in the overall education and rehabilitation of schoolchildren.

THE PRINCIPAL

The key person in the speech, language, and hearing program is the building principal. This individual's attitude toward speech, language, and hearing can make or break a program. Without the understanding and cooperation of the principal it would be extremely difficult to carry out an effective program. The principal is the administrator of the building, and in a sense, the school SLP is responsible to that person while in that building. The school SLP is a member of staff of that particular building in the same way that other teachers are staff members.

The principal is often the representative of the local education agency in the development of individualized programs for children and may serve as the coordinator of the placement team.

What can the school clinician expect from the principal? First, the principal is responsible for arranging for adequate working space and facilitating the procurement of equipment and supplies. The principal acquaints the clinician with the policies, rules, regulations, and all procedures in that school.

The principal may assist the clinician in scheduling the screening programs and in setting up the schedule for children to be seen in therapy. The principal may help the SLP in integrating the speech, language, and hearing program into the total school program.

The interpretation of the program to other members of the school staff, the parents, and the community is ongoing, and much may be done by the principal. In addition, the principal may arrange opportunities for the clinician to interpret the program to the staff and the parents as well as professional and lay groups in the community. The principal is the liaison between the school and the community and between the school clinician and the school staff. When a parent, a classroom teacher, or a member of the community has a question regarding the speech, language, and hearing program, that person will ask the principal, who may answer the query or refer it to the school SLP. Clinicians may not always be immediately available for questions that come to the school because on that particular day they may be scheduled at another school. When this occurs, the principal will be the one to handle the questions.

The principal can be expected to visit the therapy sessions and observe. Indeed, a wise clinician will invite the principal to observe therapy sessions and will encourage questions.

The principal can smooth the way for school clinicians in many situations. Perhaps one of the most important is in helping the clinician gain acceptance of the program by the school staff and the parents. The attitude of the principal may be reflected by the teachers, and the attitudes of the children may stem from the way teachers perceive the program. Because of a myriad of duties and heavy administrative responsibilities, principals cannot be expected to know everything about the therapy program, but a willing and cooperative principal with a positive attitude is excellent insurance for a good speech, language, and hearing program.

On the other side of the coin the school clinician has some important responsibilities to the principal. If the clinician is itinerant, more than one building and more than one principal will be involved; therefore, the clinician needs to know the policies and procedures in each school.

Providing information about the program to the principal is one of the most important factors in maintaining a good relationship. The principal needs to know the children in the active caseload, the children dismissed from therapy, and the children on the waiting list and have a brief statement on the progress of each child enrolled. The children on these lists should be identified by name, age, grade, room number, and teacher's name.

The clinician should also provide information to the principal on screening policies and procedures, the children screened, the criteria for case selection, and those children selected, as well as scheduling policies and procedures. In many schools the clinician will want to confer with the principal regarding each of the steps of the program. Some of the information can be conveyed through a conference, however. It is advisable to furnish the principal with periodic written reports, such as a monthly report, on the various aspects of the program.

The clinician should discuss with the principal any plans for parent conferences and should furnish a schedule of them. Any plans for in-service programs for teachers and group meetings with parents should be discussed with the principal prior to inception.

Any written reports or correspondence pertaining to a child in that school should be shown to and approved by the principal. This would include information to other professional personnel as well as letters and notices to parents.

If the school clinician keeps in mind that the principal is legally and educationally responsible for each child enrolled in the school, the answers to many of the clinician's questions will be self-evident. Generally speaking, the school clinician should keep the principal well informed on every aspect of the program.

Because clinicians work in several buildings and with several principals at one time, it is good practice to keep all the principals informed in a general way about the programs in the other schools. This practice serves to keep the principals well informed about the total program in the school system, may suggest ways of cooperation and coordination among schools, and helps keep the clinician's workload well balanced.

Administrator's Attitudes

The functions of the school SLP are ideally carried out as a member of the educational team. To provide the best possible treatment for the communicatively handicapped pupil the school pathologist must work cooperatively with other members of the education community. Sometimes this involves providing information and support and sometimes it means receiving information and support; most often it entails both.

How well have clinicians integrated themselves into the educational setting? Are school administrators and other school personnel aware of their potential contribution? Or do they need to develop this role more thoroughly?

A study was conducted by Phelps and Koenigsknecht (1977) on the attitudes of classroom teachers, learning disabilities specialists, and school principals toward speech, language, and hearing programs in the schools. The results showed that the overall disposition of these educators was moderately favorable; however, they perceived the size of the clinician's caseload as too large to effect desired behavioral change. They also found that the classroom teachers of grades four to six showed the least enthusiasm for and support of elementary-school speech and language programs.

Although the results of this study are, and should be, disturbing to the entire profession, it is evident that there are many school clinicians who are doing a good job. The study should prompt us to take a good look at some aspects of the programs in the schools and take whatever steps are necessary to remedy potentially dangerous situations and conditions.

The Principal's Understanding of the Speech-Language Program

A study by Blosser and DePompei (1984) indicated that speech-language pathology may not be a well-understood profession within the educational setting.

According to Blosser and DePompei,

> The findings appear to indicate that principals continue to view the speech-language pathologist in the traditional role. There was inconsistency in the title given to the speech-language pathologist. Principals agreed the SLPs work with children with articulation, voice, fluency and language disorders; but did not agree that they work with children with learning disabilities or identify hearing loss. Most agreed that SLPs continue to conduct therapy one to one or in small groups.
>
> Several principals indicated that SLPs do share information about their programs with them and participate in selected building level activities. A majority of the principals responded that they agreed correction of communication disorders is important. Few principals agreed that SLPs currently play a role in teaching language skills in the classroom. While 89% of the principals indicated that they understood the role of the SLP, only 37% reported they had had academic exposure to the SLP's role. This may indicate that there is limited discussion of the speech-language pathology profession in the academic preparation of administrators.
>
> In relation to recent discussions in the literature regarding changes in the role of the school speech-language pathologist, the findings of this survey demonstrate that principals do not currently support modifications of the traditional role. Principals indicated they would prefer that the SLP have more direct contact with children with communication disorders, parents, teachers, and the principals themselves. They also appear to understand those factors which interfere with the provision of more direct contact such as paperwork, the evaluation process, and the high numbers of children requiring services in contrast to the low number of SLPs available.

Considering that over 45% of the profession is employed within the school setting, these results are disturbing. It will be difficult to institute changes while school administrators continue to be content with the status quo.

Principal's Responses to Open-Ended Questions

The principals were asked to respond to the following three open-ended questions:

a. What changes would you as a principal like to see in the speech-language therapy program?
b. What changes do you feel your teachers would like to see in the speech-language therapy program?
c. Do you feel there are problems with the way the speech-language therapy program is currently operated? If yes, what are they?

The responses fell into the following categories:

1. Desired Changes: Principals indicated they would prefer more direct contact; increased services at the high school level; more parent contact; and more work with the severely and multiply handicapped. Many stated that they feel SLPs should begin their programs earlier in the year and end them later. Many noted that SLPs take too long to test and do too much testing in relation to teaching. Several remarked that SLPs don't adhere to the same accountability for their time as other teachers do and are not available when needed.
2. Teacher Contact: The majority of respondents indicated they feel their teachers would like the SLP to be more informative about their program and work more closely with teachers and other special educators. They indicated that teachers don't feel SLPs function as a part of the educational team. They would like SLPs to become more involved in school activities. Many stated that they would like to see the SLP provide in-service for the teaching staff regarding when and how to make referrals, the therapy program, and developmental norms for communication skills.
3. Problems: Principals indicated that problems which interfere with the speech-language therapy program include: the paperwork necessary for due process; high caseloads; too many building assignments; and conflicting schedules.

It was interesting to note, however, that the principals rated the SLP's individual qualities high: 91 percent of the principals rated them high in flexibility, 85 percent in organization, and 74 percent in creativity. Approximately two-thirds (65 percent) agreed that the SLP in their school demonstrates leadership.

Blosser and DePompei suggest that administrators are not likely to take steps independently to find out more about the SLP profession. They recommend that an assertive, proactive approach is needed to gain administrative support. To accomplish this, administrators must first be educated about the profession and be encouraged to work with the SLP to facilitate effective program changes. The SLP needs to establish a more visible position in the school so that administrative attention, understanding, and cooperation can be attained. Blosser and DePompei suggest that an Administrator Education Program be initiated in the following manner:

1. Conduct a quality program. No program change or growth can occur unless quality is already in operation.
2. Identify the key decision-makers within the school district. Determine who needs to be "educated." This may include principals, teachers, curriculum directors, central office administration, school board members and parents.
3. Continually supply key administrators at the building, central administration and top administration levels with facts and information that will challenge them to act on behalf of the speech-language therapy program when decisions are being made.
4. Increase the visibility of the speech-language therapy program districtwide:
   a. Join school committees and attend building activities.
   b. Participate in prevention services and in-service activities.
   c. Host invitational days. ("Board of Education Day"; "Principal's Day"; "Administrator's Day"; "Teacher's Day.") Invite important people to observe therapy sessions.
   d. Establish an on-going mechanism for communication such as a monthly newsletter.
   e. Offer to speak at Board of Education meetings, local parent groups, church groups, etc.
   f. Serve as a source of information to other educators regarding communication skills. Forward informative clippings and articles about the importance of effective communication skills and/or therapy. An "FYI" ("For Your Information") approach could be effective.
5. Inform administrators of your aspirations and goals for your program. Arrange for a meeting with district leaders to share your ideas about the program's strengths, weaknesses, and potentials.

THE CLASSROOM TEACHER

The continuum-of-service model discussed in Chapter 4 has as one of its components consultative services. In this program the SLP does not provide direct service, such as therapy, but instead is responsible for providing information, demonstrations, and training to regular or special classroom teachers, curriculum specialists, parents, and so forth to alleviate or prevent communication problems from developing. These communication behaviors may occur in social, educational, or cultural contexts.

The Committee on Language, Speech, and Hearing Services in the Schools (1984) suggested that the consultation program be used to monitor a student's communicative abilities, before enrolling him or her in a direct service program, to determine the degree of severity, rehabilitative potential, or most appropriate placement. Another application may be to review the student's progress after dismissal from a direct service program.

In the pathologist's role as a consultant to the classroom teacher, two areas should be considered: the communicatively handicapped child and all the other children in the classroom. This means that the SLP must be a generalist as well as a specialist. It also means that the SLP must know what is going on in the classroom as well as making sure that the classroom teacher understands the speech, language, and hearing program and the role of the pathologist.

In most school systems there is an administrator for curriculum development. With assistance from teachers, principals, directors of special services, or other administrators, this person is responsible for the selection of textbooks and instructional supplies and materials. The business of educators is the selection of what will be taught, at what level, and in what sequence. That which is taught is the *curriculum.* The curriculum is organized by teachers into *instructional units,* each made up of lesson plans, constituting how the curriculum is taught (Rebore, 1984).

One of the ways in which the speech and language program can be integrated into the curriculum is for the SLP to have input into the curriculum committee, either as a member or in an advisory capacity. In this way the pathologist can be perceived by the rest of the staff as someone who does more than correct frontal lisps. As a communications specialist the pathologist can provide information on pragmatics, communication in the classroom, how to help the children follow directions, how to encourage children to ask questions, and how teachers can become better communicators in the classroom. The pathologist can offer suggestions on how the teaching of improved communication skills can be integrated into language arts, social studies, science, art, physical education, math, reading, spelling, and writing.

The integration of the speech, language, and hearing program into the curriculum is a basic factor. It is essential that the classroom teacher understand the program, but it is equally important that the speech clinician understand what is going on in the classroom. It is not enough to give lip service to the idea of integrating the program into the educational framework; it must be put into practice.

How can this be accomplished? The answer is not a simple one, but let us first consider some of the things the school pathologist can expect of the classroom teacher; then let us look at some of the expectations of the classroom teacher in regard to the clinician.

The school SLP can expect the teacher to provide a classroom environment that will encourage communication and will not exclude the child with the stuttering or articulation problem or the child who is hearing impaired. A teacher who shows kindness and understanding toward the handicapped child is not only assisting that child but also is showing other children in the classroom how to treat handicapped individuals. Sometimes it takes more time and patience to deal with handicapped children, but the rewards in terms of the child's performance are many. The teacher in the classroom takes the lead in establishing the emotional climate in that setting, and the children learn by example.

The classroom teacher is also a teacher of speech and language by example. If you doubt this, watch a group of children "playing school" sometime. Teachers provide the models for communication and children imitate the teachers. Teachers must have an awareness of their use of language, the quality of speech, the rate and volume of speech, and the use of slang or dialect.

The SLP can expect the teacher to help identify children in the classroom with speech, language, or hearing problems. Some children with communication problems are not spotted during a routine screening, and teachers who see children on a day-to-day basis will have more opportunity to identify the children and refer them to the SLP.

The clinician can expect the classroom teacher to send the children to therapy at the time scheduled. The SLP will need to supply the teacher with a schedule, and both teacher and clinician should stick to it. The SLP can also expect the teacher to inform him or her of any changes in schedules that would necessitate a child being absent from therapy.

One of the most important areas of cooperation between the SLP and the classroom teacher is in the carryover, or generalization stage—when speech and language behavior learned in therapy is brought into the classroom. For this to be accomplished it will be necessary for the SLP to keep the teacher well informed about the child's goals in therapy, progress in therapy, and steps in development of new patterns. This must be done not in general terms but in very specific ones. The teacher needs precise information on the child's problem and what is being done in therapy before there can be a carryover into classroom activities. The teacher can provide the SLP with information concerning how well the child is able to utilize the new speech or language patterns in the classroom.

When confronted with the idea of helping the communicatively handicapped child in the classroom, the teacher's reaction is apt to be "I don't have time to work with Billy on his speech when I have 25 other children in the room." The SLP's role in this situation is to give the teacher specific suggestions on how this can be accomplished as a part of the curriculum. This of course means that the clinician will have to be well acquainted with classroom procedures, practices, and activities. It also means the SLP will have to know what can be expected of children of that age and on that grade level.

To integrate fully the speech, language, and hearing program into the school, there must be a continuous pattern of sharing ideas and information between the SLP and the classroom teacher.

We have considered what the SLP can expect of the classroom teacher. Now let us look at the other side of the coin—what the teacher can expect of the clinician.

If you are new in the school, starting off on the right foot is important. Being friendly and open with teachers, showing an interest in what they are doing in their classrooms, and showing a willingness to give them information are all things that can be done to help build trust and understanding. There are many ways in which this can be accomplished. One way is to plan to eat lunch with the teachers in the teachers' lunchroom. Another is to participate in some of their social activities. Because clinicians deal with many teachers in different schools it is not wise to become identified with little cliques and associate only with a very small group. Outside the school you will have your own circle of friends, but inside the school be friendly with everyone.

If you have a schedule, keep to it, and if you make changes in it, as you surely will, be sure to tell the classroom teachers who are affected. If you send a child back to the classroom late, you will have no basis for complaint if the teacher fails to send a child to you on time.

Share information with teachers through informal conferences, arranged conferences held periodically, invitations to observe therapy sessions, and observation in classrooms. Always make arrangements in advance for conferences and observations. The principal can often help make arrangements for any of these activities. In one school where I worked, the principal volunteered to take over each classroom for a half-hour so that each teacher in the school could observe in the therapy room.

Information can also be transmitted in written form. Short descriptions or definitions of the various speech, language, or hearing problems or any aspects of the program will help teachers understand the program better. *Short* is emphasized because realistically teachers are not going to take the time to read long treatises.

Providing in-service programs or short courses for credit are excellent ways of providing teachers with information about communicatively handicapped children.

Dopheide and Dallinger (1975) described a pilot in-service program in a district in Maine that had been providing language, speech, and hearing services to children for only one year. It was seen as a potential model for other schools in the state. Enrollment by the teachers was voluntary, and the course consisted of eight workshops that spanned a four-month period and carried three credits toward state recertification.

The objectives of the workshop were to: (1) design the program so that teachers and the clinician would engage in free and open professional communication; (2) deal with problems in developing teachers' support of the clinician's work; (3) help teachers understand definitions of speech problems, criteria for making referrals, procedures used by the speech pathologist to help children with communication problems, and how to assist in the change process; (4) prepare a series of videotapes to effectively stimulate discussion of improved cooperation between clinicians and teachers.

Mainstreaming means that teachers will be faced with the task of integrating exceptional children into regular classrooms. The speech, language, and hearing clinician can help teachers understand children with communication disorders by providing in-service programs.

What are some of the things that classroom teachers will need to know about communication and communication disorders? Following is a list of topics that might be included in an in-service program:

1. The relationship of speech, language, and hearing to the educational process
2. The speech, language, and hearing program in the school, including the preventive, diagnostic, and remediation aspects.
3. Normal speech and language development
4. Articulation disorders—characteristics, possible causes and related factors, diagnosis and assessment, therapy, and the role of the classroom teacher
5. Delayed language development and language disorders—characteristics, causes and related factors, therapy, and the role of the classroom teacher
6. Speech and language—characteristics of mentally retarded children, diagnosis, therapy, and the role of the classroom teacher
7. Stuttering—characteristics, possible causes and related factors, the various stages of stuttering, the role of the classroom teacher, and therapy

8. Voice disorders—characteristics, causes and related factors, medical diagnosis, assessment and diagnosis by the speech pathologist, the role of the classroom teacher, and the prevention of voice problems

9. Cerebral palsy—characteristics; diagnosis and assessment; roles of the physician, physical therapist, occupational therapist, pathologist; and suggestions to teachers

10. Cleft palate—characteristics, related factors, medical and dental intervention, importance of early diagnosis and treatment, possibility of concomitant hearing loss, therapy, and the role of the teacher

11. Hearing problems—anatomy of the ear, nature of sound, types of hearing loss, causes of hearing loss, identification and measurement of hearing loss, role of the classroom teacher, rehabilitation and habilitation of hearing deficiencies.

In working with classroom teachers the school SLP is a partner in effecting the best possible services for the communicatively handicapped child. The more help that is given to the teacher, the more opportunity there will be for integrating the speech, language, and hearing program into the schools.

The book *Speech and Language Services and the Classroom Teacher* by Gerald G. Freeman (1977), was written specifically for teachers and provides much useful information regarding classroom management of communicatively handicapped children; it emphasizes the team approach.

Some universities require students majoring in elementary education to take a course in speech, language, and hearing problems.

In a study conducted by Gelfand and Horwitz-Danzinger (1984) a 50-item questionnaire was sent to 229 teachers (K–12) in a suburban midwestern school district. The purpose of the study was to determine how successfully SLPs have become involved in interdisciplinary efforts with parents, learning disability specialists, administrators, guidance counselors, classroom teachers, and other educational colleagues in efforts to alleviate communication handicaps. Another purpose of the survey was to assess implications for a teacher's in-service training program. The areas of information sampled included general information; laws and requirements; due process procedures; referral, evaluation, and placement; program scheduling; caseload and therapy; general information about therapy; and subjective evaluation of program effectiveness.

The investigators found that the elementary-school staff had a better overall understanding of the school pathologist's duties and responsibilities than did the secondary teachers, and in addition, they were more knowledgeable about specific areas. In other words, what the elementary-school staff knew, the secondary-school staff also knew but to a lesser degree. The study also revealed that there are implications for in-service training programs for teachers and administrators to help them understand the changing role of the SLP in the school, as well as the increased responsibilities, brought about by PL 94-142.

How does the SLP bridge this gap in understanding? First, it must be emphasized that understanding is a two-sided coin and that although clinicians seek to be understood, they must also understand the roles and responsibilities of school administrators and personnel. Second, this is a continuous, ongoing process requiring a vigorous and assertive stance on the part of the SLP. Administrators and teachers are not about to invite us as SLPs to tell them who we are or what we can do. The pathologist must be like the Fuller Brush salesperson of the past and start by getting a foot in the door. Third, this responsibility should have the support and active participation of the American Speech-Language-Hearing Association, over 45 percent of whose members are employed in schools, as well as state and local professional organizations such as the Council for Exceptional Children.

SUPPLEMENTARY LANGUAGE THERAPY IN THE CLASSROOM

Fujiki and Brinton (1984) have provided some valuable suggestions on how the SLP can work with the classroom teacher on supplementing language therapy in the classroom. For example, the technique of talking with children can be used for language-normal as well as language-disordered children. The teacher should

1. Create a climate of emotional acceptance in the classroom that emphasizes communication
2. Become an attentive listener
3. Avoid complexity in conversation by using shorter utterances, avoiding ambiguous words, using direct requests, and adjusting the degree of conceptual difficulty and abstractedness of words
4. Use extra stress on important words
5. Utilize context as an aid to comprehension
6. Utilize specific techniques for talking with children
7. Encourage the child to make an unintelligible message more intelligible, while at the same time not allowing the child to become too frustrated

The consultation role made may be useful when servicing students who are severely or profoundly mentally handicapped or multiply handicapped.

The report further stated that the consultation program should be based on the needs of the student and is not to be considered second best or used when direct intervention by the SLP is not possible. The program is suitable for all degrees of disorders, from mild to severe. It may be appropriate for students who are homebound, students with multiple handicaps, or young children who can best be served in their natural environment.

Many pathologists have been using the consultation program in a variety of ways, depending on the needs of the school program. It should not be considered an adjunct to the communicative disorders program but should be an integral part of it, the students enrolled should be part of the clinician's caseload, and an appropriate amount of time should be allotted for it.

Preventing Vocal Abuse in the Classroom

Nilson and Schneiderman (1983) described a preventive classroom program to make second- and third-grade children aware of the function and proper use of the vocal folds to prevent vocal abuse and misuse. The program was also designed to determine if the children could retain the skills learned and to educate the teachers regarding good vocal hygiene and their part in referring children with possible voice disorders.

The results of the investigation were positive. According to Nilson and Schneiderman,

> . . . Because the speech-language pathologist is responsible for serving all communicatively handicapped persons, the efficient use of time and help from other staff members is imperative. Using such programs to prevent vocal abuse and hoarseness, with the aid of classroom teachers as facilitators and to carryover information, helps the speech-language pathologist be more responsible and provides a method of serving the milder problems not eligible for direct therapy. By involving the teachers in the prevention program, the speech-language pathologist can also educate the teachers in the identification and management of communication disorders. By using such a management program, one can fulfill the consultative responsibility of the clinician.

WORKING WITH TEACHERS ON THE READING PROCESS

The relationship between reading and speech has been recognized for some time by classroom teachers, reading teachers, and speech and language clinicians. Often they find that the child with a speech or language problem also has difficulty with reading. The precise relationship between the problems, however, has thus far eluded many researchers. Some studies show a relationship between speech and reading and between language and reading, but whether the problems are in a causal relationship or whether they exist concomitantly has not been established. Nonetheless, there is much evidence to indicate that the speech-language clinician can contribute significantly to the treatment of reading problems. The reading teacher, likewise, will be able to offer much valuable information to the speech-language clinician in regard to the child with both a reading and communication problem.

Research suggests that children with reading failure need to learn the rules of spoken language. Stark (1975) indicated that they need to develop strategies for processing morphophonemic and syntactic units and learn the logic of the language system. He suggested that teaching so-called *word attack* skills, teaching sound and letter correspondences and blends, and improving perceptual-motor skills must be questioned. He also felt that an overwhelming amount of attention is being given to visual motor testing and training despite the fact that in 21 of 25 studies from 1960 to 1975 it was found that concomitant improvement in reading cannot be expected as a result of systematic visual motor training.

According to Stark,

> . . . we believe that there is a significant amount of evidence to indicate that speech and language pathologists can make a very important contribution to the prevention and treatment of reading problems. Assisting parents, teachers, and other specialists by providing information about the nature of language acquisition and training children in linguistic processing may produce highly desirable results. At the least, speech and hearing clinicians may be able to modify cur-

rently used teaching techniques and materials so that teachers can more effectively understand the role that language development plays in reading.

Rees (1974) stated,

The speech pathologist has an essential contribution to make to the process of reading acquisition, in normal and learning-disabled children. The speech pathologist can make this contribution when he functions as a language specialist rather than in the limited role of articulation therapist. As a language specialist, the speech pathologist makes use of research findings and theoretical accounts of the foundations of reading in language and speech. The speech pathologist has the responsibility to assess and develop the linguistic prerequisites for reading, as well as to assist the child in developing the specific linguistic awareness required for reading. Specific training in auditory perception is probably of limited value.

According to Sanders (1977),

The arguments concerning whether or not auditory perceptual problems arise from deficiencies in specific auditory skills has its corollary in the area of reading difficulties. There is little doubt that auditory perception plays an important role in learning to read. Certainly, the widely used phonic approach to reading depends heavily on the child's ability to process patterns of speech sounds and their linguistic values. Examination of existing theories about how a child learns to read reveals a surprising parallel to theories . . . concerning how the spoken word is perceived. Many of the same questions are asked and many similar hypotheses are made concerning how the process might operate. It seems quite logical to assume that a common basis exists for an understanding both of speech perception and reading.

Sander's book *Auditory Perception of Speech* provides reference information on neurophysiological, psychoacoustic, and psycholinguistic aspects of the auditory processing of speech. He also discusses auditory learning difficulties as a language-processing dysfunction and the correlation between auditory perceptual skills and the process of reading.

Discussions on auditory processing and the assessment of cognitive and linguistic skills, as well as suggestions for remediation, are included in Wiig and Semel's (1976) book *Language Disabilities in Children and Adolescents.* Muma's (1978) book, *Language Handbook: Concepts, Assessment, Intervention* also contains information helpful to the clinician.

Gruenewald and Pollak (1973) described the clinician's role in helping primary classroom teachers develop strategies for teaching the auditory skills necessary in learning to read. They suggested that the clinician utilize knowledge of auditory processes in diagnosing and analyzing auditory skills such as listening attention, identification and localization, discrimination, auditory sequencing and memory, and auditory association and closure. According to Gruenewald and Pollak the appraisal of reading readiness is often weighted heavily toward visual discrimination tasks or the combination of visual and auditory tasks, to the exclusion of auditory learning tasks.

Gruenewald and Pollak stated that although speech clinicians are generally not trained to teach reading as a process, they are trained in the auditory aspects of speech and language development and must not isolate themselves from the total learning process:

> We are suggesting that the clinician use knowledge of auditory processes to assist the primary teacher in diagnosing needs and implementing group and individual programs in the developmental aspects of reading. Our unique contribution to the educational team can be the analysis of speech, language, and auditory learning upon which further symbolic and academic skills are built.

Following is a diagnostic outline showing auditory activities involved in reading readiness (starred items). The outline was developed by Gruenewald and Pollak, along with the developmental reading specialist in the Madison, Wisconsin, public schools to provide a framework for the classroom teacher in assessing reading readiness skills (starred items indicate auditory activities):

1. Some components of reading readiness assessment
    A. Following directions
        *(1) Attending behavior (visual and auditory contact)
        *(2) Language of instruction (comprehension of task)
        (3) Performance of task (at what level?—motor, perceptual, conceptual, verbal)
    *B. Language
        (1) Nonverbal
        (2) Social
        (3) Comprehension (nonverbal-verbal)
        (4) Verbal (structure and content)
        (5) Conceptual parameters (classification and relationship)
    *C. Auditory behavior
        (1) Listening behavior
        (2) Recognition, identification, and localization of sound
        (3) Discrimination
            a. Concept: same-different
            b. Nonverbal: sound, pitch, rhythm
            c. Verbal: letter sounds, words
        (4) Auditory memory and sequencing (nonverbal and verbal)
        (5) Auditory association
        (6) Auditory closure
    D. Visual behavior
        (1) Visual reception
        (2) Visual recognition and identification
        (3) Visual discrimination
        (4) Visual memory and sequencing
        (5) Visual association
        (6) Visual closure
    E. Motor behavior
        (1) Gross motor performance
        (2) Fine (visual-motor)
            a. Hand-eye functioning
            b. Eye focus
            c. Tracking
            d. Midline structure

Wray and Watson-Florence (1984) suggested that SLPs demonstrate activities and strategies for classroom teachers to improve reading proficiency in the classroom. These strategies are based on a language theory paradigm and are in concert with the daily curriculum. In this type of model the SLP shares information on the "language-reading connection" with the teacher, and together they plan the structuring and achieving of goals for the language-delayed child at risk for reading development.

According to Wray and Watson-Florence,

> Guidelines are provided to aid the speech-language pathologist in creating an integrated communication curriculum to be used to teach reading skills. Activities designed to improve oral language development and usage will be related to exercises stressing reading development and usage. To avoid fragmented learning experiences, the child's language program in areas such as writing, spelling, reading, speech and auditory training will be coordinated and based on overall language acquisition. These ideas will be based on the assumption that demonstration for the teacher will initially take place with the speech-language consultant gradually assisting the teacher to independently implement these ideas in the daily curriculum.

Language Procedures to Facilitate Reading Skills

Wray and Watson-Florence suggest activities that

Stress discrimination among speech sounds to teach grapheme/phoneme correspondence

Teach listeners to discriminate various stress patterns across words

Teach auditory awareness of where one word stops and another begins

Develop semantic awareness of word labels and functions

De-emphasize accuracy and encourage rhythm and melody during oral reading

Acknowledge the child's dialect

Write stories composed by the children using their language patterns

Have adults read various types of materials to children

Involve the children as active participants in meaningful language/reading activities

Demonstrate how stories are typically organized

Demonstrate how to ask questions to obtain additional information

Introduce vocabulary concepts systematically using grouping techniques

Stress comprehension skills

Select vocabulary and reading material from the child's basal reader making certain the reading level is easy

Apply compare/contrast techniques to language instruction

Present the reading words in the context of a phrase using a modifier or verb, not in isolation

Reading is one of the most important skills taught in the school. Classroom teachers in the primary and early elementary grades are responsible for teaching reading, and the reading specialist in the school system is responsible for helping the child with a reading problem. Sometimes this is done directly with the child and sometimes it is accomplished indirectly through the teacher.

Classroom teachers often use quick screening instruments to place students at appropriate reading levels. Children having reading difficulties are referred for a thorough reading analysis, which may be done by the reading specialist.

The speech clinician and the reading specialist should strive to learn one another's professional terminology. Often they are talking about the same things but using different terms.

The reading specialist and the SLP have much in common and much to offer one another. A close working relationship between them is an important aspect of the speech, language, and hearing program.

THE LEARNING DISABILITIES TEACHER

Speech-language pathologists and audiologists relate to all the providers of special instructional services in the schools, including teachers of the emotionally disturbed, the learning disabled, the mentally retarded, the physically handicapped, the visually handicapped, and the deaf. All these groups provide special instructional services as defined by PL 94-142, which does not define the areas of professional specialization involved in the delivery of services. The result is frequent confusion concerning the scopes of practices, especially between SLPs and learning disabilities specialists. *Learning disabilities* is a generic term that comprises a heterogeneous group of disorders, the majority of which are disorders of language. Originally, PL 94-142 did not even refer to disorders of language; however, this was corrected during oversight hearings.

The American Speech-Language-Hearing Association in a position statement (*Child Services Review System,* 1982) noted that

> a major concern of speech-language pathologists are those individuals whose primary learning disabilities are characterized by disorders of language acquisition, comprehension and production. It is the position of the American Speech-Language-Hearing Association that qualified professionals, including speech-language pathologists must participate actively in the:
>
> 1. assessment of individuals suspected of having learning disabilities to determine the presence or absence of a language disorder;
> 2. assessment, program planning, and program development for individuals who have language disorders and language-based learning disabilities;
> 3. delivery of programs and services to language disordered individuals on a direct or indirect basis as appropriate.
>
> Therefore, the American Speech-Language-Hearing Association advocates that agencies having responsibility for providing programs and services to these individuals ensure that qualified speech-language pathologists are members of the multidisciplinary assessment and instructional team.

At this writing the interacting roles of the learning disabilities specialist and the SLP are not yet clearly defined. The working relationship is dependent on the local school and the individual professional persons involved, including the principal and the classroom teacher. Some issues are clear: The SLP has the academic background, interest, and competence in language development and disorders. Also, the fields of speech-language pathology and audiology have a solid backing of research in language disorders.

The Committee on Language Learning Disabilities of the American Speech-Language-Hearing Association supports the following activities:

It is the position of ASHA that speech language pathologists be included as members of the multidisciplinary team involved in the management of individuals with learning disabilities. More specifically:

1. The speech-language pathologist must be included in the review of referral data. Regular classroom teachers, parents, and other specialists are not always aware of the importance of language skills to successful learning. Some prerequisite academic problems are manifestations of language problems.
2. The speech-language pathologist must be included in the assessment process. PL 94-142 suggests that a speech-language pathologist be a member of the assessment team. However, many local educational agencies do not require a language assessment to identify children with specific learning disabilities.
3. As members of the multidisciplinary team, the responsibility of speech-language pathologists must be expanded to include educational planning. For children whose handicapping condition is primarily a communicative disorder or a language and learning disability, the speech-language pathologist must be a participant in the development and review of individual educational programs. For students with other handicapping conditions, the speech-language pathologist must be a participant when the child has an accompanying communicative disorder.
4. The speech-language pathologist must be able to provide both direct service and consultative functions by helping teachers with language programs for LD children in classrooms, analyzing the language of the curriculum, and conducting language therapy sessions for students where appropriate.

Despite the difficulties in defining areas of work, the learning disabilities specialist and the SLP on the local level have in many instances achieved satisfactory working relationships. This has been the result of each specialist recognizing and relying on the expertise of the other. The consequence has been more effective programming for children with language-learning disabilities.

Under the continuum-of-services model, liaison with learning disabilities teachers may be provided under several different plans. These delivery-of-service models are not mutually exclusive. The SLP may function as a member of the diagnostic team during the initial evaluation procedures or on an ongoing staffing basis. Specific remediation may be provided to children placed in full-time special classes or transition classes. The SLP may function as the resource room professional for the language-learning disabled child or as a consultant to the learning disabilities specialist in relation to general or specific problems. Obviously, different delivery-of-service models would depend on each local school system's situation. The possibilities have not been fully exploited, and the creativity of the SLP may be utilized in determining innovative approaches to helping pupils with language-learning disabilities.

Crabtree and Peterson (1974), through a case study, described the role of the speech pathologist as a resource teacher for the child with a language-learning disability. They stressed the idea that the speech pathologist, to function successfully as a communication specialist, must have a theoretical background in language development; must be able to identify and develop prescriptive techniques for problems related to phonology, syntax, and semantics; and should be able to relate these aspects of linguistics to all levels of oral and written language. In addition, the speech pathologist must be a generalist as well as a specialist. In other words, the speech pathologist must know how academic learning is developed and the effect of sensory deprivation, from any cause, on learning.

Simon (1977) described a program in which the SLP worked closely with the learning disabilities teacher in a developmental program in expressive language. The essentials of the program involved cooperation, communication, and programming. Both professionals focused on how they could best combine their talents, expertise, and schedules to increase the linguistic sophistication of the children in the program.

THE EDUCATIONAL AUDIOLOGIST

The most evident interrelationship between specialists in education to the hearing handicapped and members of the speech-language profession is in audiology. Educational audiology, a comparatively new specialization in the field of communication disorders, was born out of a need for improved services for the hearing-impaired child in the school and the mainstreaming component of PL 94-142, which mandates that the child be placed in the least restrictive educational environment possible. An educational audiology program was pioneered at Utah State University in 1966 (Alpiner, 1970). Since that time some states have followed suit in providing training programs for educational audiologists, and several universities have established curricula. This specialization is still in its infancy, and there is still much to be done if hard-of-hearing children in classrooms are to receive the kind of care that will enable them to perform at optimal levels in the school.

The adverse effects of hearing loss on schoolchildren has been well documented. The Ad Hoc Committee on Extension of Audiology Services in the Schools (1983) focused on three major issues:

1. It causes delay in the development of receptive and expressive communication skills (speech and language).
2. It causes learning problems that result in poor academic achievement.
3. It causes a reduced ability to understand the speech of others and to speak clearly which often results in social isolation and poor self-concept.

The educational audiologist plays a primary role in identifying hearing-impaired children through mass screenings and/or teacher or parent referrals. The children who fail the screening are given a complete audiological assessment. Air and bone conduction pure-tone tests are administered as well as speech-reception and speech-discrimination tests. Imittance or impedance testing evaluates the function of the middle ear and can provide valuable information about the presence or absence of middle-ear pathology (for example, otitis media).

Additional evaluative and/or therapeutic recommendations may be made by the audiologist if indicated by the tests. If audiological and medical evaluations reveal that amplification is necessary, the educational audiologist helps the parents to obtain the aid and to continue to monitor the child's behavior and hearing ability to ensure its acceptance and proper use (Townsend, 1982).

In addition to parent counseling, it is necessary to provide regular classroom teachers with information to help them deal with hearing-handicapped students. The audiologist also monitors classroom acoustics, measures noise levels, makes recommendations for sound treatment, and calibrates audiological equipment.

Ideally, all these functions are performed by the educational audiologist. Unfortunately, they are in short supply and often must spread themselves very thin.

In a study by Wilson-Vlotman and Blair (1984) the roles and attitudes of professionals serving the hard-of-hearing child in the regular classroom revealed some areas of concern. According to the study there is no one dealing with case management for the child to ensure optimum coordination of services. The educational audiologist appears to be in the best position to be a case manager if the optimization of residual hearing is the starting point for learning. Moreover, the monitoring of hearing aids is typically done at present by the classroom teacher or an itinerant teacher of the hearing impaired, although the educational audiologist is the best-equipped person for this function.

Direct services provided for the hearing-impaired child in the classroom are often termed *aural (re)habilitation* and are essential if the child is to develop skills that will enhance learning opportunities. The Wilson-Vlotman and Blair study found that 64 percent of educational audiologists did not engage in aural habilitation with any hearing-impaired students, and a further 18 percent provided direct service for only one-half day per week.

Other areas of concern include the availability of counseling for parents and for the child as well as consultative services for teachers, administrators, and other resource personnel. According to Wilson-Vlotman and Blair, there must be a united effort and coordination of services among the professions serving the hard-of-hearing student.

Another factor that may hinder the delivery system of audiological services is that primarily, educational audiologists were trained as, were functioning as, and viewed themselves as clinical audiologists who were based in the school. They carried excessively large caseloads, which is in keeping with the medical model. In effect, educational audiologists had limited impact on the classroom and were not taking full responsibility for the total management of the hearing-impaired child.

In considering the role of the SLP in relation to the educational audiologist there are many possible areas of cooperation. The SLP is specifically prepared to provide a program of language and speech therapy and is the best qualified person to do so. As information is obtained from the audiologist concerning the child's need for auditory development, it can be incorporated into that speech and language program. Because most audiologists service a wide geographical area and are not in a specific building with the same regularity as the SLP, the latter is considered to be the critical link between the student in the classroom and comprehensive audiological services.

The SLP may work with the educational audiologist in the evaluation of the hearing-disabled child. Consultation with classroom teachers and visits to the classroom may be scheduled by both the SLP and the educational audiologist in an effort to better assess the needs of the student.

To summarize, it may be said that to provide the hearing-impaired child with the best possible services, the SLP and the educational audiologist must work together in the evaluation, remediation, and psychosocial adjustment of the child.

School SLPs would do well to encourage the employment of educational audiologists who are either by training or experience familiar with schools and the process of education. Educational audiologists must utilize their clinical knowledge and awareness of the educational and communicative needs of the hearing-impaired child in the classroom.

Although the number of educational audiologists employed in the schools is increasing, there are still many schools with partial or limited audiological services. The school SLP may be playing a larger role in the delivery of services in these situations. Without an educational audiologist in the school system the task of caring for the hearing-impaired child falls to the SLP.

Northcott (1972) described the role of the speech clinician as an interdisciplinary team member in regard to the hearing-impaired child. The term *hearing impaired* was used to include every child with a hearing loss that was developmentally and educationally handicapping. The importance of early intervention was stressed. Northcott describes the school clinician's role as (1) providing appropriate components of supplemental services directly to hearing-impaired children; (2) serving as a hearing consultant to teachers, administrators, and resource specialists, helping them make reasonable accommodations to meet the special needs of the hearing-impaired child in the integrated class setting; and (3) serving as a member of an interdisciplinary team developing new components of comprehensive hearing services within the school district.

THE SOCIAL WORKER

A major role of the social worker is to facilitate referrals among tax-supported and voluntary agencies. This individual's thorough knowledge of social agencies in an area can be of considerable aid to the school clinician. The social worker is a key person in helping families find places where they may receive needed help. The social worker may do some counseling, both individually and in groups, may make home visits, and can be the liaison between the school and the family. When financial assistance is required for supplemental services, the social worker is the one who can be of assistance to the family in locating that aid.

Not all school systems are fortunate enough to have a social worker on the staff, but if there is one, the school clinician should explore ways in which they may work cooperatively.

THE PSYCHOLOGIST

The school psychologist is a member of the team of professional persons helping the communicatively handicapped child. The school clinician may make referrals to the psychologist to obtain additional information about educational diagnosis, school adjustment, personality, learning ability, or achievement. The child's speech, language, or hearing problem may be closely related to any of these factors, either as a result, a cause, or an accompanying factor.

The school clinician and the psychologist will find that a close working relationship is mutually beneficial. The school clinician will want to know the kinds of testing and diagnostic materials the psychologist uses. On the other hand, the clinician may be helpful to the psychologist in interpreting the child's communication problem so that the best possible tests may be used. In making a referral to the psychologist the clinician should ask specific questions in regard to the kind of information being sought. The school clinician can also furnish the psychologist with helpful information that would facilitate working with the child.

The school psychologist's role differs from one school system to another, so the clinician should make a note of that role and find out what additional kinds of psychological help are available in the community.

THE GUIDANCE COUNSELOR
AND VOCATIONAL REHABILITATION COUNSELOR

The guidance counselor works with students with adjustment or academic problems, helps students plan for future roles, and makes available to them information pertinent to their situation. This individual may also do individual counseling.

The guidance counselor is especially helpful in dealing with students in the junior high and high school. Students with communication problems are often known by the guidance counselor, so the school clinician may depend on this person for referrals, supplementary information, and cooperative intervention.

The vocational rehabilitation counselor is usually employed by a district or state agency. This individual assists students 16 years of age and older in overcoming handicaps that would prevent them from being employable at their highest potential. The vocational rehabilitation counselor, although not a member of the school staff, may work in conjunction with the school system.

THE SCHOOL NURSE

Depending on the size of the system, there may be a number of school nurses, only one, or one working part time. In some localities the school nurse may be part of the staff of the city, county, or district health department and work either part time or full time with the school. The new school clinician will want to know in which of these arrangements the school nurse functions.

The school nurse maintains the health and medical records of the children in the school. Children with hearing loss, cleft palate, cerebral palsy, and other physical problems are already known by the school nurse. The nurse is the one who arranges for medical intervention when it is needed, makes home visits, and knows the families. The school nurse is a storehouse of medical and health information. It goes without saying that the school nurse and the speech-language pathologist work closely together and need to share information on a continuing basis.

In some states, Ohio for example, the school nurse is legally responsible for conducting hearing screenings. The nurse, the school clinician, and the educational audiologist may work together in organizing and administering the hearing-conservation program of detection, referral, and follow-up. Medical referrals and follow-ups involving family doctors, otologists, and other medical specialists may be carried out by the school nurse. Medical problems in addition to those connected with hearing loss would be included.

The school nurse is one of the best sources of information for the school clinician and should be one of the clinician's closest working allies.

THE PHYSICAL THERAPIST

By definition a trained physical therapist works in the general area of motor performance. The services may focus on correction, development, and/or prevention of motor-related problems. Physical therapists are more likely to be found in hospitals or home health care agencies than they are in public schools. They no longer work under a doctor's prescription but often under medical referral. Physical therapists usually develop a written treatment plan for each patient, which is countersigned by a physician.

Physical therapists work with persons with ambulatory problems, focusing on the improved use of the lower extremities in sitting, standing, walking, and movement with and without aids.

The school SLP and the physical therapist may work together in serving children with orthopedic and neurologic problems and on developmental programs for high-risk infants. Physical therapists may also provide information and assistance to SLPs in achieving good posture for optimal breath support and control and in the stabilization of extraneous movements for cerebral palsied children. In addition, physical therapists may evaluate motor abilities for students who are possible candidates for communication boards or augmentative communicative equipment.

The speech-language pathologist can provide the physical therapist with assistance in the establishment of methods of communication modes with their clients.

THE OCCUPATIONAL THERAPIST

Because the work of the occupational therapist covers such a wide range it is difficult to define the scope of activities. The profession of occupational therapy is concerned with human lives that have been disrupted by physical injury, accident, birth defects, aging, or emotional or developmental problems. The programs in occupational therapy are designed to help persons regain their well-being and their "occupation." The word *occupation* does not necessarily refer to the individual's employment but rather to being occupied in meaningful day-to-day activities, including work, leisure, and play.

Occupational therapists work in a variety of settings, and today an increasing number is employed in public school systems. The occupational therapist and the SLP will find many areas of cooperation that will enhance the disabled student's potential. These same areas, however, may also give rise to conflicts regarding professional responsibility as well as differences in therapeutic approaches. The answer to this problem seems to be the establishment of a truly cooperative working relationship. Each profession has unique skills, and the recognition and respect for each other's expertise will only serve to help the handicapped individual.

Occupational therapists may work with the severely disabled child, especially in the development of adaptive devices, such as conversation boards, that aid greater independence. They may work with children with visual-spatial perceptual problems or with children who are having trouble adjusting to handicaps. They may work with a child individually or with groups of students in such activities as role playing, games, work adjustment sessions, and discussion groups.

WORKING WITH PHYSICIANS IN THE COMMUNITY

A good relationship with the physicians in the community enhances the speech, language, and hearing program. School clinicians should take every opportunity to establish such relationships by conducting their programs in a professional manner—following established local protocol in referral procedures, writing letters and reports that are professional in content and style, and giving talks to local medical groups if invited to do so.

A competent school clinician never oversteps professional bounds by giving medical advice or advice that could be construed as medical in nature. For example, the school clinician may think that a child's persistent husky voice may be the result of either vocal abuse or vocal nodules, or possibly a combination of both conditions. After collecting as much information as possible from parents and teachers and the child, the clinician then follows local referral policies established by the school system. These policies will differ from school system to school system. In some places all medical referrals are done through the school nurse, the school social worker, or some designated administrator. The school policy may allow the clinician to discuss the contemplated referral with the parents, who then follow through by taking the child to the family physician. The referral is accompanied by a letter from the clinician and includes results of diagnostic procedures, general impressions, and specific questions, as well as any other helpful information. The clinician should also include a request for the results of the physician's diagnosis and suggestions. It is best to request that the physician's results should be sent to the SLP, with a copy to the parents.

When parents ask the clinician to suggest a physician in the event they don't have a family doctor, the acceptable policy is to give the family the names of at least three doctors from which they can choose.

The question of who pays for the medical services has, at this writing, been addressed by PL 94–142. According to Dublinske and Healey (1978) the following interpretations of the law were made:

Must Medical Services Be Provided at no Cost to the Parents?

Yes and No. If the medical services are diagnostic in nature and necessary to determine if a child is handicapped, the cost of such services are to be provided at no cost to the parent. For example, medical diagnostic services could include assessments by laryngologists to determine that a child has a voice disorder or otologic assessments to diagnose hearing disorders if not available as part of the regular school program hearing conservation services. Medical services that are restorative or rehabilitative in nature cannot be funded under PL 94-142.

Nothing is more important than good health. The child who is ill or in need of medical attention cannot be expected to perform well in school. School clinicians should be alert to the child's physical condition. If there are any behaviors or symptoms that might be related to a health condition, the school clinician should discuss this with the school nurse and/or the principal, who would then take the proper referral steps.

THE HEALTH AND PHYSICAL EDUCATION TEACHER

One staff member who may be in closer contact with pupils than the classroom teacher is the health and physical education (HPE) teacher. This individual sees students in an environment where movement is stressed, where pupils are engaged in activities in which they may be more relaxed, and where talking may be more spontaneous. School SLPs may be able to work with the HPE teacher in generalized activities for the pupil with an articulation problem. The HPE teacher can also help with the pupil with a voice problem who yells too much. The HPE teacher is competent in teaching relaxation strategies and may help the mild cerebral palsied or dysfluent pupil. The HPE teacher on the elementary or secondary level can be a valuable resource person for the SLP.

WORKING WITH THE DENTIST

There are a number of areas of specialization within the dental profession, among them pedodontists, who are concerned with children's dental care; orthodontists, who are concerned with dental occlusion; and prosthodontists, who are concerned with designing and fitting appliances to compensate for aberrations within the oral structure. SLPs may make referrals to, or may be the recipient of referrals from, these dental specialists as well as the dentist in general practice within a community. The referrals may be children whose articulation problems are related to dental or oral cavity problems, such as cleft palate or other craniofacial anomalies. Children with dysarthrias associated with cerebral palsy, as well as developmentally disabled children, may require special handling by dentists. Thus the professional relationship between the dentist and the SLP requires cooperation.

WORKING WITH PARENTS

Throughout this book references are made regarding the importance of working with parents. Public Law 94-142 has mandated the inclusion of parents and/or guardians in the IEP process. This is not a new role for the SLP; most have always worked with the parents of children on their caseloads and the parents of children at risk. In this section the term *parents* shall be used to include guardians.

There is no one set of rules on how the school SLP works with parents, but for the beginning clinician it might be helpful to have some general ideas. As clinicians gain experience they develop their own "style" of working with parents.

The first thing to remember is that parents are people, and the basic ingredients in working with people are understanding and respect. The inexperienced clinician sometimes approaches parents with a preconceived idea of how they are going to react and behave and, therefore, expects resistance. At the same time the parents may anticipate the clinician's role as that of the "expert" who has at hand all the information and know-how to "cure" their child's problem. Obviously, then, everyone gets off on the wrong foot. But if the clinician approaches the parents in a friendly open way and lets them see her or him as a person whose task is to apply the most appropriate principles of rehabilitation (or habilitation) to the situation, the clinician will set the stage for the next step in the process. It is the clinician's responsibility to establish the ground rules and create the climate. A knowledge of body language would be helpful to allow the clinician to "read" the parents more accurately. Many useful books are written on this topic.

Also important is the ambience of the parent conference. For example, is there a desk between the clinician and the parents? How are the chairs arranged and are they comfortable? (They can sometimes be too comfortable!) Are they all an equal height? Is the light from the window directly on the clinician's or the parents' faces?

In addition to discussing these questions in the university classrooms, it is helpful for prospective SLPs to use role playing as a vehicle for rehearsing situations commonly encountered by the school clinician. For example, here are a few role-playing situations involving parents:

1. Parents ask whether having their child's tonsils removed will help his speech problem.
2. Parents ask how long Johnny will be in therapy to cure his stuttering.
3. Parents ask how they can stop the neighborhood children from teasing their child because she "can't talk right."
4. A parent asks if her smoking during pregnancy caused her child to be hard of hearing.

Role playing allows the prospective clinician to act out situations in front of a critical but friendly audience. In this way future clinicians can share observations and feelings with their contemporaries and discuss various ways the comments and questions may be dealt with in real situations. Students shouldn't expect agreement on what may be considered the "right" answer, and it is not fair to use the evasive phrase, "It depends on the situation"!

Parent Groups

As the school clinician you will be working with parents on a group basis as well as in individual situations. Parent groups may be organized by the school clinician as support groups or by the parents themselves out of a felt need. The professional in this kind of relationship assumes the "helping" role in which parents can be encouraged to express both positive and negative feelings without being judged. Parents of handicapped children often have feelings of guilt, as if something they did or didn't do caused the child's handicap. Professionals need to understand this and to help parents use the group situation as an opportunity for change, growth, and personal development. The use of the words *ought* and *should* are best dropped from the SLP vocabulary when dealing with anxious parents.

Parents, especially mothers, can be the most reliable sources of information concerning the child's speech, language, and hearing behavior. For example, if a parent insists that her child stutters when playing with an older sibling, accept her word for it. Subsequent observation will often prove her correct.

Changing Family Patterns

Family patterns are changing in the modern world. There are many single-parent families, latchkey children, children who are cared for on a daily basis by someone other than a parent, and divorced and remarried parents in families in which the children are "his," "hers," and "ours." The effect of these family situations may often have negative effects on the child. The speech-language clinician needs to be sensitive to this possibility.

There are other family situations that the school clinician may have never encountered in his or her own experience but nevertheless should be prepared for. One is that of the child from the poverty-level or lower-income family. Unfortunately this condition is becoming more and more common. The school clinician should keep in mind that many of these children come to school hungry, malnourished, and inadequately clothed. The cutback in the school lunch programs by the federal government will cause even greater problems in the future. Children who are hungry have needs greater than the refinement of minor articulation problems. However, the school clinician should not assume that children from poverty-level families are children who are not cared for and loved. These children may have a rich and loving family life and may receive superior parenting.

Abused And Neglected Children

Another unfortunate condition that seems to be more widespread is that of the battered or neglected child, who may also have communication problems. The maltreatment of children usually falls into one or more four general areas:

1. Physical abuse
2. Neglect
3. Emotional maltreatment
4. Sexual abuse

Some forms of abuse and neglect are easily recognized, such as beatings that leave facial bruises or being repeatedly locked out of the home for long periods of time. The more subtle forms of abuse may include verbal abuse, poor supervision, or overly strict discipline. What is the school clinician's role in regard to abused and neglected children? First, the SLP should be alert to the signs of abuse. It is important to keep in mind that abuse occurs among the rich and well educated as well as the impoverished. The next step is to report your suspicions to the principal, backed up with as much evidence as possible. Your suspicions may be wrong, but you may also be saving a life.

Working effectively with parents is a challenging and sometimes frustrating part of the SLP's program. It can also be the most rewarding and fruitful.

NONTEACHING PERSONNEL IN THE SCHOOLS

Nonteaching personnel are the clerical staff, custodians, bus drivers, cafeteria workers, gardeners, and others who make the school function. These individuals, who often know the students in different ways than does the teacher, are important people without whom the school could not run smoothly. The SLP can rely on them for information on where to get things and where to find things as well as information on the school buildings, equipment, and classroom housekeeping. The custodian may be the only one who knows that in back in a storage closet there are some files or some chairs or a portable chalk-board that the clinician could use.

A good relationship with the nonteaching personnel is essential. These persons, as well as the teaching and administrative staff, have pride in their work and deserve respect and admiration for their efforts.

COMMUNITY INFORMATION PROGRAM

Keeping the community informed about the speech, language, and hearing program in the schools has a number of advantages. First, it interprets the program of prevention, assessment, and remediation to the public at large and may remove any possible stigma attached to having a child enrolled in the program. It also builds a feeling of trust and confidence in the program and toward the school system in the community.

A community information program should not be a haphazard affair; it should be well planned and executed. It should not be a "one-shot" deal but rather continuous, consistent, and persistent. It should also be varied, informative, and interesting.

The school clinician may want to survey the types of media available within the community. The most commonly utilized are newspapers, radio, television, service clubs, lectures and presentations, and displays.

The clinician may wish to make arrangements with the local newspaper to run a series of articles on such topics as types of communication problems, how parents can help children learn to talk, the school therapy program, dos and don'ts for families of children with fluency problems or hearing-impaired children, the importance of early referral, and the many other topics of interest to parents and community members.

In preparing articles for release in the local newspapers, it is best to inquire of the editor how long the article should be and then stick to the length suggested. If an article submitted is too long the editor is likely to trim it and may inadvertently cut out an important part. Most editors like to have articles submitted, but they should be well written and interesting. The school clinician can usually obtain from a member of the newspaper staff the pertinent facts on style and length. If pictures are used and they contain any children, it is an absolute *must* first to obtain written consent of the parents.

Some school systems have a person in charge of community information or public relations, and this individual will often assist the clinician in preparing articles for publication.

Radio interviews or other types of radio programs are a good way of getting information across to the public. Local radio stations often welcome suggestions on programs of special interest. Clinicians can utilize such timely events as Better Speech and Hearing Month in May to focus attention on the needs of persons with speech, language and hearing disorders.

The same can be said of television programs. Often local television stations have programs during which various community figures are interviewed. Or the television station may cooperate in preparing a program on various aspects of the speech, language, and hearing program.

Talks to community service clubs, professional organizations, and other groups can yield innumerable benefits. Many of these groups sponsor special projects or programs as part of their community service activities. Another effective way of informing the community about the program is through displays at health fairs and similar events. Public libraries are often willing to add to their shelves books of interest to parents of handicapped children. The school clinician can make suggestions for specific books, which could then be made available to the public.

DISCUSSION TOPICS AND PROJECTS

1. Invite an elementary principal in to talk to the class on how he or she views the speech, language, and hearing program.
2. Interview a learning disabilities teacher on how he or she works with the school SLP.
3. Find out what your state requires in the certification of educational audiologists.
4. List ways the SLP in the school can work with the classroom teacher on the teaching of reading. How would you implement these strategies?
5. How would the SLP in the schools schedule time for consultation?
6. Plan an in-service session or a group meeting with elementary-school principals to acquaint them with the speech, language, and hearing program.
7. Do a survey of the health and rehabilitation agencies in your community. What are their referral policies and their criteria for accepting clients?
8. Ask a practicing school pathologist what the policies are concerning medical referrals in that school system.

TEN
ORGANIZING AND MAINTAINING RECORDS AND REPORTS FOR ACCOUNTABILITY AND EVALUATION

INTRODUCTION

There are good reasons for maintaining a comprehensive record and report system on the language, speech, and hearing program. Although it has always been done by clinicians, the reasons today are somewhat more compelling and the goals more inclusive.

Public Law 94-142 places a tremendous emphasis on accountability in the school system. Accountability has made it urgent that special services in the schools develop a method of reliably and accurately reporting data on handicapped children.

Historically, the school clinician maintained written records to inform, to keep track of the services provided, to provide continuity both to the program and to the child's progress in therapy, to serve as a basis for research, to coordinate the child's therapy with the child's school program, and to serve as a basis for program needs and development. These reasons remain valid; however, there are additional reasons why an accounting system is needed today. One is a legal reason. Many states at the present time have licensing for speech pathologists and audiologists. This factor implies a legal responsibility, and the need for accountability becomes greater (Caccamo, 1973).

Another reason, according to Caccamo, is in the fiscal area. Several court decisions in education have carried financial damages for failure of the school to teach the child to read. The precedent for money damages in this type of case has already been set. Also, with the increasing competition for tax dollars, government agencies are requiring statements of accountability prior to funding. Local, federal, and state agencies want to know what results are being obtained for the tax money spent.

O'Toole (1971, pp. 24–25) posed some questions for school speech-language pathologists in regard to accountability:

How appropriate is speech therapy for each student in your program? Does each one belong in therapy? Have you established goals which, if accomplished, will make a difference? Is therapy time so well used as to justify taking students away from their academic subjects? Do you know how much progress each of your cases is making? Is that recorded? Are you aware of the rate of change? If progress is very slow or nonexistent, are you seeking additional help? How many cases have you followed through either to complete remediation or to the greatest degree of compensation that can be expected? If not very many, why not? Are you using therapy time as efficiently as possible? Is your coordination time justifiable because it is being used for the ultimate benefit of your student? Are you making use of all the knowledge and resources available? Are you moving children along as fast as they can go, or only as fast as is comfortable for you? Are you adapting to student needs, or are they suiting yours? Does your immediate supervisor understand what you do and the type of students you can and should see in therapy? Does he understand that if results are expected, the quality as well as the quantity of therapy is important?

In addition to the impetus added by PL 94-142 for record and report keeping, it makes good sense for the clinician to keep an account of a child's progress in therapy simply because the clinician is dealing with a large number of children and it would be impossible to remember all the facts and details pertinent to each of them.

CASE MANAGEMENT RECORDS

One of the problems in record and report systems is the quick retrieval of information regarding the status, disposition, and intervention of individual students as well as the collective data that must be recorded to report program statistics. Wing (1975) developed a concise form to help itinerant school clinicians who are responsible for managing caseloads of between 75 and 150 children throughout a school year. Wing reports that although the caseloads, exclusive of mass screenings, have been reduced, there is increasing demand for accurate record keeping, case management reporting, and statistical data for accountability to school administrators, boards of education, and state departments of education. Figure 10-1 shows the data-recording form used in the Great Falls, Montana, speech, language, and hearing program.

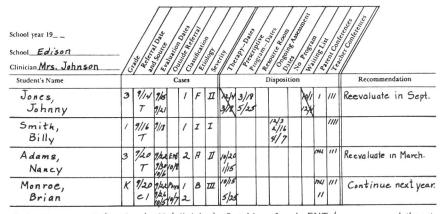

School year 19_ _

School **Edison**

Clinician **Mrs. Johnson**

Student's Name	Grade	Referral Date and Source	Evaluation Dates	Outside Referral	Classification	Etiology	Severity	Therapy-Dates	Prescriptive Program-Dates	Resource Room	Ongoing Assessment Dates	No Program	Waiting List	Parent Conferences	Teacher Conferences	Recommendation
		Cases						Disposition								Recommendation
Jones, Johnny	3	9/14 T	7/6 7/21		I	F	II	12/4 3/8 3/8 5/25				10/1 12/1	I		///	Reevaluate in Sept.
Smith, Billy	1	9/16 T	7/13		I	I	I			12/3 2/16 4/7					////	
Adams, Nancy	3	7/20 T	9/22 ENT 9/30 10/8 10/6	2	A	II	10/20 1/15				mu	///	Reevaluate in March.
Monroe, Brian	K	7/20 C/	9/22 Phys 9/26 10/7 10/5 10/7 2	1	B	III	10/15 5/25				mu //	///	Continue next year.

Referral source: T (teachers), CI (clinician). *Outside referral:* ENT (ear, nose, and throat specialist), phys. (physician), sch. psyl. (school psychologist), and so on. *Classification:* 1, articulation; 2, phonation; 3, rhythm; 4, language; 5, no problem (any appropriate classifications may be used, listed in order of significance). *Etiology:* A, organic pathology; B, cleft palate; C, cerebral palsy; D, mental retardation; E, hearing loss; F, dental anomalies; G, emotional factors; H, environmental factors; I, developmental factors; J, undetermined (any appropriate classifications may be used, listed in order of significance). *Severity:* I, mild, II, moderate; III, severe. *Note:* slash marks are used to indicate change of status in any category. This form can be stenciled on standard 8½x11" paper with spaces to accommodate seven to nine student names.

FIGURE 10-1   Data recording form for speech and hearing services

A school clinician going into a program that has been established will probably find a record and report system already set up and in operation, whereas a clinician who starts a program will have to develop his or her own. In both instances it will be necessary to evaluate and monitor the system continuously and make the necessary changes in the forms. The confidentiality of information makes it imperative that the storage of records and reports be a major consideration. The policies regarding security measures should be established and in writing. The same is true of the availability of such records and reports to other school personnel, administrators, other clinicians on the staff, and parents. Policies should be in writing and should be adhered to once agreed upon.

The abundance of records and reports essential to a program should be taken into account on the clinician's weekly schedule. One of the most time-consuming tasks is filling out reports, keeping up to date on information recorded, and filing and retrieving material. The task is a daily one for much of the information, and when weekly, monthly, or yearly reports are involved, a large chunk of time is needed. Some of the work can be assigned to an aide and some of it might be given to the school secretary; however, there are usually many demands on their time as well. A large program may need some secretarial help, either on a part-time or full-time basis, depending on the size and scope of the program. Most of it, however, will be up to the school clinician, and if this is the case, scheduled time should be allotted for it.

Most school systems provide a central office for the school clinicians and in this way a uniform filing, retrieval, recording, and security system can be utilized. A central office system has another advantage in that secretarial or aide assistance can be pooled.

School clinicians will have to abide by the policies of the school system in regard to how long records and reports on individual children should be retained, which records should be retained, and how records are transferred from school to school as well as from school system to school system. Statistical information in relation to program management and incidence figures can be very useful to clinicians in planning future programs and serving as a basis for research. The retaining of this type of information might be decided by the school clinical staff. Provisions for the storage of such information would have to be made.

In an effort to improve information systems for the school speech, language, and hearing programs, a Task Force on Data Collection and Information Systems (Healey, 1973) was appointed to study the issue. Among recommendations made to school systems, the following steps were considered essential:

1. Formulate a school-wide policy.
2. Develop a general framework for planning.
3. Determine a policy relating to information gathering and distribution.
4. Provide a clearinghouse and a meaningful circulation system.
5. Assure checks for control of information.
6. Protect individual privacy and insure confidentiality.
7. Develop uniform nomenclature.
8. Select computer language if necessary.
9. Determine what output is desired.
10. Insure accuracy and quality of the data input.
11. Determine the categories of information needed for measurement.
12. Ascertain the action that will be taken once the data have been collected.

The task force also suggests an outline for basic data collection which could be adapted to educational and professional agencies at the local, state, and national levels. (See Figure 10–2.) The school speech, language, and hearing clinician might consider this outline as a framework for developing the record and report forms necessary to the program. Such as outline also could be used as a framework for evaluating clinician behavior in the clinical process as well as analyzing the total program management data to effect changes in program design and practices.

FIGURE 10-2 Recommended Outline for Data Collection Systems

DEMOGRAPHIC DATA	PROGRAM PLANNING AND MANAGEMENT DATA

I. Case
  A. Indentification
    1. Vital statistics (social security number; birth data; chronological age; sex; grade; parent's name, address, and telephone number)
    2. History (health history of child and family, type of problem, treatment provided or offered)
    3. Referent (name of referral agency—teacher, parents, others; date of referral; history of evaluations)
  B. Diagnostic information
    1. Type of problem
    2. Test administered
    3. Psychological information

Diagnostic information
  Behavior observed (anecdotal records by teacher/clinican) Comparative speech behavior
    Formal
      Normative data
      Test of articulation
      Test of language
    Informal
      Estimate of child's ability based upon clinician's experience and training

  C. Educational
    1. Preschool
    2. Regular
    3. Special
  D. Services needed
    1. Screening
    2. Diagnostic
  E. Treatment
    1. Speech
      a. Articulation
      b. Voice
      c. Rhythm
    2. Hearing
      a. Audiological
      b. Rehabilitation audiology
    3. Language
      a. Phonologic
      b. Auditory discrimination

(continued)

FIGURE 10-2   (continued)

DEMOGRAPHIC DATA	PROGRAM PLANNING AND MANAGEMENT DATA
c. Auditory sequencing d. Memory span e. Morphologic f. Syntax	
II. Clinician A. Current case load B. Waiting list C. Attendance records of children D. Amount of time spent in travel	Clinician Effectiveness of treatment techniques Behavioral objectives Criteria for case selection, therapy techniques based on the needs of the child, individualizing instruction (group or individual session, frequency and length of sessions)
III. Program (supervisory) A. Number of clinicians B. Number of children to be served	Program Plan for recording and evaluating treatment techniques Program objectives Assessment of clinician and need for continuing education Evaluation of progress Planning of research Long and short-term objectives
IV. Administration (local, state, federal) A. Child-clinician ratio B. Statistical summary C. Dissemination D. Conversion to ADP E. Projected population growth patterns F. Projected program growth G. Facilities available	Administration Cost benefit analysis Pattern of expenditures Projected need for services Projected need for facilities

COMPREHENSIVE ASSESSMENT AND SERVICE EVALUATION INFORMATION SYSTEM (C.A.S.E.)

The C.A.S.E. information system was developed by the American Speech and Hearing Association to provide a method of recording information concerning speech, language, and hearing services in the schools (American Speech and Hearing Association, 1976). The prototype describes a formal system for collecting, storing, and retrieving essential information categorized under the following processes: referral, screening, diagnostic assessment, placement decisions, intervention programs, coordination of service delivery, and program management.

One of the important aspects of the system is that it has computer potential. This would make it valuable to both local and state educational agencies interested in developing a data system that would help determine the actions necessary to improve the program, analyze operating costs, facilitate research, furnish information on which to base future program planning, improve record-keeping practices, and free the school SLP and educational audiologist for more client contact and intervention.

The C.A.S.E. manual contains detailed and extensive forms that were designed to assist a large number of data collectors in school districts, state education departments, and related agencies. In addition the forms permit data collection across a number of different processes that occur at different times during the year. Only those forms relevant to a given process are used at any one time. For example, the individual placement form is used only during the placement process, and the end-of-period progress report is completed at the close of the local agency's reporting period, which may be several months after the initiation of intervention.

Another feature of the system is that one staff member generally would not be required to complete all the forms. For example, the audiologists performing the diagnostic audiologic work would complete the audiological assessment forms, whereas the specialist responsible for providing ongoing educational and clinical services would use the response data form, or the session summary data form, throughout intervention. Many of the summary forms can be completed by the clerical staff.

The C.A.S.E. Manual is available from DLM-Teaching Resources, P.O. Box 4000, One DLM Park, Allen, Texas 75002.

CHILD SERVICES REVIEW SYSTEM (CSRS)

The American Speech-Language-Hearing Association has developed a system for evaluating the effectiveness of services provided to handicapped children. The Child Services Review System (CSRS) (1982) meets the requirements of PL 94-142 for documentation of appropriate and effective services, review of outcomes specified on individualized education plans (IEPs), team management of handicapped pupils, and continuing personnel development in accordance with objectively assessed needs.

Nine steps comprise the process of the review: (1) select audit topic, (2) draft criterion statements, (3) ratify criterion statements, (4) review records, (5) identify and analyze problems, (6) develop solutions, (7) ratify solutions, (8) implement solutions, and (9) reaudit.

The CSRS process and products are effective tools for evaluating and improving the quality of services and can also serve as a long-term quality-assurance tool, promote staff development, and enhance the communication process (Barnes & Pines, 1982).

Further information and a CSRS manual are available from the Professional Practices Division of the American Speech-Language-Hearing Association, 10801 Rockville Pike, Rockville, Maryland 20852.

COST ACCOUNTING

One way of looking at accountability is in relation to cost accounting. When the cost of a product or service is known, it is then possible to predict the cost of producing similar products or services. In applying the model to speech, language, and hearing services, one might consider the various aspects of therapy, program management, and instructional materials used. One of the first persons to apply the cost accounting method to speech therapy services was Mowrer (1972), who used it in an analysis of the cost of correcting speech misarticulation. Mowrer hypothesized that the use of a cost accounting system might make it possible to determine the economic value of different training programs such as programmed instruction, group therapy, and various time-schedule programs of instruction. Mowrer felt that the major goals should not be provided therapy services at the lowest possible cost but to provide the highest caliber services for a given amount of money.

Research projects to evaluate several aspects of a school district's program in speech and language (Work et al., 1975 and 1976) through the process of cost accounting have been reported. The first project dealt with the cost of services provided by an itinerant staff, and the second project dealt with an analysis of instructional materials.

An analysis of the data in the first project (Work et al., 1975) revealed that the itinerant program cost was less than anticipated and less than that of most clinic or private therapy programs in the same geographic area. Another finding indicated that further data are needed for school services utilizing different delivery-of-service models.

The project dealing with the evaluation of materials and their effectiveness in clinical intervention developed a prototype that could be used with phonological disorders as well as other types of disorders. The study was undertaken to assist the school clinician, who is required to answer questions and seek information on the large amount of commercially developed instructional materials. Questions facing clinicians include these: How effective are the materials? Do clinicians choose appropriate materials for the type of therapy planned? Are materials related to performance objectives and therapy goals?

A program to study the actual costs of providing quality speech and language services in Florida was reported by Ehren et al. (1984). The study was prompted by the agreement among special educators that reduced state funding was leading to a steady rise in class size ratio. A team of school finance officers and speech and language supervisors visited selected school sites and individually interviewed administrators, speech-language clinicians, budget analysts, and other district personnel. The Program Quality Review Guidelines included (1) learner achievement, (2) program quality, (3) instructional peronnel, (4) learning environment, (5) materials and human resources, (6) compliance data, and (7) specialized or optional data.

Ehren stated that a major contributing factor to inaccurate cost reports was unclear instructions for assigning costs to the appropriate programs. For example, schools might supply all speech-language clinicians with audiometers. However, the cost was not reflected at the school level since the audiometers were purchased from a central budget. Additionally, federal monies used to support personnel, transportation, classroom aides, and other services were not included in the direct costs of the program at the school level.

A recommendation was that all school districts should develop cost review procedures. The complexity of cost data; cost reporting; state, federal, and local requirements; and local school practices makes it imperative that program costs support and are sensitive to quality standards.

Further suggestions by Ehren were the following (1) professional program review of costs and cost analysis procedures; (2) periodic review of data-collection practices and thorough ongoing study; (3) in-service training for personnel responsible for collecting cost data; and (4) identification of all costs, indirect and direct, that can be attributed to a program.

COMPUTER-BASED INSTRUCTION VERSUS TRADITIONAL INSTRUCTION: A MODEL FOR COMPARING THE COST BENEFITS

Speech-language pathologists may ask themselves, Are instructional benefits from microcomputers worth the cost when compared to the traditional form of instruction (which may or may not include a paraprofessional)?

A model used to evaluate computer applications in the form of a cost-benefit analysis was developed by Flaherty (1984). The model was developed to determine the comparative costs of computer-based instruction (CBI) versus traditional treatment (TT).

According to Flaherty,

> The itinerant speech/language specialist must juggle many responsibilities. Specialists diagnose potential caseload candidates, develop and sometimes translate IEPs, treat disorders, and evaluate that treatment. Software is available for all of these duties. Computer-based instruction (CBI) varies in efficiency and effectiveness with traditional treatment (TT). The costs of the two methodologies also vary. As budgetary constraints are always present, it is essential to compare the costs and benefits of CBI against that of traditional treatment in order to determine the one more cost-beneficial.

Benefits of CBI and TT

Benefits with numerical measures (i.e., quantitative benefits) are important as well as descriptive measures (i.e., qualitative benefits). Some monetary measure is expected among the quantitative benefits in a cost-benefit analysis. "Shadow pricing" is one way to come up with the needed monetary measures.

Quantitative benefits   The estimated value of pull-out speech/language services as well as of CBI classroom tutors may be determined through "shadow pricing". A change in school attendance by the speech/language handicapped student and a change in hours spent in treatment before correction are also important. Test score changes, computer literacy, and acquisition of touch typing skills are measureable benefits for the student. Of benefit to the specialist may be the change in time devoted to IEP preparation.

Qualitative benefits   Less easily measured is the change in specialist or student morale after the CBI experience. Surveys may assist in defining this variable.

Cost of CBI and TT

A short-term estimate of costs is required by this model. Long-term estimates (beyond three years) are beyond the scope of this model.

Quantitative costs   Obviously the hardware, software, and specialist training may require expenditures by the speech/language department. Traditional materials are required in treatment by traditional means as well as by computer. Likely CBI will require fewer traditional materials, however.

Occasionally computer systems are purchased to take the place of speech aides. The CBI program increases the student-trainer ratio in such a case. Yet the cost of the computer system may be less that that of the aide's services.

Qualitative costs   Burdens may be placed on certain participants in the educational process of the handicapped student. Opportunity costs to the student may also occur and need to be described in this model.

Net Difference

When traditional treatment includes a speech aide and CBI includes a portable computer system, CBI of speech/language services is the more cost-beneficial according to this model.

Conclusion

There is an increase in the use of CBI in speech and language services in the schools. A model has been developed to describe the costs and benefits of CBI. The model can best be utilized in an assessment of the appropriateness of CBI in the treatment of a speech or language disorder. Qualitative variables and quantitative variables are included in the model (see Tables 10-1 and 10-2).

TABLE 10-1   Comparison of Costs and Benefits per Student per Fiscal Year Following Traditional Treatment or Computer-Based Instruction

	TRADITIONAL (TT)	COMPUTER-BASED (CBI)	CBI-TT
Costs			
Annual Costs for which monetary estimates are known			
1. Hardware	$ 0.00	$18.18	$18.18
2. Software	0.00	9.00	9.00
3. Training	0.00	0.00	0.00
4. Materials	1.80	.90	− .90
5. Speech Aide	72.72	0.00	−72.72
	$74.52	$28.08	$ − 46.44
Other Costs			
6. Burdens on others	?	?	?
a. Teacher			
b. Parents			
c. Specialist			
d. Translator			
e. Diagnostic Examiner			
7. Opportunity costs			
a. Socialization skills	+	−	−
b. Creative expression	+	−	−
c. Information vocational skills	−	+	+

Source: Carol Flaherty, "Cost-Benefit Analysis of Computer-Based Instruction of School Speech Services." Presentation at the American Speech-Language-Hearing Association Convention, San Francisco, 1984.

COMPUTER APPLICATION IN A SCREENING PROGRAM

Many school districts have central computerized files. School SLPs and educational audiologists may be able to utilize the data-processing centers in the schools for the storage of information about pupils with speech, hearing, and language problems. An example of this type of program was described by Heob et al. (1984):

> The Educational Audiology Program at the Mesa Public Schools currently employs a computerized tracking system for storing, retrieving, analyzing, and printing the pure tone and impedance screening results from approximately 25,000 students each year. Two on-line, interrelated screen applications plus 26 programs were developed by the district's Data Processing Department to reduce time-consuming paper work and errors in processing.

TABLE 10-2   Comparison of Costs and Benefits (Flaherty)

	TRADITIONAL (TT)	COMPUTER-BASED (CBI)	(CBI-TT)
Benefits			
Annual Benefits for which monetary estimates are known			
1. Classroom tutor	$ 0.00	$ 5.00	$ 5.00
2. Pull-out services	30.77	30.77	0.00
	$30.77	$35.77	$ 5.00
Other Benefits			
3. Program assessment (annualized)			
a. Diagnostic accuracy (change in disorder)	0 change	0 change	0 change
b. Standard score	baseline	+10 points	+10 points
c. Criterion-referenced test level	baseline	+ 1 level	+ 1 level
d. Skills: Computer Literacy (cl) and Touch Typing (tt)	cl: 0 tt: 0	cl: yes tt: 0	cl: yes tt: 0
e. Attendance	92%	95%	+ 3%
f. Student hours in program	18 hours	12 hours	4 hours earlier dismissal
g. Specialist hours for IEP preparation	1 hour	.5 hour	.5 hour earlier completion
4. Morale change a. Specialist b. Student	?	?	?
Summary			
Valued Benefits	$ 30.77	$ 35.77	$ 5.00
Valued Costs	74.52	28.08	−46.44
Net (Benefits-Costs)	$ − 43.75	$ 7.69	$ + 51.44

The Hearing/Audiology System is incorporated within the district's Student Data Base. The System communicates with the Student Data Base allowing retrieval of identifying information. This includes student name, birthdate, school, student number, grade, room number, parents' name, home and work phone numbers, and whether the screening is a first or second screening. The information is printed directly on each screening form and, at second screening, results from initial screening are printed on the screening form.

Screen #1   This screen stores a large number of data, including up to eight serial screenings per student. Retrieval of results is greatly facilitated by typing a student number at a terminal rather than searching through files for a result. Screening information is also accessible to personnel at remote terminals throughout the district.

Sorting options for producing printed reports are numerous. Most often used is a "cover sheet" for nurses, alphabetically listing students' results by grade and room number for a given school. Results may also be sorted according to those students enrolled in a special education program, or as a compilation of students with a given tympanogram type.

Screen #2   This screen stores follow-up information received from physicians regarding disposition of students referred for medical examinations. Diagnosis, treatment, and other relevant follow-up information are stored along with the physician's name. This program also retrieves the screening data as entered on Screen #1.

An extensive program was developed that sorts medical diagnosis entered on Screen #2 into a category describing the failed impedance result. For example, a student may fail the impedance screening because of abnormally low compliance (less than .15 cc). This result is entered in Screen #1. Medical diagnosis, otitis media, for example, might be received from the student's physician and stored in Screen #2. The program would sort the diagnosis under the heading of "Type B," or low compliance, and print the result in a row corresponding to the school.

This program eliminates time-consuming cross-checking tasks and provides accurate records of screening validity. The program also provides tallies on a continual basis, allowing time to correct errors before year-end statistical compilation.

The data processing system utilized by Mesa's Educational Audiology Program greatly facilitates record keeping and analysis of the screening results from the district's large, diverse student population.

Requests for additional information regarding this system should be directed to Bill Heob or Gail Carter at (602) 898-7871, or write to the Educational Audiology Program, 549 N. Stapley Dr., Mesa, AZ 85203.

USING THE WORD PROCESSOR IN WRITING REPORTS

Silbar (1984), a speech-language pathologist at a center for trainable mentally retarded children in Michigan, described a method of generating reports by using a word processor. She has used the word processor for writing reports, keeping a running file on students, and for letters to parents. Getting used to using the word processor initially took some time, but according to Silbar it was well worth the trouble. Figure 10–3, a sample program, includes two reports: initial status and progress. The word processor for the series was an IBM Office Systems 6.

FIGURE 10-3   A sample program using a Word Processor

Y1   Initial Speech-Language Evaluation

Y2   Three Year Speech-Language Evaluation

Y3   Year-End Speech Language Report

Y4   Student: //*//
        SLP: //*//
        CA: //*//
        Date: //*//

Y5   The development of communication is a desired and useful goal. Each
        student is considered as to communication level and ability. Programs
        which are developed, where a need is determined, are planned around the
        daily experiences and individual abilities of each student within the
        total classroom program.

Y6   The last evaluation for //*// was completed during the school year. The
        following test(s) were administered to assess present level of speech and
        language development.

Y7   //*// received a speech and language evaluation as part of the intake
        procedure to Lincoln School. This was done to assist the staff in
        placing the student in a classroom language program. The results of this
        evaluation determine which program is best suited to the student's language
        needs and how it is to be implemented.

Y8   This evaluation is part of the Multidisciplinary Evaluation Team's three
        year reevaluation to determine eligibility for special education servic-
        es.

Y9   This report is a status report on the student's progress this school
        year.

Y10   The following tests were administered.

Y11   _____   Zimmerman Pre-school Language Scale

Y12   _____   Peabody Picture Vocabulary Test

Y13   _____   Carrow Test of Auditory Comprehension of Language

Y14   _____   Sequenced Inventory of Communication Development

Y15   _____   An Articulation Test

Y16   _____   Spontaneous Language Sample

Y17   _____   Structured Photographic Language Test

Y18   _____   Pre-Speech Assessment

Y19   _____   An Oral Peripheral Examination

Y20   _____   Piagetian Comparison

Y21   The Zimmerman Preschool Language Scale assesses the student's auditory
        comprehension and expressive skills. On this test //*// received an
        auditory comprehensive age of //*// and verbal expression age of //*//.
        Below those ages //*// had difficulties with //*//.

Y22   //*// single word receptive vocabulary as measured by the Peabody was
        //*//.

Y23   The test of Auditory Comprehension of Language evaluated the student's
        ability to understand vocabulary and grammar.   On this test //*//
        received a language age score of //*//. //*// had difficulties with
        //*//.

FIGURE 10-3 (continued)

Y24   The SICD Receptive Scale measures the student's awareness, discrimination
      and understanding of sounds, speech and words. //*// received a score of
      //*//. Below the level //*// made errors with //*//.

Y25   The SICD Expressive Scale indicates the student's ability to imitate,
      initiate and respond to motor, vocal and verbal stimuli. //*// received
      a score of //*//. //*// errors occurred with //*//.

Y26   The articulation assessment indicates how well the student can use sounds
      in conversation. It encompasses the student's cognitive and language
      skill levels. At this point in time it appears as if //*// articulation
      is //*//.

Y27   A language sample was taken. This assessment allows the student to
      generate sentences and phrases which are compared with developmental
      norms. //*//

Y28   The Structured Photographic Language Test assesses the student's elicited
      expressive language. On this test //*// scored at the //*//. This
      corresponds to an expressive language age of //*//. Below that age the
      student made errors in //*//.

Y29   In comparing //*// cognitive, social, receptive and expressive language
      abilities, it appears as if //*// is at the Piagetian stage of //*//.
      //*// receptive language skills were //*// the cognitive area. Expres-
      sively, //*// language was //*// cognition.

Y30   A Pre-Speech Assessment and Scale evaluation was completed with //*//.
      The test evaluates the student's feeding skills, breathing and sound
      productions. On this test the student received scores which were normal
      in development in the area(s) of //*//. Those skills normally develop-
      ing, although delayed were in the area(s) of //*//. Behaviors considered
      abnormal were in the area(s) of //*//.

Y31   An oral peripheral observation was made to help determine the efficacy of
      tongue, lip and mouth movements. //*//'s structures and functioning
      appeared //*//.

Y32   A sentence completion task was given. This task measures the student's
      ability to accurately repeat sentences of increasing length. On this
      task //*// was able to accurately repeat a //*// word sentence.

Y33   Summary & Recommendations:

Y34   Since //*// language skills are commensurate with //*// cognitive skills,
      it is felt that a language program conducted in the classroom would best
      be //*//.

Y35   Since //*// language skills are lower than //*// cognitive skills, it is
      felt that a language program conducted in the classroom with supplementa-
      ry work provided through speech consultation be provided.

Y36   In addition, it is felt that //*// would benefit from some additional
      help in sound production and sequencing.

Y37   In addition, additional work in the following areas will be implemented
      by the classroom teacher and speech-language pathologist //*//.

Y38   In addition to the classroom programming the speech-language pathologist
      will provide direct assistance in //*//.

Y39   A pre-speech and feeding program in the classroom. This program is
      designed by the occupational therapist and speech-language pathologist

Y40   //*// is currently receiving language instruction, in the classroom,
      through the Distar Language Program. This program is designed to in-
      crease //*// vocabulary and to improve sentence construction. //*// will
      move to the next level when the current lessons are mastered.

FIGURE 10-3   (continued)

Y41   //*// is currently receiving language instruction in the classroom
through the Classroom Language Inventory Program. This program is
designed to allow the students to develop language by developing normally
occurring language patterns.

Y42   At this point in time it is felt the //*// should use/continue with //*//
augmentative communication.

Y43   Although //*// primary mode of communication is an augmentative system,
the use of oral speech is used simultaneously.

Y44   The goals and objectives contained within the current program continue to
be appropriate at this time. It is recommended the //*// continue to
receive consultive speech and language services.

Y45   //*// is currently using a communication board to express basic needs.
When these present symbols are used spontaneously, additional ones
will be placed on the board representing additional functional needs.
There are presently //*// entries on the board.

Y46   //*// is currently using manual signs to communicate basic needs. When
these signs are used spontaneously, additional signs will be taught.
Presently, //*// can use //*// signs.

Y47   //*// is currently receiving help in the classroom on speech-sound
skills. A group of words were assigned and once they are used adequately
and spontaneously more will be added. So far the words //*// have been
used.

Y48   //*// is currently receiving help in the classroom, saying consonant and
vowel combinations which follow a normal level of sound-sequencing
development. When able to repeat the current sound combinations successfully, more combinations will be selected. The student is presently on
level //*//.

Y49   //*// is currently working on increasing auditory discrimination skills.

Y50   //*// is currently working on the ability to discriminate difference in
intensity, frequency and duration of sound patterns. These skills are
needed to accurately produce and self-monitor speech.

Y51   //*// //*// //*// //*//

FIGURE 10-3   (continued)

Document Assembly Form

Segment

Job	No.		Variables	

Y   1   1._____   2._____   3._____

        4._____   5._____   6._____

___ 4   1. Ray_____   2. Jean Silbar___   3. 3-7_____

        4. October 1980___   5._____   6._____

___ 7   1. Ray_____   2._____   3._____

        4._____   5._____   6._____

___ 10 1._____   2._____   3._____

        4._____   5._____   6._____

___ 14 1._____   2._____   3._____

        4._____   5._____   6._____

___ 20 1._____   2._____   3._____

        4._____   5._____   6._____

___ 24 1. Ray_____   2. 24 mo_____   3. he_____

        4. body parts and prepositions_____   6._____

___ 25 1. Ray_____   2. 20 mo_____   3. His_____

        4. verbalizations + naming_____   6._____

___ 29 1. Ray's_____   2. he_____   3. Sensorimotor Stage V

        4. His_____   5. equal to_____   6. his   7. equal to

___ 33 1._____   2._____   3._____

        4._____   5._____   6._____

___ 34 1. Ray's_____   2. his_____   3. through a program
                                                   designed to increase
        4._____   5._____   6. his verbalizations
                                                   and one-word
    ___ 1._____   2._____   3. utterances.

        4._____   5._____   6._____

FIGURE 10-3 (continued)

Initial Speech-Language Evaluation

Student: Ray
SLP: Jean Silbar
CA: 3-7
Date: October 1980

Ray received a speech and language evaluation as part of the intake procedure
to Lincoln School. This was done to assist the staff in placing the student
in a classroom language program. The results of this evaluation determine
which program is best suited to the student's language needs and how it is to
be implemented.

The following tests were administered.

_____   Sequenced Inventory of Communication Development
_____   Piagetian Comparison

The SICD Receptive Scale measures the student's awareness, discrimination and
understanding of sounds, speech and words. Ray received a score of 24 months.
Below that level he made errors with body parts and prepositions.

The SICD Expressive Scale indicates the student's ability to imitate, initiate
and respond to motor, vocal and verbal stimuli. Ray received a score of 20
months. His errors occurred with verbalizations and naming.

In comparing Ray's cognitive, social, receptive and expressive language
abilities, it appears as if he is at the Piagetian stage of Sensorimotor Stage
V. His receptive language skills were equal to the cognitive area. Expressively, his language was commensurate with cognition.

Summary & Recommendations:

Since Ray's language skills are commensurate with his cognitive
skills, it is felt that a language program conducted in the classroom would
best be provided through a program designed to increase his verbalizations and
one word utterances.

FIGURE 10-3   (continued)

Document Assembly Form

Segment

Job	No.		Variables	

Y 2   1._____   2._____   3._____

4._____   5._____   6._____

___ 4   1._Ray_____   2._Jean Silbar_   3._6-7_____

4._Sept. 28, 1983_   5._____   6._____

___ 8   1._____   2._____   3._____

4._____   5._____   6._____

___ 10   1._____   2._____   3._____

4._____   5._____   6._____

___ 14   1._____   2._____   3._____

4._____   5._____   6._____

___ 20   1._____   2._____   3._____

4._____   5._____   6._____

___ 24   1._Ray_____   2._32 mo_ a gain of_. 10 mo from 10/80

4._he_____   5._prepositions, colo_r_ following two-step directions

___ 25   1._Ray_____   2._24 mo which was_ only a 4 mo gain

4._____   5._____   6._____

___ 29   1._Ray's_____   2._he_____   3._Early Preoperations_

4._His_____   5._equal to_   6._his_   7. below_

___ 33   1._____   2._____   3._____

4._____   5._____   6._____

___ 35   1._Ray's expressive_   2._his_____   3._provided through Project Perform with an_

4._____   5._____   6._augmentative sign language system._

___ ___   1._____   2._____   3._____

4._____   5._____   6._____

FIGURE 10-3 (Continued)

Three Year Speech—Language Evaluation

Student: Ray
SLP: Jean Silbar
CA: 6-7
Date: September 20, 1983

This evaluation is part of the Multidisciplinary Evaluation Team's three year
reevaluation to determine eligibility for special education services.

The following tests were administered.

_____   Sequenced Inventory of Communication Development
_____   Piagetian Comparison

The SICD Receptive Scale measures the student's awareness, discrimination and
understanding of sounds, speech and words. Ray received a score of 32 months,
a gain of 10 months from October 1980. Below that level he made errors with
prepositions, colors, and following two steps directions.

The SICD Expressive Scale indicates the student's ability to imitate, initiate
and respond to motor, vocal and verbal stimuli. Ray received a score of 24
months which was only a four months gain from 1980. His errors occurred with
word repetition and answering questions.

In comparing Ray's cognitive, social, receptive and expressive language
abilities, it appears as if he is at the Piagetian stage of Early
Preoperations. His receptive language skills were equal to the cognitive
area. Expressively, his language was below cognition.

Summary & Recommendations:

Since Ray's expressive language skills are commensurate with his cognitive
skills, it is felt that a language program conducted in the classroom would
best be provided through Project Perform with an augmentative sign language
system.

DISCUSSION QUESTIONS AND PROJECTS

1. Why are school programs in speech, language, and hearing accountable?
2. To whom are programs accountable?
3. Start a collection of record and report forms used in the schools. How
   would you organize report forms for a school system?
4. What is the relationship between demographic data and incidence figures? Is there a financial component in this relationship?
5. It has been suggested that cost accounting procedures used in evaluating programs do not cover all the components in the program. What
   components are not covered? Is there a method of assessing them?
6. Interview a school SLP or educational audiologist who uses computers.
   How are the computers used? What are their potential uses?
7. Do you think computer literacy should be a required part of the school
   SLP's armamentarium?

ELEVEN
STUDENT TEACHING

INTRODUCTION

Student teaching is sometimes regarded with trepidation by the prospective student teacher, probably because like all new experiences it contains the element of the unknown. The unknown is usually anticipated with a mixture of fear, curiosity, and excitement. The actual experience may bear out what was anticipated, and it may also contain some surprises.

The following comments from student teachers provide insights for contemplation, not only for prospective student teachers but for school and university supervisors as well:

> The thought that occupied my mind as I drove home after my first day of being a student teacher, was, "How will I ever make it?" I had come face to face with part of my "Sammy Snakes," "quiet sounds," "growling sounds," "frog sounds," and I foresaw ten weeks of writing lesson plans and thinking up activities. And now, here I am ten weeks later. I can look back to that first day and laugh when I think of how my ideas have changed. It doesn't seem possible that I could have experienced all that I did. My student teaching was in all aspects a total learning situation.

> Student teaching has been a great experience and has been more of a benefit, not only from the professional point of view, but also from the personal point of view, than I ever imagined it would be. It has been a lot of hard work and a lot of time invested, but the satisfaction, rewards, and learning that this has created has made it all worthwhile.

> Without having had the opportunity to student teach, the answers would have been a long time coming.

I suddenly realized that I didn't need to be unsure, for I could handle the situation that I feared, adequately and surprisingly well.

I have met with many new experiences as a member of a school system. I have met many teachers, talked with them and have gotten to know them as fellow educators. I feel much more confident being out in the schools since I am no longer regarded as a "student." When the teachers ask my professional opinion about various children, their confidence in me boosts my confidence in myself.

I feel the most important things I learned from my student teaching experience were learned through my own mistakes. I had a very intelligent school supervisor who allowed me to experiment and try new things on my own. When I failed, I learned a great deal. Instead of telling me my ideas were inappropriate, she allowed me to find out for myself through my own mistakes.

As a student teacher I have grown to understand the daily routine, unexpected problems and hassles a school clinician must go through and accept. I have also experienced the rewards a therapist obtains when a child achieves progress and success. Being able to take over many of the responsibilities has opened my eyes and allowed me to see how fulfilling it is to be able to help children improve in their speech communication.

One fact which cannot go without mentioning is that in this field we are all professionals and must uphold a certain dignity and respect for our position while complying with ethical standards. Through my student teaching experience I have had a taste of the professional dignity and hope in the future I will be able to combine the professional and personal components for a complementary balance.

My student teaching experience was the most rewarding one of my college career and I owe most of this to my school supervisor, who allowed me to experiment with my own ideas while watching me with a critical eye.

One mistake I feel that I made at the beginning of student teaching was in failure to ask questions about everything that was going on around me. I don't know if I was afraid to ask them or if I didn't know which questions to ask but either way it was a mistake. I think I went in with the attitude that I was "supposed" to know everything. This is, of course, the wrong attitude to take. The whole purpose of student teaching is to learn and what better way to learn than by asking questions?

The seminars during student teaching have been very helpful. The discussions were relaxed, free, and very relevant.

My supervising clinician was very helpful when I asked questions. She gave me her professional opinions and/or referred me to other professional sources. Although she informed me of reasons why some therapy sessions were less successful, she did not fail to commend the progress she saw and my success in therapy.

Student teaching has shown me how a school can function, how to deal with faculty, staff, and parents, and possible procedures to follow in making referrals and recommendations.

Another thing I've learned is that the activity is not terribly important. I've wasted a lot of time trying to be like Milton-Bradley or some of the other games and toy makers. What is important is getting the child to use his good speech and language as much as possible during the session.

The most valuable information I obtained was how to schedule clients and set up a therapy program.

Mrs. Harms maintained an atmosphere of organization, responsibility, cordiality and resourcefulness throughout the entire ten weeks. Because of such outstanding qualities in my supervising school clinician, I had a very fulfilling and rewarding student teaching experience.

I consider the practical experience that student teaching afforded me to be the most effective learning device in my college education. It was a positive and growing experience. Student teaching has started a growing in me, and a desire to grow more which I can continue for the rest of my life.

What is the purpose of student teaching in speech-language pathology and why is it a necessary and important part of the preparation of school SLPs? According to Anderson (1972),

The purpose of the school practicum as a part of the training program of the speech-language pathologist and audiologist is to provide certain learning experiences which the university or clinic setting cannot provide. If the practicum is to be meaningful there must be a careful delineation of those learning experiences which can and/or should be provided in each of those settings. It must be recognized that the student who begins his practicum in the schools is not a "finished" clinician but a student who needs certain types of experiences before he is ready to assume the responsibility of a job of his own.

THE STUDENT TEACHING TRIAD

Basically, three persons are directly involved in the process of student teaching. The first is the student teacher who is doing his or her practicum in an off-campus school system; the second is the pathologist employed by the school system, who is directly responsible for the day-to-day supervision of the student intern; the third is the university supervisor.

Too often the roles and responsibilities of the various participants in the student teaching process are not clearly defined and these individuals are put in a situation of not knowing what is expected of them, what to do, or how to do it. Following is a list of the roles, qualifications, and responsibilities of the persons involved in the clinical practicum in the schools. This is by no means a complete list, and others may wish to add to it or delete from it (Neidecker, 1976).

> I. *Qualifications of the University Supervisor:*
>   A. Shall have a master's degree in speech pathology and, or, audiology.
>   B. Shall have ASHA Certificate of Clinical Competence in speech pathology and, or audiology.
>   C. Shall have had experience as a full-time public school pathologist for a minimum of three years.
>   D. Shall be a competent speech-language pathologist.
>   E. Shall have had experience in teaching on a university speech pathology and audiology staff.

F.   Shall demonstrate ability in supervision techniques, evaluation methods, counseling, and in-service training.

G.   Shall have knowledge of school administration; general and special education policies and laws; physical planning of speech-language and hearing facilities; the process of developing programs for speech, language, and hearing handicapped children; available social and welfare agencies and services; and the practice and psychology of management techniques.

H.   Shall be aware of the current issues facing educators and contemporary trends in education.

I.   Shall have the following personal characteristics:
   1.   Shall be an effective communicator.
   2.   Shall be objective and flexible and able to adapt to change.
   3.   Shall have the capacity for self-evaluation and the ability to profit from mistakes.

II. *Responsibilities of the University Supervisor:*

A.   Shall be responsible for establishing criteria in regard to the time when a student is ready for practicum in the public schools.

B.   Shall be responsible, in part, for selection of the cooperating pathologist.

C.   Shall assume that the university still has the ultimate responsibility for the student's practicum experience.

D.   Shall be responsible for conducting in-service training for cooperating pathologists.

E.   Shall act as consultant to the cooperating pathologist.
   1.   Shall provide time for conferences to keep the cooperating pathologist informed of the university program and policies.
   2.   Shall provide written materials concerning the university policies and procedures.
   3.   Shall provide information on the background of the student teacher, both general and specific.
   4.   Shall be able to provide a wide variety of resource materials, approaches, and techniques which are based on sound theory, successful therapy, or documented research.

F.   Shall establish goals with the student teacher which are realistic and easily understandable.
   1.   Shall prepare informational material about the expectations of the student teacher and policies of the university regarding the school practicum.
   2.   Shall observe the student teacher during the practicum.
   3.   Shall confer with the student teacher each time a visit is made to the school.
   4.   Shall provide opportunity for the students to give feedback on their practicum experiences both during and after the practicum experience, either in writing or through conferences.

G.   Shall promote communication between the university and the public school setting.

H.   Shall act as mediator between the student teacher and school administration.

I.   Shall act as mediator between the cooperating pathologist and the student teacher.

J.   Shall participate in conferences with the student teacher and the cooperating pathologist individually and collectively.

K.   Shall establish that the responsibility for the student teacher's prac-

ticum is shared equally by the university supervisor and the cooperating clinician, but that the daily supervision of the student is the responsibility of the cooperating pathologist.
- L.   Shall be able to demonstrate therapy for both the student and the cooperating pathologist during the therapy session.
- M.   Shall share with the cooperating clinician in making the final evaluation of the student teacher.

III.   *Qualifications of the Cooperating Clinician:*
- A.   Shall have had at least three years experience in the public schools as a speech, language, and hearing pathologist.
- B.   Shall have the appropriate credentials as a speech-language pathologist in the schools.
- C.   Shall be recognized by colleagues as a competent professional person.
- D.   Shall be willing to have a student teacher.

IV.   *Responsibilities of the Cooperating Clinician to the Student Teacher:*
- A.   Shall be responsible for the day-to-day supervision of the student teacher.
- B.   Shall acquaint the student teacher with available materials and equipment for screening and diagnostic procedures.
- C.   Shall acquaint the student teacher with materials available for therapy.
- D.   Shall encourage the student teacher to create and develop his or her own materials.
- E.   Shall supplement the student teacher's background information through reading lists and other references.
- F.   Shall provide the student teacher with information regarding the school system in reference to school policy, location of schools, the community, dismissal and fire drill procedures, and other appropriate information.
- G.   Shall provide the student teacher with opportunities to:
  1.   Observe the cooperating pathologist doing therapy.
  2.   Assist in screening and diagnostic programs.
  3.   Plan for and evaluate therapy sessions.
  4.   Visit classrooms where speech, hearing, and language handicapped children are enrolled.
  5.   Meet other school personnel informally and also confer with them about specific chidren.
  6.   Write progress reports, case history reports, letters, therapy logs, and individual educational programs.
  7.   Become familiar with the reporting, recording, filing and retrieval systems used by the cooperating pathologist.
- H.   Shall provide feedback to the student teacher regarding strengths and weaknesses. The feedback shall be done on a regular basis and may take the form of verbal communication, written communication, tape recordings, video taping and, or, demonstration therapy.
- I.   Shall encourage the student to develop behavioral objectives regarding himself and the children with whom he works.
- J.   Shall encourage and assist the student to utilize supportive personnel and aids when available.
- K.   Shall encourage the student to become increasingly independent in thinking and problem solving.

V.   *Responsibilities of the Cooperating Clinician to the University Supervisor:*
- A.   Shall inform the university supervisor immediately of any problems that arise.

B. Shall be aware of and assist the student in fulfilling university requirements.
C. Shall provide the university supervisor with feedback concerning the student's progress.

VI. *Qualifications of the Student Teacher:*
A. Shall, after completion of practicum, be no more than one quarter or semester away from completing the degree program in speech-language pathology and, or, audiology at an accredited university.
B. Shall have completed the required clinical practicum.
C. Shall have had observation experience in a school setting prior to school practicum.
D. Shall demonstrate physical, mental, and emotional stability.
E. Shall possess acceptable speech and language patterns and adequate hearing.

VII. *Responsibilities of the Student Teacher:*
A. Shall be aware of and adhere to the Code of Ethics of the American Speech-Language-Hearing Association.
B. Shall be aware of and carry out the university requirements during school practicum.
C. Shall adhere to the policies and practices of the school to which assigned.
D. Shall comply with the directives of the cooperating pathologist as to working in the school therapy program.
E. Shall expect to be treated as a professional person and act accordingly.
F. Shall demonstrate ability to be dependable and assume responsibility while realizing that the cooperating clinician is legally responsible for the children being treated.
G. Shall contribute to the fullest extent to the school therapy program based on academic background and university clinical practice.
H. Shall demonstrate ability to establish and maintain appropriate interpersonal relationships with school personnel.
I. Shall demonstrate ability to establish and maintain appropriate rapport with children.
J. Shall demonstrate ability to evaluate self in therapy and a willingness to accept and utilize constructive criticism.
K. Shall be aware of the criteria for evaluating the practicum experience.
L. Shall recognize status as a learner and regard the practicum as a learning situation from which much is to be gained.
M. Shall expect the practicum experience to assist in the development of skills enabling one to function as an independent professional person.
N. Shall demonstrate interest in continued professional growth by making use of resource centers, attending in-service meetings, workshops, and professional meetings.

THE STUDENT TEACHING PROGRAM

Universities have many ways of carrying out the student teaching program in speech, language, and hearing. Obviously, there are many different patterns that are followed successfully depending on conditions and factors present in local areas and on the philosophy of the university concerned. There are, however, some commonalities that we will consider.

Schedules   It is important that the student teacher submit a day-by-day schedule to the university supervisor. Because many school therapy programs are on intermittent program schedules, several centers may be involved in the student teacher's assignment. Important also is the obligation of the student teacher to keep the university supervisor informed of the hours he or she will be at the schools, as well as times when therapy may not be going on as a result of interruptions to the school's daily schedule.

Log of clinical clock hours   In addition to fulfilling the university's requirements for daily attendance, the student clinician must also consider the future possibility of verification of clinical clock hours for certification by the American Speech-Language-Hearing Association, licensing in various states, and certification by state departments of education. Most universities use a weekly reporting system, and the forms used to record this information vary. Besides the identifying information, the forms should include places to record the age range of the children; the various types of communication problems; and the amount of time actually spent in diagnosis, audiometric testing, screening, and group and individual therapy sessions. The student teacher and the cooperating pathologist should sign the completed form. A summary form may be filled out at the conclusion of student teaching.

Lesson plans   A daily written plan of intervention for each child with whom the student teacher works is a necessary tool of therapy. The plan should include both long- and short-range goals for each child, procedures, materials used, and evaluation of the therapy session. The evaluation is done by both the cooperating pathologist and the student teacher and may include the progress of each child, the effectiveness of the procedures and the materials used, and the effectiveness of the approach used by the student teacher. There is no one universally accepted form for a lesson plan, but most forms include the same basic elements.

Seminars   It is common practice to hold seminars for the student teachers on a periodic basis. These seminars may be held weekly or less often, depending on the philosophy of the university. Frequently, the seminar time may be used for discussions and sharing of information and problems; speakers may be invited to discuss pertinent issues, panels may be utilized to familarize student teachers with current information, demonstration therapy or diagnosis may be carried out, visits may be made to agencies or centers, and one seminar may be devoted to an explanation of school policies and practices. It is valuable for student teachers in speech, language, and hearing pathology to attend at least several seminars that include all student teachers in a school system.

Evaluations   Assuming that self-evaluation and evaluation by supervisors is an ongoing procedure, it also may be useful to have a more formal type of written evaluation at the midpoint and at the conclusion of student teaching. The form used for these evaluative procedures should be in the hands of the student teachers during the first week of student teaching, or even prior to it, so that they know exactly what will be expected of them.

The midpoint evaluation should let the student teacher know his or her weak points, strengths, areas needing improvement, and how these improvements may occur. The student teacher then has the responsibility to act on the suggstions.

The final evaluation may be an evaluation of the student teacher during that experience, and it may also contain the perceived professional potential of that individual. It is important to differentiate between these two items. No student teacher emerges from the experience a "finished product," and this should be conveyed in the final evaluation report.

Additional Requirements for Student Teaching

There are additional requirements for student teaching that many university training centers have found productive and valuable in assisting student teachers to become full-fledged, competent professional persons. One is a checklist of experiences the prospective student teacher has had before the teaching experience. Such a checklist submitted to the cooperating pathologist is helpful in acquainting that person with the student teacher's capabilities. It might include information on any experience in child care such as baby-sitting or teaching church school; observational experience; clinical practicum experience; diagnostic experience; academic experience; and experience with tape recorders, audiometers, auditory training units, video tape machines, duplicating machines, and typewriters.

Student clinicians should know something about the community in which they are doing their teaching. Knowing the socioeconomic backgrounds of the families in the school districts helps student teachers to understand better the children with whom they will be working. This may be especially important for student teachers whose own backgrounds are different from those of their prospective clients.

This is only a partial list of possible requirements for student teaching, and understandably, each university training center will develop its own set.

COMPETENCY-BASED EVALUATION
OF THE STUDENT TEACHER

Competency-based evaluation systems can be used to evaluate the student teaching experience. Johnson et al. (1982) developed a form comprised of 89 competencies which was field-tested on 34 student teachers and 30 supervising clinicians for two semesters (see Figure 11-1). The results indicated that the

By the end of the student teaching experience, the student teacher will be able to:

Laws and Standards—Demonstrate knowledge of laws and standards. He or she will demonstrate the competency by:

YES NO N/A

1. Explaining the mandates of PL 94-142 (HB 455)

2. Outlining the procedures for due process safeguards as determined by the school district.

3. Preparing Individualized Educational Plans (IEP) for at least five children.

4. Participating in a placement team conference.

5. Explaining the state standards for speech therapy services in the school.

COMMENTS:

Screening—Plan and implement an efficient and effective speech-language and hearing screening program. He or she will demonstrate the competency 85% of the time by:

YES NO N/A

1. Explaining the procedures of screening and referral.

2. Select and utilize appropriate screening materials.

3. Screening the speech, language, and hearing of pupils with 85% agreement with the supervising clinician:

    a. Articulation disorders

    b. Language disorders

    c. Voice disorders

    d. Fluency disorders

    e. Hearing disorders

4. Recording results accurately on school records.

5. Interpreting and communicating screening results.

COMMENTS:

Diagnosis—Diagnose speech, language and/or hearing problems. He or she will demonstrate this competency 85% of the time by:

YES NO N/A

1. Selecting appropriate diagnostic instruments and procedures.

2. Administering effectively:

    a. An oral peripheral examination

    b. 2 diagnostic tests for articulation

    c. 2 diagnostic tests for language

FIGURE 11-1   Competency-Based Objectives for Student Teaching in Speech and Hearing

FIGURE 11-1 (continued)

d. A diagnostic assessment for voice

e. A diagnostic assessment for fluency

f. Diagnostic test for auditory perceptual skills.

g. Hearing thresholds

3. Recording diagnostic results accurately on school records.

4. Interpreting and communicating diagnostic results to speech pathologists and key persons/other professionals.

COMMENTS:

Scheduling—Effectively schedule public school therapy programs. He or she will demonstrate this competency 85% of the time by:

YES NO N/A

1. Selecting case load based upon eligibility criteria established by school district.

2. Scheduling program in relation to the needs of the children to be served.

3. Communicating with school personnel about schedule.

COMMENTS:

Planning Procedures—Write effective and appropriate objectives and therapy plans. He or she will demonstrate this competence 85% of the time by:

YES NO N/A

1. Utilizing diagnostic information to determine long-term objectives.

2. Utilizing diagnostic information to determine short-term objectives.

3. Planning a service strategy to meet long-term objectives.

4. Planning a service strategy to meet short-term objectives.

5. Using information and evaluations from previous therapy sessions.

6. Preparing lesson plans in advance.

COMMENTS:

Materials—Demonstrate the ability to select, produce, and utilize a variety of appropriate materials. He or she will demonstrate the competency 85% of the time by:

YES NO N/A

1. Selecting a variety of commercial materials.

2. Making new materials.

FIGURE 11-1   (continued)

3.   Utilizing materials appropriate to client's interests, abilities, and age level.

4.   Learning how to manipulate equipment and materials before therapy sessions.

COMMENTS:

Therapy—Conduct effective therapy sessions. He or she will demonstrate this competency 85% of the time by:

YES NO N/A

1.   Providing the rational for selection of specific therapy techniques.

2.   Using therapy procedures appropriate to child's age level.

3.   Establishing and maintaining good rapport with client.

4.   Giving directions clearly.

5.   Handling child's behavior effectively.

6.   Demonstrating creativity in materials and techniques.

7.   Beginning and ending therapy on time.

8.   Providing for carry-over to classroom and home.

9.   Communicating goals and techniques to parents.

10. Communicating goals and techniques to teacher.

COMMENTS:

Articulation Therapy—Conduct effective articulation therapy sessions. He or she will demonstrate this competency 85% of the time by:

YES NO N/A

1.   Explaining the theories and demonstrating ability to conduct two types of articulation therapy techniques:

  a.   List name of technique: _____

  b.   List name of technique: _____

2.   Conducting therapy consistent with goals.

3.   Discriminating correct/incorrect sound production with 85% agreement with supervising clinician for 85% of the articulation caseload.

4.   Obtaining maximum number of responses per therapy session.

5.   Providing appropriate and consistent reinforcement.

6.   Demonstrating flexibility in therapy situations.

7.   Evaluating the pupil's performance with respect to moving on to the next therapy step.

COMMENTS:

FIGURE 11-1   (continued)

Language Therapy—Conduct effective language therapy session. He or she will demonstrate this competency 85% of the time by:

YES NO N/A

1. Eliciting a spontaneous language sample.

2. Analyzing a spontaneous language sample.

3. Demonstrating ability to conduct 2 types of language therapy techniques:

   a. List name of technique: _____

   b. List name of technique: _____

4. Conducting therapy consistent with goals.

5. Recognizing correct/incorrect language productions with 85% agreement with the supervising clinician.

6. Obtaining appropriate number of responses per therapy session.

7. Utilizing a variety of appropriate activities.

8. Providing appropriate reinforcement.

9. Demonstrating flexibility in therapy situations.

10. Evaluating the pupil's performance with respect to moving on to the next session.

COMMENTS:

Stuttering Therapy—Conduct effective stuttering therapy session. He or she will demonstrate this competency 85% of the time by:

YES NO N/A

1. Conducting therapy consistent with goals.

2. Explaining the procedures of one therapy program.

3. Teaching fluency techniques.

4. Demonstrating flexibility in therapy situations.

COMMENTS:

Voice Therapy—Conduct effective voice therapy sessions. He or she will demonstrate this competency 85% of the time by:

YES NO N/A

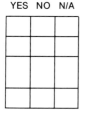

1. Conducting therapy consistent with goals.

2. Counseling pupils about causes of vocal abuse.

3. Discriminating correct/incorrect voice production with 85% agreement with the supervising clinician for 85% of the voice cases.

4. Explaining the procedures of one therapy program.

FIGURE 11-1   (continued)

5. Demonstrating flexibility in therapy situation.

6. Explaining the steps of making a medical referral.

COMMENTS:

Other Disorders—Conduct effective therapy sessions. He or she will demonstrate this competency by:

YES NO N/A

1. Explaining the procedures of one aural rehabilitation technique.

2. Explaining the procedure of a program for improving auditory perception skills.

COMMENTS:

Observation and Self Evaluation—Observe and evaluate him- or herself. He or she will demonstrate this competency by:

YES NO N/A

1. Evaluating therapy through audio or video tapes.

2. Compiling data on child's performance in order to plan future session.

3. Following through on suggestions from the supervising clinician.

4. Setting personal objectives for change as a result of self evaluation.

COMMENTS:

Professionalism—Demonstrate a professional attitude. He or she will demonstrate this competency by:

YES NO N/A

1. Attending professional meetings.

2. Exhibiting interest and enthusiasm about his/her work.

3. Interacting with parents.

4. Interacting with school personnel.

5. Dealing appropriately with supervising clinician.

6. Arriving at school on time.

7. Demonstrating regular attendance.

8. Demonstrating initiative.

9. Demonstrating dependability.

10. Dressing appropriately.

11. Demonstrating correct articulatory skills.

12. Utilizing appropriate vocal quality, rate, and intonation.

COMMENTS:

two groups favored the competency-based form to that of the traditional numerical form to evaluate knowledge, skill, and value objectives.

According to Johnson et al., the procedures are as follows:

At the beginning of the semester, the university supervisor distributes the competency-based forms to both the supervising clinican (the public school speech-language pathologist to which the student is assigned in the schools) and the student teachers. The university supervisor meets with the supervising clinician and student teachers to discuss the use of the form. At this time, several aspects of the competency-based form are explained:

1. An explanation of a minimal competency is given. This is the minimal requirement that the student must meet by the end of the student teaching experience.
2. For each competency a choice of yes, no, or not applicable is given. A review of competency-based systems throughout the education field utilizes a yes/no format. According to a strict competency-based format, the student either demonstrates the competency (by meeting the criteria) or does not. The N/A category was included to cover the skills and cases the student does not experience (e.g., type of caseload).
3. A competency is achieved if the student demonstrates a skill with 85% accuracy by the end of the semester.
4. At mid-term the supervising clinician is to review the form with the student teacher and discuss the student's strengths and weaknesses in various areas.
5. At the end of the semester the supervising clinician is to complete the competency-based objectives form and discuss these results with the student teacher. (At Miami University student teaching is graded on a pass/fail basis.)

In conjunction with the competency-based objectives form, a traditional numerical rating form was used at both mid-term and at the end of the semester. The numerical form, which utilized a scale from 1 to 7, rates the same skills evaluated on the competency-based form with the exception of those skills that could not be rated on a 1–7 basis, that is, the entire laws and standard section.

A WORD OF ADVICE TO STUDENT TEACHERS

Are you ready to start your student teaching? Here are some suggestions that might be helpful:

1. Work in harmony with your cooperating pathologist and university supervisor. Their job is to help you become a better speech-language pathologist and/or audiologist.
2. Be enthusiastic about your work and sincerely interested in the children with whom you will be working.
3. Keep healthy; get plenty of rest and eat the right foods.
4. Take advantage of every opportunity to become involved in the unique experiences a school has to offer.
5. Ask questions when you aren't sure, and ask questions even if you *are* sure.
6. Know what you can expect of children at various age and ability levels.
7. Be firm, fair, consistent, and compassionate in all your dealings with children. Every human being deserves respect.

8. Know the ground rules of the various schools and adhere to them.
9. When making professional decisions always ask yourself, "Is this in the best interests of the child?"
10. Enjoy your student teaching experience!

GUIDELINES FOR THE COOPERATING CLINICIAN

In a chapter dealing with student teaching it is appropriate to include information useful to the person who plans and directs the student internship. That person is the cooperating clinician in the schools.

An article by Hess (1976) contains many excellent suggestions. According to Hess,

> It is vital for the cooperating clinician working with a student clinician to realize the importance of student teaching. The student deserves the chance to be involved in a worthwhile program, and it will be worthwhile if he is met with leadership, an opportunity for growth, and a well-planned program.

Hess discusses the responsibilities of the cooperating clinician in the first week of student teaching. They are

1. Communicate with the student clinician before the first week, by telephone call or letter, or an invitation to visit the school ahead of time.
2. On the first day provide orientation for the student by having him meet with the program director and other school pathologists and student teachers to discuss school policies, complete necessary forms, map out routes to the schools, and generally to minimize anxieties. He could also be informed of time schedules of the various schools, as well as the school calendar.
3. During the first week the student teacher should be given a tour of the school buildings and should be introduced to the principal and secretary of each building to which he has been assigned, as well as the teachers, school counselor, nurse, and psychologist.
4. The cooperating pathologist should prepare the children enrolled in therapy for the arrival of the student teacher in such a way that they understand his role in relation to them.
5. The cooperating pathologist and the student teacher should discuss the university's materials, requirements, and suggestions so they are mutually understood.
6. The major goals for the student teaching program, as well as assignments and weekly goals, should be discussed. The cooperating pathologist should discuss his expectations of the student teacher and encourage the student to express his own expectations.
7. The student teacher should be made aware of rules, regulations and policies of individual schools, the school system as a whole, and of the speech-language and hearing program in the state.
8. The first week of student teaching should include the opportunity to observe therapy sessions and to become acquainted with the children. During the first week the student teacher may assist with segments of the therapy sessions.

9. If the student teacher is assigned at the beginning of the school year he may assist in the screening programs.

According to Hess, the assigned weeks of student teaching should be utilized effectively and efficiently, but the student teacher should not be overloaded.

There are numerous school activities the student clinician can take part in during the weeks of student teaching. It is important for the cooperating clinician to have a list of priorities or activities that seem most valuable for the student. The list can be compiled from various sources: university information, other clinicians, published articles, and discussions with the student clinician. The student should have the opportunity to take part in as many phases as possible of the school therapy program. Besides learning to organize and carry out a therapy program, the student clinician will want to become familiar with related activities. For instance, it is helpful for the student to attend meetings of the clinicians as well as those meetings held in the individual schools.

The cooperating clinician should discuss with the student clinician how to begin and how to terminate the school year. The clinician will want to include the student in obtaining referrals for therapy and in conferences with teachers and parents. Furthermore, the cooperating clinician can discuss with the student clinician bulletin board ideas, newsletters for parents, parent conferences, and special therapy ideas that have proven successful. The student should learn to use the copy machine and any other office equipment that is applicable to the therapy program. Also the student clinician will want to have information about the many sources of therapy materials.

The publication *Introduction to Clinical Supervision in Speech Pathology* by Schubert (1978) contains such information that would be of interest to the supervisor of the student teacher in the school. In addition, there are numerous articles on supervision in professional journals. Another suggested reading is *Proceedings: Conference on Training in the Supervisory Process in Speech-Language Pathology and Audiology,* ed. Jean L. Anderson, Conference Director, Indiana University, Bloomington, July 20–24, 1980.

DISCUSSION QUESTIONS AND PROJECTS

1. Interview a current student teacher on his or her suggestions to beginning student teachers.
2. Invite a principal to talk to your class on what he or she expects of the student teacher.
3. What is the student teacher's role when a child must be punished for misbehavior?
4. What is the student teacher's role in relation to children in therapy? Defend your choice.
    a. A buddy
    b. Mother or father figure
    c. "One of the gang"

    d.   Authority figure

    e.   Permissive big brother or big sister

    f.   Teacher

    g.   Counselor

    h.   One who "lays down the law"

    i.   Referee

5. What do you hope to learn from student teaching?

6. Interview a school SLP on what he or she expects from a student teacher.

7. Ask a first-, second-, or third-grade child what he or she likes best about a favorite teacher. Ask a junior high and high-school student the same question. Did you find any differences or similarities in their answers?

TWELVE
LIFE AFTER COLLEGE

INTRODUCTION

Changes in the field of speech-language pathology and audiology are occurring rapidly. As Heraclitus once said, one may not step in the same river twice, not only because the river flows and changes, but also because the one who steps into it changes, too, and is never at any two moments identical.

What does this mean to you as a beginning SLP? And more specifically, what does it mean to those of you who will be employed in education? First, it means that this is an incredibly interesting time to be alive and in the field of communications. This era has been called the "age of communication," and the SLP or audiologist will be in the thick of it. You will need to be knowledgeable and involved in the world, not only the world of the therapy room and the classroom, but also the community beyond.

In this chapter we will look at some of the ways you will be able to keep abreast of current information through professional journals and continuing education programs. Your role as a researcher will also be examined. Collective bargaining and the school SLP is an issue of importance to you. We will also look at ways you may provide interviewers and prospective employers with information about your skills, knowledge and attitudes, in order to enhance your employment opportunities.

PROFESSIONAL PUBLICATIONS AND RESOURCES

As the roles of the school SLP and audiologist expand, there is a need to keep abreast of current information. This is particularly crucial for school clinicians working in remote areas or in areas where there is no access to academic libraries, medical libraries, or even public libraries. School libraries usually do not have publications pertinent to a school pathologist's needs.

Throughout the United States regional resource centers have established a statewide network system with regional centers that have among their services the collecting and distributing of special education materials as well as providing information about the materials. They also help school personnel create new materials when commercially produced products are not available. Information is provided by newsletters concerning the services and materials available.

The publications of the American Speech-Language-Hearing Association are available to members. They are the *Journal of Speech and Hearing Disorders;* the *Journal of Speech and Hearing Research, Asha;* and *Language, Speech & Hearing Services in Schools.*

Public libraries in almost all communities have an interlibrary loan service whereby library materials are made available by one library to another for use by an individual. In addition to books, materials may include audiotape, videotape, film, and microfilm. The community public library can be of great assistance to the school clinician, and librarians are always helpful in obtaining materials. The school clinician may want to visit the library and find out what kinds of services are available.

Language and Language Behavior Abstracts is published quarterly and examines the contents of approximately 1,000 publications for articles to be summarized. The subject categories are speech and language pathology, special education, verbal learning, and psycholinguistics. Subscriptions can be obtained by writing to P.O. Box 22206, San Diego, California 92122.

The Council for Exceptional Children publishes *Exceptional Child Education Resources (ECER),* a quarterly journal that contains abstracts of books, articles, research, and conference proceedings. It also offers reprints of selected computer searches from *ECER* and ERIC (Educational Resources Information Center). *Resources in Education* is published monthly and contains abstracts of research reports and materials, with the exception of journal articles.

Following is a list of publications of interest to the school SLP and audiologist. School clinicians may want to examine the publication before subscribing. Some publications will be of interest to other school personnel as well, and it might be worthwhile for the school system to subscribe for the teachers' library collection.

Speech Pathology and Audiology (Professional)

Journal of Speech and Hearing Disorders (JSHD), American Speech-Language-Hearing Association, 10801 Rockville Pike, Rockville, Maryland 20852. Essential for the speech-language pathologist and audiologist.

Journal of Speech and Hearing Research; quarterly; same publisher as above (*JSHD*).

Asha; monthly; same as *JSHD.*

Language, Speech & Hearing Services in Schools; quarterly; same as *ASHA.* Excellent publication for clinicians in the schools.

Journal of the Academy of Rehabilitative Audiology; biannual; *JARA,* Department of Audiology, Wayne State University, Detroit 48201. Good for information and research on aural rehabilitation.

Journal of the Acoustical Society of America; monthly; Acoustical Society of America, 335 East 45th Street, New York 10017. Mainly a research book in audiology.

Cerebral Palsy Journal; bimonthly; Institute of Logopedics, Wichita, Kansas 67219. Interesting journal, especially for the speech pathologist who works with cerebral palsied individuals.

Topics in Language Disorders; quarterly; Aspen Systems Corp., 16792 Oakmont Avenue, Gaithersburg, Maryland 20877. Excellent publication for SLPs and audiologists.

Language and Speech; quarterly; Robert Draper, Kerbihan House, 85 Udney Park Road, Teddington, Middlesex, England. A British journal that covers such things as transmission, perception, and patterns of speech. Also includes articles on abnormalities of language and speech.

Journal of Linguistics; semiannually; F. R. Palmer, Cambridge University Press, 32 East 57th Street, New York 10022. Concerned with all branches of linguistics including phonetics. May be useful.

Today's Speech; quarterly; Eugene Vasilew, State University of New York, Binghamton 13401. Touches on all phases of speech communication, including speech therapy. Also one of the best in its field, but geared more toward speech departments on high-school level.

Journal of Child Language; Cambridge University Press, Bentley House, 200 Euston Road, London, England. International research regarding development and usage of language by children.

American Speech; quarterly; Columbia University Press, 440 West 110th Street, New York 10025. Concerned with language and linguistics. Majority of articles concentrate on pronunciation, dialects, current usage, new words, and phonetics. It could be useful to a speech pathologist who works with dialectical differences.

Journal of Childhood Communicative Disorders; quarterly; Council for Exceptional Children, 1411 South Jefferson Davis Highway, Building 1, Suite 900, Arlington, Virginia 22202. Official journal of the Division for Children with Communication Disorders, CEC. Excellent publication for school pathologists.

Cleft Palate Journal; quarterly; American Cleft Palate Association, Waverly Press, Mt. Royal and Guilford Avenues, Baltimore, Maryland. Reflects research and clinical activities in the study and treatment of cleft lip and cleft palate.

Journal of Communication Disorders; quarterly; North Holland Publishing Co., P.O. Box 3489, Amsterdam, Holland. A journal of research and information from different countries; interesting and informative.

Education

Today's Education; quarterly; Mildred Fenner, National Educational Association of the United States, 1201 16th Street N.W., Washington, D.C. 20036. Official journal of the largest educational association in the United States. Valuable to anyone in the teaching profession.

Journal of General Education; quarterly; The Journal of General Education, Pennsylvania Street, University Park, Pennsylvania 16802. Filled with articles that are informative and interesting to anyone in the field of teaching.

Journal of Education; quarterly; Adolph Manoil, Boston University School of Education, 765 Commonwealth Avenue, Boston 02100. Devoted to the in-service education of school teachers. Each issue focuses on a particular theme and is concerned with elementary and secondary education.

Elementary School Journal; monthly; University of Chicago Press, 5750 South Ellis Avenue, Chicago 60636. Keeps elementary school teachers abreast of new developments and provides them with practical in-service education.

Childhood Education; monthly; Association for Childhood Education, 3615 Wisconsin Avenue N.W., Washington, D.C. 20016. Directed to both parent and teacher of the child from prenursery through the elementary grades. An all-around education/childhood magazine.

Instructor; monthly; Ernest Hilton, Instructor Park, Dansville, New York 14437. Primarily for elementary-school teachers and special staff.

Grade Teacher; monthly; Harold Littledale, Professional Magazines, 22 West Putnam Avenue, Greenwich, Connecticut 06830. Provides practical how-to articles for the elementary-school teacher. Covers all subjects and activities of the elementary-school program.

Reading Teacher; monthly; Lloyd Kline, International Reading Association, Tyre Avenue, Newark, Delaware 19711. Deals with all aspects of the teaching of elementary and secondary reading—useful for the teacher who is searching for new methods of improving reading.

Journal of Reading Behavior; quarterly; National Reading Conference, Clemson University, Clemson, South Carolina 29150. Includes articles of research on reading skills. Some articles pertinent to the field of communication disorders.

Learning; monthly; Education Today Co., 530 University Avenue, Palo Alto, California 94300. Directed to elementary and junior high-school teachers looking for new ideas on how to teach more effectively.

Education Digest; monthly; Lawrence Prakken Publications, 416 Longshore Drive, Ann Arbor, Michigan 48103. Has a broad scope of new information from the elementary grades to graduate school.

Resources in Education; monthly; Educational Resources Information Center, Superintendent of Documents, U.S. Government Printing Office, Washington, D.C. 20402. Important for the speech pathologist to keep abreast of the current research in the field of education, speech, and language pathology.

PTA Magazine; monthly; Eva Grant, 700 North Rush Street, Chicago 60611. Although not a source of educational information, it is useful and beneficial for parents and teachers.

Journal of Educational Psychology; bimonthly; American Psychological Association, 1200 17th Street N.W., Washington, D.C. 20036. Interesting but not pertinent for speech and language pathologists in schools.

Special Education

Mental Retardation Journal; bimonthly; available to members of American Association on Mental Deficiency; Boyd Printing Co., 49 Sheridan Avenue, Albany, New York 12210. Interesting journal, especially for those who will work with the mentally retarded.

Education and Training of the Mentally Retarded; quarterly; Council for Exceptional Children, 1411 South Jefferson Davis Highway, Building 1, Suite 900, Arlington, Virginia 22202. Journal of the Council for Exceptional Children's Division on Mental Retardation. A combination of theory and practical advice. Could be beneficial to school pathologists, especially in regard to mainstreaming.

Journal of Special Education; quarterly; Editorial Board, Buttonwood Farms, Inc., 3515 Woodhaven Road, Philadelphia 19154. Good for keeping on top of issues pertaining to special education.

Special Children; P.O. Box 168, Fryeburg, Maine 04037. Covers wide areas from development to fitness to toys, games, and other recreational activities. Excellent for parents of retarded children.

dsh Abstracts (Deafness, Speech and Hearing Abstracts); annually; Deafness, Speech and Hearing Publications, Gallaudet College, Washington, D.C. 20002. Abstracted periodical literature on deafness and speech disorders.

Volta Review; bimonthly; The Volta Review, 3417 Volta Place N.W., Washington, D.C. 20007. Helpful articles on teaching communication skills to hearing-impaired children.

Education of the Visually Handicapped; quarterly; Association for Education of the Visually Handicapped, 1604 Spruce Street, Philadelphia 19103. Interesting journal; has a broad scope from research to practice. May be interesting and helpful to the school pathologist who has a visually handicapped child on caseload.

Exceptional Children; 8/yr.; Grace T. Warfield, Council for Exceptional Children, 1411 South Jefferson Davis Highway, Jefferson Plaza Building, Suite 900, Arlington, Virginia 22202. Includes articles on curriculum planning, organization of programs and classroom hints, research, mainstreaming, current topics, etc.

Exceptional Parents; bimonthly; Editorial Board, Box 101, Back Bay Annex, Boston 02117. Information bulletin to parents of exceptional children.

Journal of Learning Disabilities; bimonthly; P. E. Lane Professional Press, 5 North Wabash Avenue, Chicago 60602. Represents 24 disciplines from anthropology to speech. Each is supported by a member of a large editorial advisory board. For the professional educator and specialist, yet will have interest for the elementary-school through college teacher.

Children's Periodicals

Children's Digest; 10/yr.; Elizabeth R. Mattheos, Parents' Magazine Enterprises, Inc., 52 Vanderbilt Avenue, New York 10017. A magazine for children ages seven to 12 presented in a format of 100 pages of material. Activities could be utilized in therapy.

Highlights; 11/yr.; Dr. and Mrs. Garry C. Myers and Dr. Walter B. Barbe, 2300 West Fifth Avenue, Columbus, Ohio 43216. Edited to assist the preschool and elementary child to "gain in creativeness, ability to think and reason, and to learn worthy ways of living." Would be good to stimulate language-delayed child.

Child Life; 10/yr.; B. R. SerVaas, 1100 Waterway Boulevard, Indianapolis, Indiana 46202. For children from prereaders to sixth-graders. Equally divided among fiction, arts, crafts, and miscellaneous. The activity pages could be used by a speech pathologist in therapy.

Humpty Dumpty Magazine for Little Children; 10/yr.; Thomas Roberts, Parents' Magazine Enterprises, 52 Vanderbilt Avenue, New York 10017. Written and illustrated for children from three to seven years of age. Stories, articles, and features are written to develop reading and vocabulary.

Jack and Jill; 10/yr.; Nelle K. Bell, Jack and Jill Publishing Co., 1100 Waterway Boulevard, Indianapolis, Indiana 46202. A variety magazine to suit the reading ability and interests of children ages five to 12. The games, projects, recipes, and picture features could be used by speech pathologists in therapy.

Sesame Street; monthly; Jane O'Connor, Children's Television Workshop, 1 Lincoln Plaza, New York 10023. Intended for the preschool child. Each issue has four posters, activities, stories, and a parent's guide section. Would be excellent for visual and auditory discrimination and language therapy.

Children's Playmate; 10/yr.; Rita A. Cooper, Children's Playmate Magazine, 1100 Waterway Boulevard, Indianapolis, Indiana 46207. Directed to ages three to eight; features games and things to make and do.

Kids; 10/yr.; Valentine Smith Co., Dept. TB-1, 777 Third Avenue, New York 10017. A magazine written and illustrated by children aged five to 13 for each other. There are sections on things to make and do. Could give clinician activity ideas for therapy.

Golden Magazine; monthly; Beth Thomas, Review Publishing Co., 1100 Waterway Boulevard, Indianapolis, Indiana 46202. A special form of reading matter for boys and girls from ages nine to 13. Includes a "things to do" section, which would be helpful to a clinician with older children in therapy.

CONTINUING EDUCATION

Another way in which the SLP keeps up to date on professional matters is through continuing education, in the form of workshops, short courses, seminars, miniseminars, in-service training courses, professional meetings highlighted by competent speakers, university courses, extension courses, teleconferences, televised courses, and presentations by film and videotape. Continuing education can be carried on by a structured program or on a more informal basis. It is a lifelong process for an individual expecting to remain accountable and qualified. It is a process by which one keeps one's skills and knowledge up to date.

Continuing education is not only necessary to the individual currently practicing but also helps those persons who interrupt their professional lives and wish to reenter at a later date.

Continuing education is not the responsibility of any one institution or agency but should represent the coordinated efforts of a number of groups. Universities cannot offer extension courses in a geographical area unless there is an expressed need concerning the content area of such a course. For the university to plan for such courses, the need should be expressed to the university staff by the school clinicians. By the same token, universities should be willing to offer courses at a time that would be convenient to the school clinicians and in a location that would be accessible to them.

Members and nonmembers of the American Speech-Language-Hearing Association who are holders of the Certificate of Clinical Competence may apply for an award called the ACE (Award for Continuing Education). Credits are earned through continuing education activities under ASHA-approved sponsors. A specific number of CE units are awarded to the participant for each instructional activity, and a national CE registry is maintained; on the completion of the required number of units the ACE is awarded.

RESEARCH

It is doubtful that anyone would argue against the need for research about public school speech, language, and hearing programs. Neither is there any question that the public school is a fertile field for research in communication disorders. To add further emphasis, PL 94-142 has created pressure to find answers to questions about prevalence of speech, language, and hearing problems; comparison of delivery systems; efficacy of therapeutic methods; and other important issues.

Brett (1976), in a report of the Public School Caucus, cited as one of its 11 goals attention to research in the schools. Fisher (1977) outlined ten critical issues affecting the School Services Program of ASHA. One of the issues was the need to promote research in schools with universities.

Unquestionably a fertile field for possible research, the school programs have produced little in the past. There are a number of possible reasons given by school clinicians. Among them are lack of time, lack of funding, lack of support by school boards, lack of cooperation by university staff members, and lack of interest by journals. The fear of performing statistical analyses, the lack of training in research methods on the university level, and the lack of rewards have also been suggested as reasons for the lack of research in the schools. Another reason may be that SLPs may simply be more interested in being clinicians than researchers. This is understandable in light of their employment setting. On the other hand, school clinicians are always eagerly reading journals and attending professional meetings in the hope of finding answers to questions.

A profession must be based on a body of knowledge, and this body of knowledge is accumulated by research. There must be interested individuals to pose questions and interested individuals to seek answers and solutions. Collaboration by researchers in universities, specialists in departments of education and special education on both the state and federal levels, and school SLPs is one of the methods for generating research on the public school level.

The publications *Language, Speech & Hearing Services in Schools* and the *Journal of Childhood Communicative Disorders* contain reports of collaborative research between school SLPs and university faculty members. Public schools provide a good base for research projects, and university personnel are a good source of information for consultation on research design. It should be kept in mind by school-based SLPs, however, that university faculty members are also busy people; the SLP can't just call the local university for help with research and expect an immediate response.

Other sources of collaboration are state and local departments of education and special education and area speech, language, and hearing professional organizations.

Single-subject studies are especially amenable to research projects by the school SLP. The clinician can carry out this type of research without disruption of schedule and without ethical constraints on using school-age clients for research. Parents and school administrators need only to be advised. Single-subject studies can yield information on therapy methods and case management options. The two previously mentioned publications contain numerous examples of single-subject studies by school SLPs.

Longitudinal studies, in which a single subject or a group of subjects are followed for months or even years, are ideally suited for public school researchers in speech-language pathology. An example of this type of study involved a 15-year follow-up of 50 children initially diagnosed as communicatively impaired (King et al., 1982). Although the study was not conducted by school-based investigators, it has implications for the school SLP in terms of methodology and research. According to King et al.,

> The kind of results collected in this study suggest that some alteration in the expected outcome of academic, social, and emotional difficulties seen along with speech and language problems can be observed. This alteration may be related to early and long-term speech-language services. What appears to be critical is a need for careful records from standardized and documented nonstandardized evaluation procedures, progress toward stated therapy goals, progress and/or lack of progress in the classroom setting, results of standardized academic achievement tests, and results of teacher rating scales ranking the child's social and emotional development. It is hoped that the clinic will work diligently with school personnel to collect these data. Although the task requires some additional time on the part of all concerned, the information is desperately needed.

The school clinician of the future will undoubtedly be involved in research on the local level, the state level, or as part of a national research project. The questions are everywhere, and the need to find answers is urgent. The questions of the school clinician in Mississippi may be the same ones asked by the clinician in Montana. Not only is the search for answers important, but equally important is the need to exchange professional information. By recording data on standardized forms they can then be computerized and related to data collected and recorded in other geographical areas. The use of computers has already proven to be effective in speech, language, and hearing, and will continue to grow as a valuable method of storing, retrieving, and displaying data.

COLLECTIVE BARGAINING AND THE SCHOOL SPEECH-LANGUAGE PATHOLOGIST

The unmistakable trend toward collective bargaining in the public sector clearly indicates that school speech-language pathologists and audiologists need to develop procedures for negotiations. Collective bargaining has a long history in the private sector and since 1962 when New York City teachers negotiated a collective bargaining agreement it has become a significant factor in American education. Collective bargaining is an outgrowth of the desire to have a say in such issues as salary, fringe benefits and working conditions.

Whether the American Federation of Teachers and the National Education Association call themselves labor unions or professional organizations is a moot point. If they bargain collectively with management they are functionally labor unions. The American Speech-Language-Hearing Association and the various state speech, language and hearing associations are professional organizations because they do not negotiate salaries, contracts, and fringe benefits.

Many, but not all, states have collective bargaining laws and the laws differ from state to state. Your state's labor relations board can give you information on your state's collective bargaining law. Whether you, as a speech-language pathologist or audiologist, are considered management or labor will depend on your state's collective bargaining law. If your state classifies you as management, during a strike you may be called on to staff a classroom. If you are classified as labor, it is important to become involved in and work with the union or unit at the local level to make sure the issues and concerns important to you are brought to the bargaining table.

The decision of whether or not to affiliate with a local collective bargaining unit depends on the local situation. If you belong to the local unit of either AFT or NEA you must also belong to the state and national organization. If you do not join the locally designated unit it is required by law that the unit must bargain for you regardless.

School speech-language pathologists and audiologists are at a disadvantage primarily because they comprise a very small percentage of persons covered by the bargaining unit. During negotiations when concessions are made it would be easier for a unit to give up a demand affecting the few speech-language pathologists in favor of a demand affecting all the classroom teachers.

According to Dublinske (1986): "It appears that speech-language pathologists can have the most impact in the collective bargaining process if:

1. ASHA works with the NEA and AFT at the national level to make them aware of the general needs related to the working conditions of speech-language pathologists and audiologists employed in the schools;

2. state speech-language-hearing associations work with the NEA and AFT affiliates at the state level to make them aware of specific state needs and to work on state legislation that will improve working conditions; and if

3. individual speech-language pathologists and audiologists get involved in the collective bargaining process at the local level. If speech-language pathologists and audiologists are going to be able to use the collective bargaining process to improve their working conditions it is important to become knowledgeable about their state's collective bargaining law and how negotiations are handled locally."

According to Johns (1974):

A strong local teachers' organization can offer representation before the school board, county board, or state legislature; communications including action reports, news releases, and media coverage for educational problems; professional services and developments such as negotiations with the school board (concerning salary), arbitration of grievances, attainment of better employment conditions, and greater voice in curriculum matters; and such advantages as tax-sheltered annuities, notary service, legal service or legal defense, housing placement, civic representation, and discounts with local merchants.

GETTING YOUR FIRST JOB

In this section of the chapter I am indebted to Bowling Green State University, Bowling Green, Ohio, and JoAnn Kroll, director of Placement Services. The information herein is based on and has been adapted from the university's publication *Job Search: A Guide for Success in the Job Market.*

Where to Start

The job search for you, as a beginning SLP, may start any time during the last year of college. The best place to start is your university placement office. The service is available at most universities and is usually free to students and alumni. The first step in your job search will be to visit your university placement office to find out what specific services are available. Generally speaking, this is what they have to offer:

1. Individual counseling
2. Vacancy listings
3. Credential services
4. On-campus interviews
5. Placement seminars and guest speakers
6. Library with information concerning employment strategies, career opportunities, alumni placement services, videotapes, and slide/sound presentations
7. Mock interview training and critique sessions
8. Staff referrals of qualified candidates

After you find out what services are available, which ones are applicable to you, and which ones you want to utilize, it is time to plan your strategy. Timing is important here. You will want to visit the placement office after you have completed most of your academic work and clinical practice but before you start your student teaching.

The Credential File and Portfolio

School personnel administrators expect to see well-organized and up-to-date credential files on prospective SLPs. The credential file you accumulate must document your past achievements and support your candidacy for a position. It is important to begin early to complete the necessary forms required by your university's placement office and gather the appropriate letters of recommendation from faculty members and past employers.

A complete credential file should include the following:

1. *Credential form.* Each university has its own form, which may be obtained at that office.
2. *Letters of recommendation.* Most university placement services have a reference form on which the student writes his or her name, address, social security number, and so on. There is a place on the form for the reference writer to make statements regarding your professional or personal relationship and how long the writer has known you. There should be a description of your academic or career growth and potential, a review of your principal achievements, an estimate of future promise at this point, a paragraph on your personal qualities, and a final summary paragraph.
3. *Student teaching evaluation.* An evaluation is made by the student teaching supervisors during the experience. This may also include the perceived professional potential of the student teacher in the final evaluation report.
4. *Transcript of grades.* This is obtained from the registrar of the university.

If you intend to use someone's name as a reference it is always necessary to request that person's permission in advance. The reference letter may be sent directly to the university placement office or to you. If it is sent to the placement office it is desirable to request a copy for yourself. Always enclose self-addressed stamped envelopes.

Regardless of immediate or long-range plans, establishing a credential file at the university placement office is strongly advised for all students and alumni. Be sure you keep it up to date by informing the office of current professional addresses and positions and by periodically including letters of reference from employers.

One of the most successful "marketing tools" is the use of the student teaching portfolio. Your résumé, samples of lesson plans, photographs of displays or bulletin boards, and statements verifying your participation in educational projects both before and during the student teaching should be placed in the portfolio. Your student teaching supervisor can offer excellent recommendations concerning the content and layout of the portfolio.

The Interview

One of the keys to successful interviewing is preparation. It is also one of the best ways to combat nervousness during the interview. The beginning point of your preparation is to know yourself. Review your personal inventory and background thoroughly and always in light of the position you are seeking. Be prepared to answer questions regarding your education, grades, courses, jobs, extracurricular activities, goals, strengths, weaknesses, and other information. Keep in mind that the interviewer is asking himself or herself the question, "Why should I hire you?" In answering this question be prepared to give examples and illustrations of your abilities, skills, leadership, effectiveness, and potential.

Successful preparation for the interview also entails knowing the school system. Your placement office may be able to assist you. Other sources for general information include newspaper articles, school board minutes, parent-teacher organizations, or your university education department. However, you would also be interested in learning about the speech, language, and hearing programs, information you would be able to obtain by asking the interviewer questions. Pertinent questions would include the following: How many SLPs are presently on the school staff? How long has the program been in existence? What is the school population? How many buildings and grade levels are being serviced by the speech-language program? To whom is the speech-language clinician directly responsible?

Another important way to prepare for the interview is to practice. With a friend, relative, another candidate, or a placement staff counselor, role-play a mock interview. Pay especially close attention to questions that may deal with some weaknesses or problem areas in your background. Don't wait until you reach the interview to think about responding to a question concerning a weakness.

Another facet of interview preparation is appropriate dress. First impressions are often lasting impressions, and you must look as if you fit the role before an employer will let you act the role. How you dress is a statement about how you feel about the significance of the interview and who you will be meeting. Careful attention to dress and grooming is a way of putting your best foot forward. When in doubt it is best to be conservative in your dress.

What can you expect the interviewer to be like? Because you really don't know in advance you will need to take your cues from the content of the interview. If the interviewer wants you to do most of the talking and wants to assess your ability to communicate and reason, this individual's style will be nondirective. If the interviewer is concerned with eliciting specific and precise responses, the style will be more formal and structured. Sometimes interviewers will create some stress to ascertain how the candidate will react.

How you handle the interview is important. Avoid short responses, as they tell the interviewer little or nothing or perhaps the wrong things, about you. Use this opportunity to capitalize on your assets. Use anecdotal information to demonstrate your strong points, for example, "During my spring vacation I helped the school clinician in my hometown with the preschool screening program. We screened over 500 children for speech, language, and hearing problems. She was pleased with my work and wrote a letter describing my contribution. The letter is in my portfolio and I would like to have you read it." This tells the interviewer not only that you were able to function well in a professional situation and that you have gained some experience but that you were also interested in improving your skills by spending your spring vacation doing so.

Be prepared for questions like these: What is your philosophy of education? How would you plan to work with the learning disabilities teacher? What do you think a speech, language, and hearing program can add to a school system?

Inappropriate behaviors elicit negative impressions during an interview. They include candidates who show up late, chew gum, smoke without permission, bring uninvited guests, have poor hygiene, are braggarts and liars, are overly aggressive or too shy, lack confidence and poise, fail to look the interviewer in the eye, show lack of interest and enthusiasm, and ask no questions or poor questions.

Follow-up on the interview is important. Write a thank-you letter, noting anything that was said that you want to reemphasize; thank the interviewer for the opportunity to discuss your mutual interests and clarify any questions or ambiguities from the meeting. If you are interested in this position restate your desire to work for this particular school system. If you are undecided write a thank-you letter anyhow.

The Résumé

Another important tool is the résumé, a written document that introduces your education, background, skills, and experience to the prospective employer. It is a document that is used not only for the first job but also for subsequent employment searches throughout your professional life. The résumé, whether we like it or not, has become a cornerstone of the job-hunting process. Its worth is seldom questioned; its necessity is simply assumed. However, despite its importance as a marketing tool, many people express anxiety and frustration about preparing it.

A résumé is neither an autobiography nor merely a listing of your employment history. When properly done, it is an advertisement which excites an employer's interest in a particular product—*namely, you*. Because there are no absolutes in résumé writing, you will ultimately decide how it looks and what it says. Its style, format, and length should be determined by your employment interests or target markets and your background and qualifications.

An effective résumé can be prepared in different styles or formats and contain widely diverse information. Making the strongest presentation of your unique and individual qualifications will contribute to the kind of distinction that will set your résumé apart from others. So although there are no absolute rules on what "all" resumes should contain—except who you are and how you can be contacted—the following general rules address issues of honesty, accuracy, neatness, grammar, layout, and content that should be carefully observed:

Do not exaggerate your accomplishments to give the impression that you did more than you did. Employers know the difference between a restaurant hostess and an executive vice president for customer relations.

Be reasonably brief. You are writing a résumé, not an autobiography. Tailor your information to fit the employer's needs.

Be careful with your grammar and the design and layout of your résumé. There is no excuse for sloppy writing and poor grammar.

Do not include information that will work to your disadvantage. Negative or harmful information is best handled in a personal interview.

Use strong action verbs to make your résumé as impressive as possible. This is essential since employers will most often see your résumé before they see you.

Always present accurate information. Honesty really is the best policy.

The following résumé is designed to help you produce a document that strongly reflects your interests, qualifications, and potential. By itself, a résumé cannot get you the job you want; yet without it, you most likely will not even get started.

Marrisa Cheney

Current Address: Permanent Address:
302 Jackson Hall   179 Elm Street
Bowling Green State Univ.   Hudson, Ohio 44100
Bowling Green, Ohio 43403   (000) 000-0000
(000) 000-0000

PROFESSIONAL   This is usually the most difficult section to write. Many
OBJECTIVE   people believe that listing a job objective on a résumé is too
                    limiting. However, if you have a clear objective that applies to
                    many organizations, it is to your advantage to include it. You may
                    also state your professional objective in your cover letter rather
                    than on the résumé. Include the job function desired and the type of
                    organization. For example: Position as a speech-language pathologist
                    in an inner city, medium size school system that will allow me to
                    work with bicultural, speech, and language handicapped adolescents.
                    Or: Position as a speech-language pathologist in a rural school
                    system that will allow me to do diagnostic and remediation work with
                    K-12 students, as well as consultative and preventive work with
                    preschoolers and their parents.

EDUCATION   List highest or most recent degree first. Include name of college(s),
                    major(s) (minor optional), date(s) of graduation. Add any special
                    emphasis in your studies, such as relevant courses or research
                    projects. If your grade point average is noteworthy include it.
                    College expenses earned also can be included here.

EXPERIENCE AND
WORK HISTORY   This is a summary of your work experience, highlighting your most
                    recent or most relevant employment first. Include descriptions
                    of your responsibilities, titles of positions held, names of
                    companies or organizations, and dates you were employed. Summer
                    employment, volunteer work, student teaching, and internships
                    may be included. If you are a recent college graduate without
                    experience, do not be concerned; you are in the majority. Stress
                    the level of responsibility, achievement, and motivation you
                    demonstrated in previous jobs. This section should be an active
                    statement of what you can do. How you describe the experience
                    is the key.

ACTIVITIES/   Extracurricular involvement hightlights your leadership skills,
INTERESTS   sociability, and energy level. Thoose activities that support
                    your professional objective by demonstrating your leadership or
                    organizational skills. If you have many activities, select the
                    ones in which you were most involved and describe your degree of
                    responsibility. If you have limited activities, point out that
                    you worked and include hours worked per week as well as the per-
                    centage of school expenses earned.

FIGURE 12-1

FIGURE 12-1 (continued)

REFERENCES

It is not necessary to include names and addresses of references. If requested, these can be provided on a separate sheet or included on an application form. State either "Available upon request" or "Available upon request from (<u>your university placement service address</u>)."

OPTIONAL
INFORMATION

This includes honors and awards, publications, professional association, research projects, study abroad, and personnal information. It is illegal for an employer to solicit personal data (age, weight, height, marital status, number of children, or disability) unless a genuine occupational requirement. Include this information only if pertinent to the job you are seeking.

A FINAL WORD

Not all interviews result in a job offer. Sometimes the supply of SLPs exceeds the demand, especially if you are interested in obtaining a position in a particular geographical area. The individual who is willing to locate anywhere has a much better chance of finding a job.

The classified section of *Asha* magazine lists open positions. And don't neglect the classified pages of the newspapers although these are unlikely to yield a great amount of information about positions in school systems.

The newsletters of state speech, language, and hearing associations often list job openings in schools, and the state consultants in speech, language, and hearing know of job openings within that state. The names and addresses of the state consultants can be obtained by writing to the state departments of public instruction, division of special education. They are located in or near the state capital cities. Information can be found in educational directives.

Begin now to build a network of persons who may be able to provide you with information concerning job possibilities. This will be valuable not only for your first job but also for subsequent job searches.

DISCUSSION QUESTIONS AND PROJECTS

1. Check a school library and a public library against the lists of publications in this chapter. How many did you find from the list in each facility?
2. Which universities, organizations or other facilities in your state are ASHA approved sponsors of continuing education programs leading toward the ACE? Do you think continuing education should be mandatory?
3. Do you think it is feasible for school SLPs to conduct research studies? What is the rationale for your answer?

4. Using the résumé form in this chapter write your résumé.

5. Interview a school SLP or audiologist working in the schools to find out what they do on a typical day.

6. If the school SLP is paid more than classroom teachers will the collective bargaining union argue the SLP's cause with zeal even if they accept the SLP for membership?

7. In the case of a strike should the SLP man a classroom even though he or she is not a member of the teacher's union?

8. If the school SLPs align themselves with the classroom teachers, cannot the school administrators realistically expect them to have playground or lunchroom duties?

9. Should the state speech-language and hearing association provide assistance to SLPs whose local school district is on strike?

10. Caseload size could conceivably be a negotiable issue. What other issues of interest to the school SLP might be negotiable?

APPENDIX

Speech and Language Criteria, Union School District, Escondido, California. Developed by a Task Force of program specialists; speech and language specialists; integrated special day class teachers, communicatively handicapped; speech and language therapists; special day class teachers, communicatively handicapped; and Thomas N. French, director, Special Education Services. Reprinted by special permission of the Escondido, California, Union School District, Special Education Services Department.

TABLE OF CONTENTS

I. ARTICULATION DISORDER

A. DEFINITION: The articulation of phonemes and clusters in words or connected speech. The reduced intelligibility significantly interferes with communication and attracts adverse attention.

B. CRITERIA: Identification of an "Articulation Disorder" will be based upon a numerical point system with a maximum point potential of 87 points. The sum of an individual candidate's points will be interpreted in the following manner:

Total Points	*Interpretations*
0 – 62	Does not qualify.
63 – 87	Qualifies as having an Articulation Disorder.

C. POINTS: Based upon evidence of the following, prospective candidates will receive points in the following manner:

Data Indicate	*Points*

*1. *Articulation/Phonology:* The articulation of phonemes and   63
clusters in words or connected speech. The reduced intelligibility
significantly interferes with communication and attracts adverse
attention, as determined by one or more of the following:

   a. The child scores one year or more below his/her C.A.
expectancy on a developmental assessment.

   b. The child scores 15% or below on a nonstandardized
measurement (G-F, Arizona, DASE, APP, CELF, T-MAC,
La Meda, etc.).

   c. The child scores 2 S.D. below or more on a standardized
measurement (T-D, TOLD, PAT, etc.).

2. *Self-Awareness:* The child indicates awareness of his/her articu-   12
lation disorder by modifying his/her communication interactions as determined by:

   a. Observation by teacher or specialist.

   b. Self-referral.

3. *Parental Concern:* The parent expresses feelings about the   9
child's articulation disorder indicating that the disorder appears
to affect the parent-child relationship.

4. *Staff Concerns:* The articulation disorder interferes with com-   3
munication and adversely affects teacher-child-peer relationships
as evidenced by:

   a. Staff observation.

   b. Specialist observation.

II. VOICE DISORDER

A. DEFINITION: Abnormal voice. A pupil has an abnormal voice which is characterized by persistent, defective vocal quality, pitch or loudness.

B. CRITERIA: Identification of a "Voice Disorder" will be based upon a numerical point system with a maximum point potential of 96 points. The sum

*Required for identification.

of an individual candidate's points will be interpreted in the following manner:

Total Points	Interpretations
0 – 82	Does not qualify.
83 – 96	Qualifies as having a Voice Disorder.

C. POINTS: Based upon evidence of the following, prospective candidates will receive points in the following manner:

Data Indicates	Points

1. *E.N.T. Evaluation:* A written report shall be obtained from an appropriate doctor diagnosing the voice disorder. — 34

2. *Defective Vocal Quality, Pitch, or Loudness:* May be measured by: — 49
   a. Observation and judgment by specialists using standardized or nonstandardized measurements (Wilson Voice Profile, checklists, etc.).
   b. Observation by staff or specialist that the voice disorder adversely affects teacher-child-peer relationships.

3. *Parental Concern:* The parent expresses feelings about the child's vocal quality, pitch, or loudness indicating that the disorder appears to affect the parent-child relationships as evidenced by:
   a. Staff observation.
   b. Specialist observation. — 7

4. *Staff Concern:* The child's voice disorder interferes with communication and adversely affects teacher-child-peer relationships as evidenced by:
   a. Staff observation.
   b. Specialist observation. — 6

III. FLUENCY DISORDER

A. DEFINITION: A pupil has a fluency disorder when the flow of verbal expression including rate and rhythm adversely affects communication between the pupil and listener.

B. CRITERIA: Identification of a "Fluency Disorder" will be based upon a numerical point system with a maximum point potential of 108 points. The sum of an individual candidate's points will be interpreted in the following manner:

Total Points	Interpretations
0 – 11	Does not qualify.
12 – 108	Qualifies as having a Fluency Disorder.

C. POINTS: Based upon evidence of the following, prospective candidates will receive points in the following manner:

Data Indicates	Points

1. *Self-Awareness:* The child indicates awareness of his/her fluency disorder by modifying his/her communication interactions with others as determined by: — 18

Data Indicates   *Points*

     a. Observation by specialist, teacher or parent.

     b. Self-referral.

     c. Personality/Attitudinal checklist (Shames, etc.).

2. *Secondary Characteristics:* The child may have additional physi-   15
cal characteristics such as facial grimace, eye blinking, lips
pressed tightly, mouth open and breath holding, lip tremors, etc.,
as measured by:

     a. Observation by specialist, teacher, or parent.

     b. Assessment measures (Shine, Zwitman, data counts, etc.).

3. *Blocking:* The child may have silent prolongations.   14

     a. Observation by specialist, teacher, or parent.

     b. Assessment measures (Shine, Zwitman, data counts, etc.).

4. *Avoidance Reactions:* The child avoids communication with oth-   13
ers, will not interact in group situations, or avoids certain words,
as measured by:

     a. Observation by specialist, teacher or parent.

     b. Assessment measures (Shine, Zwitman, data counts, etc.).

5. *Sound or word repetitions or prolongations:* The child has repeti-   12
tions of a syllable or sound or voiced prolongations as measured
by:

     a. Observation by specialist, teacher or parent.

     b. Assessment measures (Shine, Zwitman, data counts, etc.).

6. *Rate:* The child's rate of speech (i.e., halting, extremely slow, ex-   12
tremely rapid, etc.) adversely affects communication between the
child and listener, as measured by:

     a. Observation by specialist, teacher or parent.

     b. Assessment measures, data counts, etc.

7. *Home Environment:* The child's home environment displays cau-   12
sitive or contributing factors as measured by:

     a. Parent questionnaires.

     b. Parent interview.

8. *Parental Concern:* The parent expresses feelings about the child's   9
fluency which indicates that the disorder appears to affect the
parent-child relationship.

9. *Staff Concern:* The fluency disorder interferes with communica-   3
tion and adversely affects teacher-child-peer relationships as evidenced by:

     a. Staff observation.

     b. Specialist observation.

IV. LANGUAGE DISORDER

A. PRAGMATICS

1. DEFINITION: The practical and appropriate use of language in a communicative context. Pragmatic disorders may be characterized by some or all of the
following:

    a. The child uses limited forms to express a variety of conversational functions.

    b. The child does not use utterances that are appropriate for the context.

    c. The child does not answer questions appropriately.

    d. The child does not initiate new utterances in new contexts.

2. *CRITERIA:* Identification of a "Pragmatic Disorder" will be based upon a numerical point system with a maximum point potential of 98 points. The sum of an individual candidate's points will be interpreted in the following manner:

Total Points	*Interpretations*
0 – 37	Does not qualify.
38 – 98	Qualifies as having a Pragmatic Disorder.

3. POINTS: Based upon evidence of the following, prospective candidates will receive points in the following manner:

Data Indicates   *Points*

*a. Children of eight years of age or older evidence deficits in one   21 or more pragmatic functions as measured by one or more of the following:

    (1) Language sample.

    (2) Classroom observation.

    (3) Pragmatic checklist.

    (4) Pragmatic assessment devices (ILSA, etc.).

*b. Children under eight years of age will evidence deficits of one year or more in one or more pragmatic functions as measured by one or more of the following:

    (1) Language sample.

    (2) Classroom observation.

    (3) Pragmatic checklist.

    (4) Pragmatic assessment devices.

c. *Educational Performance-Social:* The child's pragmatic disorder   17 adversely affects how the child relates in the school environment (classroom, playground, lunch, etc.) with his teachers and/or peers and may be measured by:

    (1) Observation.

    (2) Teacher interview.

    (3) Data counts.

d. *Potential:* A discrepancy exists between a child's potential and   15 his language disorder as measured by:

    (1) A psychologist on an approved assessment instrument (WISC-R, LIPS, SOMPA, Merril-Palmer, Kaufman, etc.).

    (2) A specialist when deemed appropriate using an approved instrument (Ordinal Scales, Uzgiris-Hunt, etc.).

e. *Self-Awareness:* The child indicates awareness of his/her prag-   12

---

*Required for identification.

Data Indicates   *Points*

matic disorder by modifying his/her communication interactions as determined by:

    (1)   Teacher or specialist observation.

    (2)   Self-referral.

f. *Home Environment:* The child's home environment displays   10
causitive or contributing factors as measured by:

    (1)   Parent questionnaires.

    (2)   Parent interviews.

g. *Staff Concerns:* The pragmatic disorder interferes with commu-   8
nication and adversely affects teacher-child-peer relationships as
evidenced by:

    (1)   Staff observation.

    (2)   Specialist observation.

h. *Educational Performance-Academic:* The child's pragmatic dis-   7
order adversely affects academic performance as measured by
one or more of the following:

    (1)   Achievement tests.

    (2)   Academic tests.

    (3)   Report cards.

    (4)   Teacher observation.

i. *Parental Concern:* The parent expresses feelings about the   7
child's pragmatic disorder, which indicates that the disorder
appears to affect the parent-child relationship.

B. SEMANTICS

1. DEFINITION: The understanding of words and word relationships. Semantic
disorders may be characterized by some or all of the following:

  a. The child's language doesn't contain objects, actions, and events in a variety of semantic relationships.

  b. The child has many revisions when talking.

  c. The child uses similar semantic combinations over and over to the exclusion of other combinations.

  d. The child doesn't use a variety of qualifiers and descriptors, such as terms of time, space, dimension, quantity, or other attributes.

  e. The child has word-finding problems, verbal perseveration, echolalia.

2. CRITERIA: Identification of a "Semantic Disorder" will be based upon a numerical point system with a maximum point potential of 96 points. The sum
of an individual candidate's points will be interpreted in the following manner:

Total Points   *Interpretations*

    0 – 35   Does not qualify.

    36 – 96   Qualifies as having a Semantic Disorder.

3. POINTS: Based upon evidence of the following, prospective candidates will
receive points in the following manner:

Data Indicates   *Points*

*a. The child scores 1.5 S.D. below the mean, or below the 7th   **22**
    percentile, or receives an age equivalent score 2 years below
    his/her C.A. or developmental level on one or more of the
    following:

    (1) Standardized Tests: PPVT, TOAL, TOLD-P, TOLD-I,
          Woodcock-Johnson Language Battery, BOEHM, ITPA,
          Detroit, Word Test, Fullerton, Expressive One Word,
          Bankson, Zimmerman, TACL, Del Rio, PEOPLE, Dos
          Amigos, etc.

    (2) Nonstandardized Tests: Wiig-Semel, CELF, SPELT,
          Merril, etc.

  b. The child displays inappropriate or inadequate usage of seman-
    tic functions/features in expressive language as measured on a
    representative spontaneous sample of a minimum of 50 utter-
    ances.

    (1) Special Day Class—Communicatively Handicapped: Must
          have a minimum of 50 utterances that are analyzed:
          (a) Standardized: DSS, Tyack, MLU, etc.
          (b) Nonstandardized: Bloom-Lahey, checklists, etc.

    (2) Special Day Class—Other: Language sample may be given
          when deemed appropriate.

    (3) Designated Instructional Service: Language sample of 10–
          25 utterances that indicate type of disorder.

  c. *Potential:* A discrepancy exists between a child's potential and   **20**
    his/her language disorder as measured by:

    (1) A psychologist on an approved assessment instrument
          (WISC-R, LIPS, SOMPA, Merril-Palmer, Kaufman, etc.).

    (2) A specialist when deemed appropriate using an approved
          instrument (Ordinal Scales, Uzgiris-Hunt, etc.).

  d. *Educational Performance-Academic:* The child's semantic disor-   **14**
    der adversely affects academic performance as measured by:

    (1) Achievement tests.
    (2) Academic tests.
    (3) Report cards.
    (4) Teacher observation.

  e. *Self-Awareness:* The child indicates awareness of his/her se-   **11**
    mantic disorder by modifying his/her communication interac-
    tions as determined by:

    (1) Observation by teacher or specialist.
    (2) Self-referral.

  f. *Staff Concerns:* The semantic disorder interferes with commu-   **10**
    nication and adversely affects teacher-child-peer relationships as
    evidenced by:

    (1) Staff observation.
    (2) Specialist observation.

*Required for identification.

Data Indicates | *Points*

g. *Educational Performance-Social:* The child's semantic disorder   7
adversely affects how the child relates in the school environment (classroom, playground, lunch, etc.) with his/her teachers
and/or peers as measured by:
   (1) Observation.
   (2) Teacher interview.
   (3) Data counts.

h. *Parental Concern:* The parent expresses feelings about the   6
child's semantic disorder, which indicates that the disorder appears to affect the parent-child relationship.

i. *Home Environment:* The child's home environment displays   6
causitive or contributing factors as measured by:
   (1) Parent questionnaires.
   (2) Parent interview.

C. SYNTAX

1. DEFINITION: The appropriate word order in sentences. Syntactical disorders
may be characterized by some or all of the following:
   a. The child uses inappropriate grammatical constructions.
   b. The child demonstrates inadequate sentence complexity for his developmental age.
   c. The child uses inappropriate word order in sentences.

2. CRITERIA: Identification of a "Syntactical Disorder" will be based upon a
numerical point system with a maximum point potential of 96 points. The sum
of an individual candidate's points will be interpreted in the following manner:

Total Points	*Interpretations*
0 – 21	Does not qualify.
22 – 96	Qualifies as having a Syntactical Disorder.

3. POINTS: Based upon evidence of the following, prospective candidates will
receive points in the following manner:

Data Indicates | *Points*

*a. The child scores 1.5 S.D. below the mean, or below the 7th   22
percentile, or receives an age equivalent score 2 years below
his/her C.A. or developmental level on one or more of the
following:
   (1) Standardized Tests: NSST, TOLD-P, TOLD-I, CELI,
   TOAL, Del Rio, PESST, Clark-Madison, etc.
   (2) Nonstandardized Tests: TSA, OLSIST, SPELT, CELF,
   MILI, etc.

*b. The child displays inappropriate or inadequate usage of syntac-
tic functions/features in expressive language as measured on a
representative spontaneous language sample of a minimum of
50 utterances.

*Required for identification.

Data Indicates   *Points*

    (1) Special Day Class—Communicatively Handicapped: Must
        have a minimum of 50 utterances that are analyzed:

        (a) Standardized: DSS, Tyack, MLU, etc.

        (b) Nonstandardized: Bloom-Lahey, etc.

    (2) Special Day Class—Other: Language sample may be given
        when deemed appropriate.

    (3) Designated Instructional Service: Language sample of 10–
        25 utterances that indicate type of disorder.

c. Potential: A discrepancy exists between a child's potential and   17
his/her language disorder as measured by:

    (1) A psychologist on an approved assessment instrument
        (WISC-R, LIPS, SOMPA, Merril-Palmer, Kaufman, etc.).

    (2) A specialist when deemed appropriate using an approved
        instrument (Ordinal Scales, Uzgiris-Hunt, etc.).

d. Educational Performance-Academic: The child's syntactical dis-   13
order adversely affects academic performance as measured by:

    (1) Achievement tests.

    (2) Academic tests.

    (3) Report cards.

    (4) Teacher observation.

e. Self-Awareness: The child indicates awareness of his/her syn-   13
tactical disorder by modifying his/her communication interactions as determined by:

    (1) Teacher or specialist observation.

    (2) Self-referral.

 f. *Educational Performance-Social:* The child's syntactical disor-   9
der adversely affects how the child relates in the school environment (classroom, playground, lunch, etc.) with his/her
teachers and/or peers may be measured by:

    (1) Observation.

    (2) Teacher interview.

    (3) Data counts.

 g. *Parental Concern:* The parent expresses feelings about the   9
child's syntactical disorder which indicate that the disorder appears to affect the parent-child relationship.

 h. *Staff Concerns:* The syntactical disorder interferes with commu-   8
nication and adversely affects teacher-child-peer relationships as
evidenced by:

    (1) Staff observation.

    (2) Specialist observation.

 i. *Home Environment:* The child's home environment displays   5
causitive or contributing factors as measured by:

    (1) Parent questionnaires.

    (2) Parent interview.

*Required for identification.

D. MORPHOLOGY

1. DEFINITION: The appropriate use of word forms (i.e., pluralization, past tense, comparatives, superlatives, negatives, etc.). Morphological disorders may be characterized by some or all of the following:

   a. The child uses inappropriate, or omits, grammatical morphemes at his age expectancy level.

   b. The child uses inappropriate, or omits, negatives at his age expectancy level.

   c. The child uses inappropriate, or omits, interrogatives at his age expectancy level.

   d. The child uses inappropriate, or omits, pronouns at his age expectancy level.

2. CRITERIA: Identification of a "Morphological Disorder" will be based upon a numerical point system with a maximum point potential of 96 points. The sum of an individual candidate's points will be interpreted in the following manner:

Total Points	*Interpretations*
0 – 20	Does not qualify.
21 – 96	Qualifies as having a Morphological Disorder.

3. POINTS: Based upon evidence of the following, prospective candidates will receive points in the following manner:

   Data Indicates   *Points*

   a. Speech and Language Assessment   21

        (1) Using more than one assessment procedure, the pupil scores at least 1.5 S.D. below the mean, or below the 7th percentile, or receives an age equivalent score 2 years below his/her C.A. or developmental age on:

           (a) Standardized Tests: ITPA, Fullerton, TOLD-P, TOLD-I, TACL, CELI, NSST, etc.

           (b) Nonstandardized tests: OLSIST, OLSIDI, etc.

        (2) The child displays inappropriate or inadequate usage of morphological features/units in expressive language as measured on a representative spontaneous language sample of a minimum of 50 utterances.

           (a) Special Day Class - Communicatively Handicapped: Must have a minimum of 50 utterances that are analyzed:

              (i) Standardized: DSS, Tyack, MUL, etc.

              (ii) Nonstandardized: Bloom-Lahey, etc.

           (b) Special Day Class - Other: Language sample may be given when deemed appropriate.

           (c) Designated Instructional Service: Language sample of 10 - 25 utterances that indicate type of disorder.

   b. *Potential:* A discrepancy exists between a child's potential and   17
   his/her language disorder as measured by:

---

*Required for identification.

Data Indicates   *Points*

      (1) A psychologist on an approved assessment instrument (WISC-R, LIPS, SOMPA, Merril-Palmer, Kaufman, etc.).

      (2) A specialist when deemed appropriate using an approved instrument (Ordinal Scales, Uzgiris-Hunt, etc.).

  c. *Educational Performance-Academic:* The child's morphological   14
disorder adversely affects academic performance as measured by:

      (1) Achievement tests.

      (2) Academic tests.

      (3) Report cards.

      (4) Teacher observation.

  d. *Self-Awareness:* The child indicates awareness of his/her mor-   14
phological disorder by modifying his/her communication interactions as determined by:

      (1) Teacher or specialist observation.

      (2) Self-referral.

  e. *Educational Performance-Social:* The child's morphological dis-   9
order adversely affects how the child relates in the school environment (classroom, playground, lunch, etc.) with his/her
teachers and/or peers as measured by:

      (1) Observation.

      (2) Teacher interview

      (3) Data counts.

  f. *Parental Concern:* The parent expresses feelings about the   8
child's morphological disorder, which indicates that the disorder
appears to affect the parent-child relationship.

  g. *Staff Concerns:* The morphological disorder interferes with   7
communication and adversely affects teacher-child-peer relationships as evidenced by:

      (1) Staff observation.

      (2) Specialist observation.

  h. *Home Environment:* The child's home environment displays   6
causitive or contributing factors as measured by:

      (1) Parent questionnaires.

      (2) Parent interview.

V. LIMITED ENGLISH PROFICIENT (LEP)

A. EVALUATION REQUIREMENT: Monolingual non-English speaking children
will be assessed by a competent individual in their native/primary language
and if the results indicate a need for remediation, recommendations will be
made to the responsible E.S.L. staff.

B. CRITERIA: Identification of a "Limited English Proficient Student with a
Speech and/or Language Disorder" will be based upon a numerical point system with a maximum point potential of 91 points. The sum of an individual
candidate's points will be interpreted in the following manner:

Total Points	*Interpretations*
0 – 31	Does not qualify.
32 – 91	Qualifies as having a Speech and/or Language Disorder.

C. POINTS: Based upon evidence of the following, prospective candidates will receive points in the following manner:

Data Indicates   *Points*

1. *Potential:* A discrepancy exists between a child's potential and   8
   his/her language disorder as measured by:
   a. A psychologist on an approved assessment instrument (WISC-R, LIPS, SOMPA, Merril-Palmer, Kaufman, etc.).
   b. A specialist when deemed appropriate using an appropriate instrument (Ordinal Scales, Uzgiris-Hunt, etc.).

*2. *Contrastive Analysis:* The comparison of testing done in Language 1 to the testing done in Language 2 indicates that a language disorder exists in both languages.   7

*3. *One Year of Educational Experience:* Child has had at least one year of educational experience in the U.S.A. or another country. The background and history of prior school experience may be obtained from: 7
   a. School records.
   b. Parent interview.

4. *Pragmatics:* The practical and appropriate use of language in a   7
   communicative context. (See IV. A.)
   a. Children of eight years of age or older evidence deficits in one or more pragmatic functions as measured by:

English:	*Spanish:*	*Other:*
(1) Language sample	Language sample	Language sample
(2) Classroom observation	Classroom observation	Classroom observation
(3) Pragmatic checklist	Pragmatic checklist	Pragmatic checklist
(4) Pragmatic assessment devices (ILSA, etc.)	Pragmatic assessment devices (ILSA, etc.)	Pragmatic assessment devices (ILSA, etc.)

   b. Children under eight years of age will evidence deficits of one year or more in one or more pragmatic functions as measured by:

English:	*Spanish:*	*Other:*
(1) Language sample	Language sample	Language sample
(2) Classroom observation	Classroom observation	Classroom observation
(3) Pragmatic checklist	Pragmatic checklist	Pragmatic checklist
(4) Pragmatic assessment devices (ILSA, etc.)	Pragmatic assessment devices (ILSA, etc.)	Pragmatic assessment devices (ILSA, etc.)

*Required for identification.

Data Indicates   *Points*

5. *Semantics:* The understanding of words and word relationships.   7
(See IV. B.)

   a. The child scores 1.5 S.D. below the mean, or below the
      7th percentile, or receives an age equivalent score 2 years
      below his/her C.A. or developmental level on:

English:	*Spanish:*	*Other:*
ACLC	ACLC	
BOEHM	BOEHM	
BSM	BSM	
BINL	BINL	
Del Rio	Del Rio	
Dos Amigos	Dos Amigos	
LAS	LAS	
Las Cruces	Las Cruces	
One Word Expressive	One Word Expressive	
TACL	TACL	
Upper Extension	Upper Extension	
Zimmerman	Zimmerman	
PPVT	Bencil	
TOLD-P	PEOPLE	
TOLD-I	PDIL	
TOAL		
Woodcock-Johnson		
ITPA		
Detroit		
Word Test		
Fullerton		
Bankson		

   b. The child displays inappropriate or inadequate usage of
      semantic functions/features in expressive language as mea-
      sured on a representative spontaneous sample of a mini-
      mum of 50 utterances.

      (1) Special Day Class - Communicatively Handicapped:
          Must have a minimum of 50 utterances that are ana-
          lyzed:

          (a) Standardized: DSS, Tyack, MLU, etc.

          (b) Nonstandardized: Bloom-Lahey, checklist, etc.

      (2) Special Day Class - Other: Language sample may be
          given when deemed appropriate.

      (3) Designated Instructional Service: Language sample of
          10 - 25 utterances that indicate type of disorder.

*6. *Developmental History-Language:* The acquisition of language   6
   milestones obtained by:

   a. Parent interview.

   b. Parent questionnaire.

*7. *Interventions:* Educational techniques, strategies, programs,   6

---

*Required for identification.

Data Indicates   *Points*

etc., that have been tried prior to Special Education referral
and address the child's Limited English Proficiency.

8. *Educational Performance-Academic:* The child's Limited   5
   English Proficiency disorder adversely affects academic performance as measured by one or more of the following:

   a. Achievement tests.

   b. Academic tests.

   c. Report cards.

   d. Teacher observation.

9. *Syntax:* The appropriate word order in sentences. (See IV. C.)   5

   a. The child scores 1.5 S.D. below the mean, or below the
      7th percentile, or receives an age equivalent score 2 years
      below his/her C.A. or developmental level:

English:	*Spanish:*	*Other:*
BSM	BSM	
BINL	BINL	
Del Rio	Del Rio	
LAS	LAS	
Las Cruces	Las Cruces	
TACL	TACL	
Zimmerman	Zimmerman	
TOLD-P		
TOLD-I		
CELI		
TOAL		
PESST		
Clark Madison		
NSST		
TSA		
SPELT		
CELF		
OLSIST		
MILI		

Data Indicates

   b. The child displays inappropriate or inadequate usage of
      syntactic functions/features in expressive language as mea-
      sured on a representative spontaneous language sample of
      a minimum of 50 utterances.

      (1) Special Day Class - Communicatively Handicapped:
          Must have a minimum of 50 utterances that are
          analyzed:

          (a) Standardized: DSS, Tyack, MLU, etc.

          (b) Nonstandardized: Bloom-Lahey, checklists, etc.

      (2) Special Day Class - Other: Language sample may be
          given when deemed appropriate.

      (3) Designated Instructional Service: Language sample of
          10 - 25 utterances that indicate type of disorder.

Points

10. *Educational Performance - Social:* The child's speech and/or   4
language disorder adversely affects how the child relates in the
school environment (classroom, playground, lunch, etc.) with
his/her teachers and/or peers may be measured by:
    a. Observation.
    b. Teacher interview.
    c. Data counts.

11. *Morphology:* The appropriate use of word forms (i.e. plurali-   4
zation, past tense, comparatives, superlatives, etc.). (See IV.
D.)
    a. The child scores 1.5 S.D. below the mean, or below the
        7th percentile, or receives an age equivalent score of
        2 years below his/her C.A. or developmental level on:

English:	*Spanish:*	*Other:*
BINL	BINL	
BSM	BSM	
LAS	LAS	
Las Cruces	Las Cruces	
TACL	TACL	
ITPA		
Fullerton		
TOLD-P		
TOLD-I		
CELI		
NSST		
OLSIST		
OLSIDI		

    b. The child displays inappropriate or inadequate usage of
        morphological features in expressive language as measured
        on a representative spontaneous language sample of a
        minimum of 50 utterances.
        (1) Special Day Class—Communicatively Handicapped:
            Must have a minimum of 50 utterances that are
            analyzed:
            (a) Standardized: DSS, Tyack, MLU, etc.
            (b) Nonstandardized: Bloom-Lahey, etc.
        (2) Special Day Class - Other: Language sample may be
            given when deemed appropriate.
        (3) Designated Instructional Service: Language sample
            of 10 - 25 utterances that indicate type of disorder.

12. *Observations:* Formal observations by competent specialist   4
which support the existence of a speech and/or language
disorder.

13. *Self-Awareness:* The child indicates awareness of his/her   4
speech and/or language disorder by modifying his/her
communication interactions as determined by:
    a. Observation by teacher or specialist.
    b. Self-referral.

Data Indicates   *Points*

14. *Articulation/Phonology:* The articulation of phonemes and   4
    clusters in words or connected speech. The reduced intelligi-
    bility significantly interferes with communication and attracts
    adverse attention.
    a. The child scores one year or more below his/her C.A. ex-
        pectancy on a developmental assessment. Some of the fol-
        lowing instruments may be used:

English:	*Spanish:*	*Other:*
T-D ARTIC	La Meda	
G-F		
Arizona		
DASE		
APP		
CELF		
T-MAC		
TOLD		
PAT		
Fisher-Logemann		

15. *Cultural Factors:* The child's speech and/or language disorder   3
    is not that individual's ethnic group.

16. *Home Environment:* The child's home environment displays   3
    causitive contributing factors as measured by:
    a. Parent questionnaires.
    b. Parent interview.

17. *Staff Concerns:* The speech and/or language disorder inter-   3
    feres with communication and adversely affects teacher-child-
    peer relationships as evidenced by:
    a. Staff observation.
    b. Specialist observation.

18. *Developmental History-Physical:* The acquisition of physical   2
    milestones as obtained by parent interview or parent question-
    naire.

19. *Parental Concern:* The parent expresses feelings about the   2
    child's speech and/or language disorder, which indicates that
    the disorder appears to affect the parent-child relationship.

VI. AUDITORY PROCESSING DISORDER

A. DEFINITION: A disability, not due to deficits in acuity, that involved attend-
    ing, localization, discrimination, memory, sequencing, analysis and synthesis
    of auditory stimuli, which significantly affects one or more of the following
    areas of language development: phonology/articulation, morphology, syntax,
    semantics, or pragmatics.

B. CRITERIA: Identification of an "Auditory Processing Disorder" will be
    based upon a numerical point system with a maximum point potential of 94
    points. The sum of an individual candidate's points will be interpreted in the
    following manner:

Total Points	*Interpretations*
0 – 58	Does not qualify.
59 – 94	Qualifies as having an Auditory Processing Disorder.

C. POINTS: Based upon evidence of the following, prospective candidates will receive points in the following manner:

Data Indicates   *Points*

*1. Speech and Language Assessment: 29

a. Using more than one assessment procedure, the pupil scores at least 1.5 S.D. below the mean, or below the 7th percentile, or received an age equivalent score 2 years below his/ her C.A. or developmental age on tests in one or more of the following areas of language development:

(1) Morphology.

(2) Syntax.

(3) Semantics.

(4) Pragmatics.

(5) Articulation/Phonology.

b. The pupil displays inappropriate or inadequate usage of expressive language as measured on a representative spontaneous language sample of a minimum of 50 utterances.

(1) Special Day Class - Communicatively Handicapped: Must have a minimum of 50 utterances that are analyzed:

(a) Standardized: DSS, Tyack, MLU, etc.

(b) Nonstandardized: Bloom-Lahey, checklist, etc.

(2) Special Day Class - Other: Language sample may be given when deemed appropriate.

(3) Designated Instructional Service: Language sample of 10 - 25 utterances that indicate type of disorder.

2. Auditory Processing: A disability, not due to deficits in acuity,   20
that involves attending, localization, discrimination, memory, sequencing, analysis and synthesis of auditory stimuli, which significantly affects one or more of the following: phonology, morphology, syntax, semantics, or pragmatics.

a. The child scores 1.5 S.D. below the mean, or below the 7th percentile, or an age equivalent score 2 years below his/her C.A. or developmental age on:

(1) Standardized measurements: ITPA, DTLA, TOLD-P, Fullerton, Token, Flowers-Costello, Auditory Pointing Test, VADS, Goldman-Fristoe-Woodcock, Auditory Integrative Abilities, Boston, etc.

(2) Nonstandardized measurements: TAAS, LAC, Wepman, T-D Discrimination, Birch-Belmont, Oliphant, etc.

3. *Potential:* A discrepancy exists between a child's potential and   13
his language disorder as measured by:

---

*Required for identification.

Data Indicates   *Points*

    a. A psychologist on an approved assessment instrument (WISC-R, LIPS, SOMPA, Merril-Palmer, Kaufman, etc.).

    b. A specialist when deemed appropriate using an approved instrument (Ordinal Scales, Uzgiris-Hunt, etc.).

*4. *Educational Performance-Academic:* The child's auditory processing disorder adversely affects academic performance as measured by one or more of the following: **10**

    a. Achievement tests.

    b. Academic tests.

    c. Report cards.

    d. Teacher observation.

  5. *Self-Awareness:* The child indicates awareness of his/her auditory processing disorder by modifying his/her communication interactions as determined by: **6**

    a. Teacher or specialist observation.

    b. Self-referral.

  6. *Staff Concerns:* The auditory processing disorder interferes with communication and adversely affects teacher-child-peer relationships as evidenced by: **6**

    a. Staff observation.

    b. Specialist observation.

  7. *Educational Performance-Social:* The child's auditory processing disorder adversely affects how the child relates in the school environment (classroom, playground, lunch, etc.) with his/her teachers and/or peers and may be measured by: **4**

    a. Observation.

    b. Teacher interview.

    c. Data counts.

  8. *Parental Concern:* The parent expresses feelings about the child's auditory processing disorder indicating that the disorder appears to affect the parent-child relationship.   **4**

  9. *Home Environment:* The child's home environment displays causitive or contributing factors as measured by: **2**

    a. Parent questionnaires.

    b. Parent interview.

VII. DEFINITIONS

A. *Articulation/Phonology*
The production of phonemes and clusters in words or connected speech.

B. *Auditory Processing*
The ability to attend, localize, discriminate, recall, sequence, analyze, and synthesize auditory stimuli.

*Required for identification.

C. *Contrastive Analysis*
The comparison of testing done in Language 1 to the testing done in Language 2.

D. *Cultural Factors*
Social behaviors that are unique to certain ethnic groups which appear to affect a child's educational performance and/or his/her teacher-child-peer relationships.

E. *Developmental History-Language*
The acquisition of language milestones obtained by parent interview or parent questionnaire.

F. *Developmental History-Physical*
The acquisition of physical milestones as obtained by parent interview or parent questionnaire.

G. *Educational Performance-Academic*
Academic performance as measured by achievement tests, academic tests, report cards and teacher observations.

H. *Educational Performance-Social*
How the child relates in the school environment (classroom, playground, lunch, etc.) with his/her teachers and/or peers may be measured by observation or parent/teacher interview.

I. *Home Environment*
The child's home environment displays causitive or contributing factors as measured by parent questionnaires or parent interview.

J. *Interventions*
Educational techniques, strategies, programs, etc., that have been tried prior to Special Education referral.

K. *Morphology*
The appropriate use of word forms (i.e., pluralization, past tense, comparatives, superlatives, etc.).

L. *Observations*
Procedure of viewing a child in various environments (home, playground, classroom) or relationships (adult-child-peer) to obtain diagnostic information.

M. *Parental Concern*
The parent expresses feelings about the child's speech and/or language disorder indicating that the disorder appears to affect the parent-child relationship.

N. *Potential*
The measurement of a child's cognitive abilities/development.

O. *Previous Educational Experience*
Background and history of prior school placements and experience. As obtained from school records, parent interview, etc.

P. *Pragmatics*
The practical and appropriate use of language in a communicative context; the social rules of language.

Q. *Self-Awareness*
The child indicates awareness of his/her speech and/or language disorder by modifying his/her communication interactions as determined by observation by teacher or specialist or self-referral.

R. *Semantics*
The understanding of words and word relationships.

S. *Staff Concerns*
   The speech and/or language disorder interferes with communication and adversely affects teacher-child-peer relationships as evidenced by staff observation or specialist observation.

T. *Syntax*
   The appropriate word order in sentences.

REFERENCES

Ad Hoc Committee on Extension of Audiological Services in the Schools, American Speech-Language-Hearing Association. "Audiology Services in the Schools Position Statement." *Asha*, 25, no. 5 (May 1983), 53–60.

AINSWORTH, STANLEY. "The Speech Clinician in Public Schools: 'Participant' or 'Separatist'?" *Asha*, 7, no. 12 (December 1965), 495–503.

ALPINER, JEROME, JOHN A. OGDEN, and JAMES E. WIGGINS. "The Utilization of Supportive Personnel in Speech Correction in the Public Schools: A Pilot Project," *Asha*, 12, no. 12 (December 1970), 599–604.

American Speech-Language-Hearing Association. "Audiologic Services in the Schools." *Asha*, 25, no. 5 (1983), 53–60.

American Speech-Language-Hearing Association Professional Services Board. *Standards and Guidelines for Comprehensive Language, Speech, and Hearing Programs in Schools*. Washington, D.C.: American Speech-Language-Hearing Association, 1973–74.

ANDERSON, JEAN L., editor. *Conference on Training in the Supervisory Process in Speech-Language Pathology and Audiology*. Bloomington, Indiana: Indiana University, 1980.

——. *Conference on Supervision of Speech and Hearing Programs in Schools*. Bloomington, Ind.: Indiana University Publications, 1970.

——. *Handbook for Supervisors of School Practicum in Speech, Hearing, and Language*. Bloomington, Ind.: Indiana University Publications, 1972.

BACKUS, OLLIE. "The Use of Group Structure in Speech Therapy." *Journal of Speech and Hearing Disorders*, 17, no. 2 (June 1952), 116–22.

BACKUS, OLLIE, and RUTH COFFMAN. "Group Therapy with Preschool Children Having Cerebral Palsy." *Journal of Speech and Hearing Disorders,* 18, vol. 4 (December 1953), 350–54.

BANKSON, NICHOLAS W. *Bankson Language Screening Test.* Baltimore, Md.: University Park Press, 1978.

BARKER, KENNETH, ROBERT BALDES, PHILLIP JENKINSON, KENYON WILSON, and JOSEPH FREILINGER. "Iowa's Severity Rating Scales for Communication Disabilities." *Language Speech and Hearing Services in Schools,* 13, no. 3 (July 1982), 156–62.

BARNES, KAROLDENE, and PATRICIA PINES. "Assessing and Improving Services to the Handicapped." *Asha,* 24, no. 8 (August 1982), 555–59.

BARRETT, MARK D., and JOHN W. WELSH. "Predictive Articulation Screening." *Language, Speech and Hearing Services in Schools.* 6, no. 2 (April 1975), 91–95.

BEALL, ADELAIDE. *Communication Disorders Program for Adolescents and Adults.* Scottsdale, Ga.: De Kalb County School System, Dept. of Special Education, 1977.

BEASLEY, JANE. "Development of Social Skills as an Instrument in Speech Therapy." *Journal of Speech and Hearing Disorders,* 16, no. 3 (September 1951), pp. 241–45.

BENDER, RUTH E. *The Conquest of Deafness.* Cleveland, Ohio: The Press of Western Reserve University, 1960.

BERG, FREDERICK S. *Educational Audiology: Hearing and Speech Management.* New York: Grune and Stratton, 1976.

BERGMAN, MOE. "Screening the Hearing of Preschool Children." *Maico Audiological Library Series,* III, report 4 (1964), Maico Electronics, Inc.

BLOSSER, JEAN and ROBERTA DePOMPEI. "How to Encourage School Administrators to Support Our Changing Roles." Presentation at the American Speech-Language-Hearing Association Convention, San Francisco, November 1984.

BRAUNSTEIN, MURIEL SUE. "Communication Aide: A Pilot Project." *Language, Speech and Hearing Services in Schools,* 3, no. 3 (July 1972), 32–35.

BRETT, RICHARD J. "The Public School Caucus: A Progress Report." *Language, Speech and Hearing Services in Schools,* 7, no. 3 (July 1976), 197–98.

BRYNGELSON, BRYNG, and E. GLASPEY. *Speech Improvement Cards.* Chicago: Scott, Foresman & Company, 1941.

BULLETT, MARYANN S. "Certification Requirements for Public School Speech-Language Pathologists in the United States." *Language, Speech and Hearing Services in Schools,* 16, no. 2 (April 1985), 124–28.

CACCAMO, JAMES M. "Accountability—A Matter of Ethics?" *Asha,* 15, no. 8 (August 1973), 411–12.

CARROW, ELIZABETH. *Screening Test for Auditory Comprehension of Language; Test Manual.* Austin, Tex.: Urban Research Group, 1973.

Child Services Review System (CSRS). Rockville, Md.: American Speech-Language-Hearing Association, 1982.

CHOMSKY, NOAM. *Syntactic Structures.* The Hague: Mouton, 1957.

CLARK, JOHN GREER. *Audiology for the School Speech-Language Clinician.* Springfield, Ill.: Charles C. Thomas, Publisher, 1980.

CODY, ROBERT C. "Hearing Screening in the Schools: The Tympano-Audiometric Approach." Paper presented at the West Virginia Speech and Hearing Association Convention, Charleston, April 1976.

Committee On Audiologic Evaluation, American Speech-Language-Hearing Association. "Guidelines for Identification Audiometry." *Asha,* 27, no. 5 (May 1985), 49–52.

Committee on Definitions of Public School Speech and Hearing Services, American Speech and Hearing Association. "Services and Functions of Speech and Hearing Specialists in Public Schools." *Asha,* 4, no. 4 (April 1962), 99–100

Committee on Language Learning Disabilities, American Speech-Language-Hearing Association. "Position Statement on Language Learning Disorders." *Asha,* 24, no. 11 (November 1982), 937–44.

Committee on Language, Speech and Hearing Services in the Schools, American Speech-Language-Hearing Association. "Guidelines for Caseload Size for Speech-Language Services in the Schools." *Asha,* 26, no. 4 (April 1984), 53–58.

Committee on Language, Speech, and Hearing Services in the Schools, American Speech-Language-Hearing Association. "Definitions of Communicative Disorders and Variations." *Asha,* 24, no. 11 (November 1982), 949–50.

Committee on Legislation, American Speech and Hearing Association. "The Need for Adequately Trained Speech Pathologists and Audiologists." *Asha,* 1, no. 4 (December 1959), 138.

Committee on the Prevention of Speech, Language and Hearing Problems, American Speech-Language-Hearing Association. "Prevention of Speech, Language and Hearing Problems Report." *Asha,* 24, no. 6 (June 1982), 425–31.

Committee on Speech and Hearing Services in Schools, American Speech and Hearing Association. "Recommendations for Housing of Speech Services in Schools." *Asha,* 11, no. 4 (April 1969), 181–82.

Committee on Speech and Hearing Services in Schools, American Speech and Hearing Association. "The Speech Clinician's Role in the Public School." *Asha,* 6, no. 6 (June 1964), 189–91.

Committee on the Status of Racial Minorities, American Speech-Language-Hearing Association. "Clinical Management of Communicatively Handicapped Minority Language Populations." *Asha,* 27, no. 6 (June 1985). 29–32.

Committee on the Status of Racial Minorities, American Speech-Language-Hearing Association. "Social Dialects Position Paper." *Asha,* 25, no. 9 (September 1983) 23–24.

Committee on Supportive Personnel, American Speech-Language-Hearing Association. "Guidelines for the Employment and Utilization of Supportive Personnel." *Asha,* 23, no. 3 (March 1981), 165–69.

Committee on Supportive Personnel, American Speech and Hearing Association. "Guidelines on the Role and Training and Supervision of the Communication Aide." *Asha,* 12, no. 2 (February 1970), 78–80.

Comprehensive Assessment and Service Evaluation Information System (CASE). Rockville, Md.: American Speech-Language-Hearing Association, 1976.

CONLON, SARA, KATHLEEN PENDERGAST, SHIRLEY JONES, VAUGHN WEBER. "Task Force Report on School Speech, Hearing and Language Screening Procedures." Language, Speech and Hearing Services in Schools, 4, no. 3 (July 1973), 109–19.

CONNELL, PHIL J., JOSEPH E. SPRADLIN, and LEIJA V. MCREYNOLDS. "Some Suggested Criterial for Evaluation of Language Programs." *Journal of Speech and Hearing Disorders,* 42, no. 4 (November 1977), 563–67.

COSTELLO, JANIS, and JUDITH SCHOEN. "The Effectiveness of Paraprofessionals and a Speech Clinician as Agents of Articulation Intervention Using Programmed Instruction." *Language, Speech and Hearing Services in Schools,* 9, no. 2 (April 1978), 118–28.

COVENTRY, W. F., and IRVING BURSTINER. *Management: A Basic Handbook.* Englewood Cliffs, N.J.: Prentice-Hall, Inc., 1977.

Council for Exceptional Children Policies Commission. "Policy Statements: Call for Response. Basic Commitments and Responsibilities to Exceptional Children."*Exceptional Children,* 37, no. 6 (February 1971), 421–23.

CRABTREE, MARGARET, and ELIZABETH PETERSON. "The Speech Pathologist as a Resource Teacher for Language/Learning Disabilities." *Language, Speech and Hearing Services in Schools,* 5, no. 4 (October 1974), 194–97.

CURRY, E. THAYER. "The Efficiency of Teacher Referrals in a School Hearing Testing Program." *Journal of Speech and Hearing Disorders,* 15, no. 3 (September 1950), 211–14.

DIEHL, CHARLES F., and CHARLES D. STINNETT. "Efficiency of Teacher Referrals in a School Speech Testing Program." *Journal of Speech and Hearing Disorders,* 24, no. 1 (February 1959), 34–36.

DONNELLY, CAROLE A. "Changing Role of the Speech-Language Pathologist in the Public Schools," University of Cincinnati, Ohio. Presentation at the American Speech-Language-Hearing Association Convention, San Francisco, 1984.

DOPHEIDE, WILLIAM R., and JANE R. DALLINGER. "Improving Remedial Speech and Language Services Through Clinician-Teacher In-Service Interaction." *Language, Speech and Hearing Services in Schools,* 6, no. 4 (October 1975), 196–205.

DUBLINSKE, STAN. "Special Reports: PL 94-142: Developing the Individualized Education Program (IEP)." *Asha,* 20, no. 5 (May 1978), 393–97.

———. "Collective Bargaining: What Can It Do for You?" *Asha,* 28, no. 5 (May 1986), 31–34.

DUBLINSKE, STAN, and WILLIAM C. HEALEY. "PL 94-142: Questions and Answers for the Speech-Language Pathologist and Audiologist." *Asha,* 20, no. 3 (March 1978), 188–205.

DUNN, HARRIET M. "A Speech and Hearing Program for Children in a Rural Area." *Journal of Speech and Hearing Disorders,* 14 (June 1949), 166–70.

Educational Technology Committee, American Speech-Language-Hearing Association. "Software Review Checklist." *Asha,* 27, no. 3 (March 1985), 71.

EHREN, TOM C., RHONDA S. WORK, and LANDIS STETLER. "Program Quality and Costs: A Study in the Schools." Broward County Schools, Ft. Lauderdale and Department of Education, Tallahassee, Florida. Presentation at the American Speech-Language-Hearing Association Convention, San Francisco, 1984.

FAIRBANKS, GRANT. *Voice and Articulation Drillbook,* 2nd ed. New York: Harper & Row, Publishers, 1960.

FINN, MARILYN S., and JUDITH B. GARDNER. "Teacher Interview—A Better Speech-Language Screening Technique," Area Education Agency AEA XI, Ankeny, Iowa, and Des Moines Public Schools. Presentation at the American Speech-Language-Hearing Association Convention, San Francisco, 1984.

FISHER, LEE J. "An Open Letter to ASHA Members Employed in the Schools." *Language, Speech and Hearing Services in Schools,* 8, no. 2 (April 1977), 72–75.

FLAHERTY, CAROL. "Cost-Benefit Analysis of Computer-Based Instruction of School Speech Services." Los Angeles Unified School District, California. Presentation at the American Speech-Language-Hearing Association. Convention, San Francisco, 1984.

FLOWER, RICHARD M. *Delivery of Speech-Language Pathology and Audiology Services.* Baltimore/London: Williams and Wilkins, 1984.

FLUHARTY, NANCY B. *Fluharty Speech-Language Screening Test.* Allen, Texas: DLM-Teaching Resources, 1978.

FREEMAN, GERALD G. "The Speech Clinician—as a Consultant." *Clinician Speech in the Schools,* 1st ed. Ed. Roland J. Van Hattum. Springfield, Ill.: Charles C Thomas, Publishers, 1969.

———. *Speech and Language Services and the Classroom Teacher.* Reston, Va.: The Council for Exceptional Children, 1977.

FREEMAN, GERALD G. and JEAN LUKENS. "A Speech and Language Program for Educable Mentally Retarded Children." *Journal of Speech and Hearing Disorders,* 27, no. 3 (August 1962), 285–87.

FUJIKI, MARTIN, and BONNIE BRINTON. "Supplementing Language Therapy: Working with the Classroom Teacher." *Language Speech and Hearing Services in Schools,* 15, no 2 (April 1984), 98–109.

GALLOWAY, HERBERT F., and C. MILTON BLUE. "Paraprofessionals in Articulation Therapy." *Language, Speech and Hearing Services in Schools,* 6, no. 3 (July 1975), 125–30.

GARRARD, KAY R. "The Changing Role of Speech and Hearing Professionals in Public Education." *Asha,* 21, no. 2 (February 1979), 91–98.

GARRISON, GERALDINE, et al. "Speech Improvement." *Journal of Speech and Hearing Disorders.* Monograph Supplement 8 (June 1961), p. 80.

GELFAUD, DOLORES, and HELEN HORWITZ-DANZINGER. "Teacher Response Questionnaire: Implications for Inservice Training Program." South Euclid-Lyndhurst City Schools, Ohio. Presentation at the American Speech-Language-Hearing Association Convention, San Francisco, 1984.

GOLDMAN, R., and M. FRISTOE. *Goldman-Fristoe Test for Articulation.* Circle Pines, Minn.: American Guidance Service, Inc., 1971.

GROSSMAN, DONNA B. "Programs and Peril: A Report on the Status of State Licensure." *Asha,* 21, no. 12 (December 1979). 1004–9.

GRUENEWALD, LEE J., and SARA A. POLLAK. "The Speech Clinician's Role in Auditory Learning and Reading Readiness." *Language, Speech and Hearing Services in Schools,* 4, no. 3 (July 1973), 120–26.

HAINES, HAROLD H. "Trends in Public School Therapy." *Asha,* 7, no. 6 (June 1965), 166–70.

HARRIS, GAIL. "Considerations in Assessing English Language Performance of Native American Children." *Topics in Language Disorders,* 5, no. 4 (September 1985).

HEALEY, WILLIAM C. "Notes from the Associate Secretary for School Affairs, Task Force Report on Data Collection and Information Systems." *Language, Speech and Hearing Services in Schools,* 4, no. 2 (April 1973), 57–65.

HEALEY, WILLIAM C., et al. *The Prevalence of Communication Disorders: A Review of the Literature.* Rockville, Md.: American Speech-Language-Hearing Association, Final Report, 1981.

HEOB, WILLIAM, RITA CARTER, JULIA A. JOCHUM, LAWRENCE DUTCHER. "Computer Application in a School Hearing Screening Program." Mesa, Arizona Public Schools. Presentation at the American Speech-Language-Hearing Association Convention, San Francisco, 1984.

HESS, RHODA. "Guidelines for a Cooperating Clinician in Working with a Student Clinician in the Schools." *Ohio Journal of Speech and Hearing,* 11, no. 2 (Spring 1976), 83–89.

HOSEA, KATHY. "Exemplary Speech Pathology Programs in Secondary Schools." Presentation at American Speech and Hearing Association Convention, Chicago, 1977.

HOWERTON, GERALD E. "What Can Be Done About Substandard Space for Speech Correction Programs." *Language, Speech and Hearing Services in Schools,* 4, no. 2 (April 1973), 95–96.

HULL, F. M., et al. *National Speech and Hearing Survey Interim Report.* (Project No. 50978.) Washington, D.C.: Department of Health, Education, and Welfare, Office of Education, Bureau of Education for the Handicapped, 1969.

HYMAN, CARL S. "Computer Usage in the Speech-Language-Hearing Profession." *Asha,* 27, no. 11 (November 1985), 25.

———. "PL 94-142 in Review." *Asha,* 8, no. 28 (August 1985), 37.

IGLESIAS, AQUILES. "The Different Elephant." *Asha,* 27, no. 6 (June 1985), 41–42.

IRWIN, RUTH BECKEY. "Speech and Hearing Therapy in the Public Schools of Ohio." *Journal of Speech and Hearing Disorders,* 14, no. 1 (March 1949), 63–68.

———. "Speech Therapy in the Public Schools: State Legislation and Certification." *Journal of Speech and Hearing Disorders,* 24, no. 2 (May 1959), 127.

JELINEK, JANIS A. "A Pilot Program for Training and Utilization of Paraprofessionals in Pre-Schools." *Language, Speech and Hearing Services in Schools,* 7, no. 2 (April 1976), 119–23.

JOHNS, ELIZABETH LAMBERT. "Teacher Organizations and the School Clinician." *Language, Speech and Hearing Services in Schools,* 5, no. 3 (July 1974), 171–73.

JOHNSON, ANN, MARIE PRUDHOMME, and ELAINE ROGERO. "Competency-Based Objectives for the Student Teaching Experience." *Language Speech and Hearing Services in Schools,* 13, no. 3 (July 1982), 187–96.

JOHNSON, WENDELL. *Children with Speech and Hearing Impairment: Preparing to Work with Them in the Schools.* Washington, D.C.: U.S. Dept. of Health, Education and Welfare, Bulletin No. 5, 1959.

JONES, SHIRLEY A. and WILLIAM C. HEALEY. *Essentials of Program Planning, Development, Management, Evaluation: A Manual for School Speech, Hearing and Language Programs.* Washington, D.C.: American Speech and Hearing Association, 1973.

———. *Project UPGRADE: Model Regulations for School Language, Speech and Hearing Programs and Services.* Washington, D.C.: American Speech and Hearing Association, 1973.

———. *Project UPGRADE: Guidelines for Evaluating State Education Laws and Regulations.* Washington, D.C.: American Speech and Hearing Association, 1975.

KARR, SUSAN, and JERRY PUNCH. "PL 94-142 State Child Counts. *Asha,* 26, no. 2 (February 1984), 33.

KING, RELLA, CYNTHIA JONES, and ELAINE LASKY. "In Retrospect: A Fifteen-Year Follow-Up Report of Speech-Language-Disordered Children." *Language Speech and Hearing Services in Schools,* 13, no. 1 (January 1982), 24–32.

KNIGHT, HELEN SULLIVAN. "Functions of the School Clinician." *Speech and Hearing Services in Schools,* no. 3 (1970), 12–23.

KODMAN, FRANK, JR. "Identification of Hearing Loss by the Classroom Teacher." *Laryngoscope.* 66, (August 1950), 1346–49.

KROLL, JOANN. *Job Search: A Guide for Success in the Job Market.* Bowling Green, Ohio: Bowling Green State University, 1985.

KRUEGER, BEVERLY. "Computerized Reporting in a Public School Program." *Language Speech and Hearing Services in Schools,* 16, no. 2 (April 1985), 135–39.

LYNCH, JOHN. "Operation: Moving Ahead." *Language, Speech and Hearing Services in Schools,* 3, no. 4 (October 1972), 82–87.

MACLEARIE, ELIZABETH, and F. P. GROSS. *Experimental Programs for Intensive Cycle Scheduling of Speech and Hearing Therapy Classes.* Columbus: Ohio Department of Education, 1966.

MADARAS, ROBERTA and JEAN WOZNIAK. "A Speech, Hearing, and Language Program in a Joint Vocational School." Unpublished article, 1978, and correspondence with author.

McCANDLESS, G. A. "Screening for Middle Ear Disease on the Wind River Indian Reservation." *Hearing Instruments* (April 1975), pp. 19–20.

MCDONALD, EUGENE. *A Deep Test of Articulation.* Pittsburg: Stanwix House, 1964.

MARTIN, EDWIN W. "The Right to Education: Issues Facing the Speech and Hearing Profession." *Asha,* 17, no. 6 (June 1975), 384–87.

MATTHEWS, ELIZABETH C., KATHLEEN A. MOORE, and AMY HARRIS. "Comparison of Screening Versus Teacher Referral in the Secondary Schools," Phoenix Union

High School District, Arizona. Presentation at the American Speech-Language-Hearing Association Convention, San Francisco, 1984.

MECHAM, MERLIN, J. L. JEX, and J. D. JONES. *Utah Test of Language Development,* rev. ed. Salt Lake City, Utah: Communication Research Associates, 1978.

MELNICK, WILLIAM, ELDON L. EAGLES, and HERBERT S. LEVINE. "Evaluation of a Recommended Program of Identification Audiometry with School-Age Children." *Journal of Speech and Hearing Disorders,* 29, no. 1 (February 1964), 3–13.

MILISEN, ROBERT. "The Incidence of Speech Disorders." *Handbook of Speech Pathology and Audiology.* Ed. Lee Edward Travis. Englewood Cliffs, N.J.: Prentice-Hall, Inc., 1971.

MONCUR, J. P., ed. *Institute on the Utilization of Supportive Personnel in School Speech and Hearing Programs.* Washington, D.C.: American Speech and Hearing Association, 1967.

MOORE, G. PAUL, and DOROTHY KESTER. "Historical Notes on Speech Correction in the Preassociation Era." *Journal of Speech and Hearing Disorders,* 18, no. 1 (March 1953), 48–53.

MOWRER, DONALD E. "Accountability and Speech Therapy in the Public Schools." *Asha,* 14, no. 3 (March 1972), 111–15.

MUMA, JOHN. *Language Handbook: Concepts, Assessment, Intervention.* Englewood Cliffs, N.J.: Prentice-Hall, Inc., 1978.

NAVARRO, M. RICHARD, and DAVID A. KLODD. "Impedance Audiometry for the School Clinician." *Language, Speech and Hearing Services in Schools,* 9, no. 1 (January 1978), 50–56.

NEAL, W. R., JR. "Speech Pathology Services in the Secondary Schools." *Language, Speech and Hearing Services in Schools,* 7, no. 1 (January 1976), 6–16.

NEIDECKER, ELIZABETH A. "Supervision in the School Clinician Practicum Situation: Roles and Responsibilities." *Ohio Journal of Speech and Hearing,* 10, no. 2 (Spring 1976), 83–89.

NIGRO, LOUIS J. *Carteret Public Schools Speech and Hearing Services.* Wooster, Ohio: The Gerstenslager Company.

NILSON, HOLLY, and CARL R. SCHNEIDERMAN. "Classroom Program for the Prevention of Vocal Abuse and Hoarseness in Elementary School Children." *Language, Speech and Hearing Services in Schools,* 14, no 2 (April 1983), 121–27.

NODAR, RICHARD H. "Teacher Identification of Elementary School Children with Hearing Loss." *Language, Speech and Hearing Services in Schools,* 9, no. 1 (January 1978), 24–28.

NORTHCOTT, WINIFRED H. "The Hearing-Impaired Child: A Speech Clinician as an Interdisciplinary Team Member." *Language, Speech and Hearing Services in Schools,* 3, no. 2 (April 1972), 7–19.

O'CONNOR, LISA, and PATRICIA ELDREDGE. *Communication Disorders in Adolescence.* Springfield, Ill.: Charles C Thomas, Publisher, 1981.

Ohio School Speech and Hearing Services. Worthington, Ohio: Ohio Division of Special Education, 1972.

Operation and Management Plan for the Northwest Ohio Special Education Regional Resource Center. Revised August 1, 1983. Northwest Ohio Special Education Regional Resource Center, 10142 Dowling Road, Route 2, Bowling Green, Ohio 43402

O'TOOLE, THOMAS J. "Accountability and the Clinician in the Schools." *Speech and Hearing Service in Schools,* no. 3 (1971), 24–25.

O'TOOLE, THOMAS, and ELINOR ZASLOW. "Public School Speech and Hearing Programs: Things Are Changing." *Asha,* 11, no. 11 (November 1969), 499–501.

PADEN, ELAINE PAGEL. *A History of the American Speech and Hearing Association 1925-1958.* Washington, D.C.: American Speech and Hearing Association, 1970.

PARKER, BARBARA L. "The Speech and Language Clinician on a Learning Center Team." *Language, Speech and Hearing Services in Schools,* 3, no. 3 (July 1972), 18-23.

PARKER, STEVE, and J. MONTAGUE. "Information Services for School Speech-Language Pathologists and Educational Audiologists." *Language, Speech and Hearing Services in Schools,* 9, no. 2 (April 1978), 103-8.

PENDERGAST, KATHLEEN, STANLEY DICKEY, JOHN SELMAR, and ANTON SODER. *Photo Articulation Test.* Danville, Ill.: The Interstate Printers and Publishers, 1966.

PHELPS, RICHARD A., and ROY A. KOENIGSKNECHT. "Attitudes of Classroom Teachers, Learning Disabilities Specialists, and School Principals Toward Speech and Language Programs in Public Elementary Schools." *Language, Speech and Hearing Services in Schools,* 8, no. 1 (January 1977), 33-42.

PHILLIPS, PHYLLIS. *Speech and Hearing Problems in the Classroom.* Lincoln, Nebraska: Cliff Notes, Inc., 1975.

———. "Variables Affecting Classroom Teachers' Understanding of Speech Disorders." *Language, Speech and Hearing Services in Schools,* 8, no. 3 (July 1976), 142-49.

PICKERING, MARISUE, and WILLIAM R. DOPHEIDE. "Training Aides to Screen Children for Speech and Language Problems." *Language, Speech and Hearing Services in Schools,* 7, no. 4 (October 1976), 236-41.

PRAHL, HARRIET M., and EUGENE B. COOPER. "Accuracy of Teacher Referrals of Speech-Handicapped School Children." *Asha,* 6, no. 10 (October 1964), Convention Abstracts, p. 392.

PRATHER, ELISABETH M., ANN BRENNER, and KAREN HUGHES. "A Mini-Screening Test for Adolescents." *Language, Speech and Hearing Services in Schools,* 12, no. 2 (April 1981), 67-73.

PTACEK, PAUL. "Supportive Personnel as an Extension of the Professional Worker's Nervous System." *Asha,* no. 9 (September 1967), 403-5.

RAIA, ANTHONY P. *Managing By Objectives.* Glenview, Illinois: Scott, Foresman & Company, 1974.

RAPH, JUNE BEASLEY. "Determinants of Motivation in Speech Therapy." *Journal of Speech and Hearing Disorders,* 25, no. 1 (February 1960).

REBORE, RONALD W., SR., *A Handbook for School Board Members.* Englewood Cliffs, New Jersey: Prentice-Hall, Inc., 1984.

REES, NORMA S. "The Speech Pathologist and the Reading Process." *Asha,* 16, no. 5 (May 1974), 258.

REYNOLDS, MAYNARD C., and SYLVIA W. ROSEN. "Special Education: Past, Present, and Future." *The Educational Forum,* 40, no. 4 (May 1976), 551-62.

RODGERS, WILLIAM C. *Picture Articulation and Language Screening Test.* Salt Lake City, Utah: Word-Making Productions, 1976.

ROE VIVIAN I., et al. "Clinical Practice: Diagnosis and Measurement." *Journal of Speech and Hearing Disorders, Monograph Supplement* 8 (June 1961), 51-57.

Rules for the Education of Handicapped Children. Worthington: Ohio Department of Education, Division of Special Education, 1982.

ROSS, MARK, with DIANE BRACKETT and ANTONIA MAXON. *Hard of Hearing Children in Regular Schools.* Englewood Cliffs, N.J.: Prentice-Hall, Inc., 1982.

RUSHAKOFF, GARY E., and LINDA J. LOMBARDINO. "Microcomputer Applications." *Asha,* 26, no. 6 (June 1984), 27-31.

SANDERS, DEREK A. *Auditory Perception of Speech: An Introduction to Principles and Problems.* Englewood Cliffs, N.J.: Prentice-Hall, Inc., 1977.

SCALERO, ANGELA M., and CONSTANCE ESKENAZI. "The Use of Supportive Personnel in a Public School Speech and Hearing Program." *Language, Speech and Hearing Services in Schools,* 7, no. 3 (July 1976), 150–58.

SCARVEL, LUCIA D. "Standardizing Criteria for Evaluating Physical Facilities and Organizational Patterns of Speech, Language and Hearing Programs." *The Journal of the Pennsylvania Speech and Hearing Association,* 10, no. 2 (June 1977), 17–19.

SCHOOLFIELD, LUCILLE. *Better Speech and Better Reading.* Magnolia, Mass.: The Expression Co., 1937.

SCHUBERT, GEORGE W. *Introduction to Clinical Supervision in Speech Pathology.* St. Louis, Mo.: Warren H. Green, Inc., 1978.

SHERR, RICHARD. "Meeting to Develop the Individualized Education Program." *A Primer on Individualized Education Programs for Handicapped Children.* Ed. Scottie Torres. Reston, Va.: The Foundation for Exceptional Children, 1977.

SIMON, CHARLANN S. "Cooperative Communication Programming: A Partnership Between the Learning Disabilities Teacher and the Speech-Language Pathologist." *Language, Speech and Hearing in Schools,* 8, no. 3 (July 1977), 188–98.

SILBAR, JEAN C., and KEVIN A. KONARSKA. "Reports With Ease: Word Processing for Fast and Easy Reports." Lincoln School, Grand Rapids, Michigan. Presentation at the American Speech-Language-Hearing Association Convention, San Francisco, 1984.

SKINNER B. F. *Verbal Behavior.* New York: Appleton-Century-Crofts, 1957.

SOMMERS, RONALD K. "Case Finding, Case Selection, Case Load." *Clinical Speech in the Schools.* Ed. Rolland Van Hattum. Springfield, Ill.: Charles C Thomas, Publisher, 1969.

STARK, JOEL. "Reading Failure: A Language-Based Problem." *Asha,* 17, no. 12 (December 1975), 832–34.

STEER, MACK D., and HAZEL G. DREXLER. "Predicting Later Articulation Abilities from Kindergarten Tests." *Journal of Speech and Hearing Disorders,* 25, no. 4 (November 1960), pp. 391–97.

STEER, MACK D., et al. "Public School Speech and Hearing Services. A Special Report Prepared with Support of the United States Office of Education and Purdue University." *Journal of Speech and Hearing Disorders, Monograph Supplement 8.* Washington, D.C.: U.S. Office of Education Cooperative Research Project No. 649 (8191), July 1961.

STEPHENS, I. *The Stephens Oral Language Screening Test.* Peninsula, Ohio: Interim Publishers, 1977.

STIMSON, ELIZABETH. "Groping or Grouping: How to Reach the Individual." *Kappa Delta Pi Record,* 16, no. 2 (December 1979), 51–53.

STRONG, BEVERLY. "Public School Speech Technicians in Minnesota." *Language, Speech and Hearing Services in Schools,* 3, no. 1 (January 1972), 53–56.

SWIFT, WALTER B. "How to Begin Speech Correction in the Public Schools." *Language Speech and Hearing Services in Schools,* 3, no. 2 (April 1972), 51–56.

TASK FORCE REPORT ON TRADITIONAL SCHEDULING PROCEDURES IN SCHOOLS." *Language, Speech and Hearing Services in Schools,* 4, no. 3 (July 1973), 100–9.

TAYLOR, JOYCE S. "Public School Speech-Language Certification Standards: Are They Standard?" *Asha,* 22, no. 3 (March 1980), 159–65.

TEMPLIN, MILDRED, and FREDERIC DARLEY. *Templin-Darley Tests of Articulation,* 2nd ed. Iowa City, Iowa: Bureau of Educational Research and Services, 1969.

TOWNSEND, DEBORAH. "Audiology in the Educational Setting." *Topics in Childhood Communication Disorders* 1 (December 1982), 12–14.

UNITED STATES DEPARTMENT OF LABOR: *Dictionary of Occupational Titles.* Washington DC, United States Government Printing Office, 1979.

VAN RIPEN, CHARLES, and ROBERT L. ERICKSON. *Predictive Screening Test of Artic-ulation,* 3rd ed. Kalamazoo: Continuing Education Office, Western Michigan University, 1973.

WALL, LIDA, GUY NAPLES, KAREN BUHRER, and CATHY CAPODANNO. "A Survey of Audiological Services Within the School System." *Asha,* 27, no. 1 (January 1985), 31–34.

WIIG, ELIZABETH H. and ELEANOR M. SEMEL. *Language Disabilities in Children and Adolescents.* Columbus, Ohio: Charles E. Merrill Publishing Company, 1976.

WILSON-VLOTMAN, ANN L., and JAMES C. BLAIR. "Educational Audiologists Working in Regular Schools: Practices, Problems and Directions." Utah State University, Logan, Utah. Presentation at the American Speech-Language-Hearing Associ-ation Convention, San Francisco, 1984.

WING, DOUGLAS M. "A Data Recording Form for Case Management and Account-ability." *Language, Speech and Hearing Services in Schools,* 6, no. 1 (January 1975), 38–40.

WORK, RHONDA S. "The Therapy Program." In *Speech-Language Programming in the Schools,* 2nd ed. Ed. R. J. Van Hattum. Springfield, Ill.: Charles C Thomas, Publisher, 1982.

WORK, RHONDA S., E. C. HUTCHINSON, W. C. HEALEY, R. K. SOMMERS, and E. I. STEVENS. "Accountability in a School Speech and Language Program: Part 1: Cost Accounting." *Language, Speech and Hearing Services in Schools,* 6, no. 1 (January 1975), 7–13.

———. "Accountability in a School Speech and Language Program: Part II: Instruc-tional Materials Analysis." *Language, Speech and Hearing Services in Schools,* 7, no. 4 (October 1976), 259–70.

WRAY, DENISE and WINIFRED WATSON-FLORENCE. "Consultative Model: Implement-ing the Language-Reading Connection in the Classroom." University of Akron, Ohio. Presentation at the American Speech-Language-Hearing Association Con-vention, San Francisco, 1984.

ZEMMOL, CAROLINE S. "A Priority System of Case-Load Selection." *Language Speech and Hearing Services in Schools,* 8, no. 2 (April 1977), 85–98.

ZIMMERMAN, J., V. STEINER, and R. EVATT. *Preschool Language Manual.* Columbus, Ohio: Charles E. Merrill Publishing Company, 1969.

ZOBACK, MARK, and DEBORAH RICHARDS. "Communication Programming: Trans-disciplinary Intervention with Severely Handicapped Preschoolers." Eastconn Regional Education Service Center, North Windham, Conn. Presentation at the American Speech-Language-Hearing Association Convention, San Francisco, 1984.

INDEX